THE PERSIANS

European history describes the Persian empires mainly through the history of the Greeks and Romans who regarded them as politically, culturally, and socially inferior. In short, to them the Persians were barbarians. Yet this Indo-European civilisation was one of the most highly developed of the ancient world. Its society, with its many different languages, cultures, and religions, had a profound and continuing influence on the West.

This study vividly introduces the reader to the history of Persia in its own right; from the heights of the Achaemenid dynasty (559–330 BC), the first monarchy to create a world empire, to the heterogeneous empire of the Parthians (247 BC–AD 224), and the powerful Sasanian empire (AD 224–651), epitomised in the rule of Khosrow Anushirvan, 'Of the Immortal Soul'.

The only book of its kind to cover both the history of the Achaemenid period and of the thousand years following Alexander's conquest, and including chapters on a wide range of separate issues such as society, economy, gender, power, and defence, this book is the essential beginner's guide to ancient Persia and ideal for students and general readers alike.

Maria Brosius is a Reader in Ancient History at the University of Newcastle. She has worked and travelled in Iran and has published several books on Persian history, including *The Persian Empire from Cyrus II to Artaxerxes I* (2000) and *Women in Ancient Persia (559–331 BC)* (1996, reprinted 1998, 2001).

PEOPLES OF THE ANCIENT WORLD

This series stands as the first port of call for anyone who wants to know more about the historically important peoples of the ancient world and the early middle ages.

Reliable, up-to-date and with special attention paid to the peoples' enduring legacy and influence, *Peoples of the Ancient World* will ensure the continuing prominence of these crucial figures in modern-day study and research.

THE PERSIANS
An Introduction
Maria Brosius

THE TROJANS AND THEIR NEIGHBOURS
Trevor Bryce

MYCENAEANS
Rodney Castleden

THE EGYPTIANS
An Introduction
Robert Morkot

THE BABYLONIANS
An Introduction
Gwendolyn Leick

THE PERSIANS

An Introduction

Maria Brosius

Routledge
Taylor & Francis Group

LONDON AND NEW YORK

First published 2006
by Routledge
2 Park Square, Milton Park, Abingdon, Oxon OX14 4RN

Simultaneously published in the USA and Canada
by Routledge
711 Third Avenue, New York, NY 10017 (8th Floor)

Routledge is an imprint of the Taylor & Francis Group, an informa business

© 2006 Maria Brosius

Typeset in Garamond 3 by
Florence Production Ltd, Stoodleigh, Devon

British Library Cataloguing in Publication Data
A catalogue record for this book is available from the British Library

Library of Congress Cataloging in Publication Data
A catalog record for this book has been requested

ISBN10: 0–415–32089–5 (hbk)
ISBN10: 0–415–32090–9 (pbk)
ISBN10: 0–203–06815–7 (ebk)

ISBN13: 978–0–415–32089–4 (hbk)
ISBN13: 978–0–415–32090–0 (pbk)
ISBN13: 978–0–203–06815–1 (ebk)

FÜR FINI

CONTENTS

LIST OF FIGURES

LIST OF MAPS

All maps were redrawn for this volume.

FOREWORD

The present book outlines the history and culture of the three Persian dynasties before the Arab conquest and the introduction of Islam in Mesopotamia and Iran in the mid-seventh century AD. Serving as an introduction to ancient Persia, the book covers general historical overviews and special issues with a view to facilitate the understanding of Persian society and culture, administration, economy and religion to non-specialists, students of Ancient History and Civilisations, as well as an interested general readership.

Within this framework I have attempted to balance the historical perspective on ancient Persia, which, due to the written sources and the classical tradition, has tended to approach the subject from a European, or western, perspective. Only recently scholarship has begun to rectify this shortcoming in the historical debate about ancient Persia and to discuss the history and culture of the ancient Persian empires in their own right.[1] This book incorporates the results of this scholarship, offering a more balanced perspective on the subject.

With this volume I hope to open a door to the fascinating world of the empires of ancient Persia to a wider audience of students and non-specialists who want to look beyond the artificial construction of the East–West divide.

ACKNOWLEDGEMENTS

For the permission to publish images of objects in their collection I wish to thank the Ashmolean Museum, Oxford, the Bibliothèque Nationale de France (Cabinet des Médailles et Antiques), Paris, the Centro Ricerche Archeologiche e Scavi, Turin, the Deutsches Archäologisches Institut, Berlin, the Hermitage Museum, St Petersburg, the Pergamonmuseum – Museum für islamische Kunst, Berlin, the Walters Art Museum, Baltimore, as well as Sir John Boardman, Hubertus von Gall, Mark Garrison, Antonio Invernizzi, Carlo Lippolis, Stephen Mitchell, Margaret C. Root, Bert Smith, Rolf Michael Schneider and Georg Gerster for making their material available to me. My special thanks go to Marion Cox for her excellent drawings. I am grateful to the School of Historical Studies of the University of Newcastle for their kind financial support for some of the illustrations.

I also would like to thank my colleagues and friends Jim Crow, Seamus Ross, Tony Spawforth and Josef Wiesehöfer, who read all or part of the manuscript, for their helpful comments and suggestions.

LIST OF ABBREVIATIONS

AA	*Archäologischer Anzeiger*
AchHist	*Achaemenid History*
Aesch.	Aeschines
AMI	*Archäologische Mitteilungen aus Iran*
AMI Ergbd.	*Archäologische Mitteilungen aus Iran, Ergänzungsband*
Amm.Marc.	Ammianus Marcellinus
App.*Syr.*	Appian, *Syriaca*
Arr.*an.*	Arrian, *Anabasis*
Avroman	E.H. Minns, 'Parchments of the Parthian period from Avroman in Kurdestan', *JHS* 35: 22–65, 1915.
Bab.	Babylonian
BM	siglum for tablets from the British Museum
Chin.	Chinese
Cic.*Manil.*	Cicero, *pro lege Manilia de imperio Cn. Pompei pro M. Marcello*
DB	Darius, Bisitun Inscription
Diakonoff, Livshits	I.M. Diakonoff, V.A. Livshits, *Parthian economic texts from Nisa*, ed. D.N. MacKenzie, vol. II, London 1977.
Diod.Sic.	Diodorus Siculus, *Bibliotheka*
DNb	Darius, Inscription from Naqsh-i Rustam (b)
DSe	Darius, Inscription from Susa (e)
DSf	Darius, Inscription from Susa (f)
DZc	Darius, Inscription from the Suez canal (c)

Elam.	Elamite
FGrH	*Fragmente griechischer Historiker*, ed. F. Jacoby, Berlin, Leiden 1923–58.
FHG	C. Müller, *Fragmenta Historicum Graecorum*, 5 vols, Paris 1841–70.
Fornara	C.W. Fornara, *Archaic times to the end of the Peloponnesian War*, Cambridge 1983[2].
Gr.	Greek
Grayson	A.K. Grayson, *Babylonian historical and literary texts*, Toronto 1975.
Hdt.	Herodotus, *Histories*
Jos.*Ant.*	Josephus, *Antiquities*
KNR	Inscription of Kirdir at Naqsh-i Rajab
Lat.	Latin
Meiggs, Lewis	R. Meiggs, D.M. Lewis, *Greek historical inscriptions*, Oxford 1989.
Minns	*see* Avroman
MP	Middle Persian
NPi	Narseh, Inscription at Paikuli
OP	Old Persian
Parth.Stat.	Isidore of Charax, *Parthian Stations*
Paus.	Pausanias
PF	siglum for Persepolis Fortification texts
PFS	siglum for Persepolis Fortification seals
Pliny, *nat.hist.*	Pliny, *naturalis historia*
Plut.	Plutarch
Art.	*Artaxerxes*
Crass.	*Crassus*
Luc.	*Lucullus*
Per.	*Pericles*
Sull.	*Sulla*
PMG	*Poetae Melici Graeci*, ed. D. L. Page, Oxford 1962.
Polyb.	Polybius
Procopius, *BP*	Procopius, *Bellum Persarum*
Procopius, *Goth.*	Procopius, *Gothica*
RC	C.B. Welles, *Royal correspondence of the Hellenistic period*, London 1934.
SEG	Supplementum Epigraphicum Graecum

ŠKZ	Šapur, Inscription at the Ka'aba-i Zardusht at Naqsh-i Rustam
Tabarī	*The history of al-Tabarī, vol. V: The Sāsānids, the Byzantines, the Lakmids, and Yemen,* transl. C.E. Bosworth, New York 1999.
Tac.*Ann.*	Tacitus, *Annales*
Theodoret, *HE*	Theodoret, *Historia Ecclesiastica*
Xen.*an.*	Xenophon, *Anabasis*
Xen.*Cyr.*	Xenophon, *Cyropaedia*
XPh	Xerxes, Inscription from Persepolis (h)

MONTH NAMES IN THE ACHAEMENID CALENDAR

	Babylonian	*Elamite*	*Old Persian*
March/April	Nisannu	Adukannash	Adukanaisa
April/May	Ayyaru	Turmar	Θuravahara
May/June	Simannu	Sakurrizish	Θaigracish
June/July	Du'uzu	Karmabatash	Garmapada
July/August	Abu	Turnabazish	——
August/September	Ululu	Karbashiyash	——
September/October	Tashritu	Bakeyatish	Bagayadish
October/November	Arahsamna	Markashanash	*Vrkazana
November/December	Kislimu	Hashiyatish	Açiyadiya
December/January	Tebetu	Hanamakash	Anamaka
January/February	Shabatu	Samiyamash	*Θwayauva
February/March	Addaru	Miyakannash	Viyax(a)na

* *reconstructed*

MONTH NAMES IN
PARTHIAN AND PAHLAVI

	Parthian	*Pahlavi*
March/April	prwrtyn	Frawardin
April/May	'rtywhsht	Ardwahisht
May/June	hrwtt	Xordad
June/July	tyry*	Tir
July/August	hmrtt*	Amurdad
August/September	xshtrywr	Shahrewar
September/October	mtry*	Mihr
October/November	'pxwny*	Aban
November/December	'trw	Adur
December/January	dtsh*	Day
January/February	whmn	Wahman
February/March	spndrmty	Spandarmad

* *reconstructed*

1

INTRODUCTION

The Persians were one of the most highly developed civilisations of the ancient world. An Indo-European people, their influence on western European civilisations is apparent not only in regard to the linguistic affinity, but also in terms of culture, society, and even the Christian religion. The Persians were the first monarchy to create a world empire which included most territories of the known ancient world, from Egypt to India, and from southern Russia to the Indian Ocean. The fall of the first Persian empire (559–330 BC), which was ruled by the Achaemenid dynasty, was followed, after a hundred-year interlude of Hellenistic rule, by a new Persian power, the Parthians, who were based in northern Iran. In a gradual process of conquest, they recovered most of the former Achaemenid empire up to the River Euphrates. The Parthians ruled for almost 500 years (247 BC–AD 224), until they were succeeded by a new Persian dynasty, the Sasanians, which rose in Persis (modern Fars) under their king Ardashir I. Their empire fell following the Arab conquest of Mesopotamia and Iran in the mid-seventh century AD, and the subsequent coming of Islam.

The following remarks may serve to highlight the political and cultural achievements of the Persian empires. The most outstanding achievement of the Achaemenids undoubtedly was their ability to maintain control over an empire of such vast and unprecedented geographic proportions for 230 years. To a large extent this was due to the Persian kings' acceptance of the political, cultural and religious diversity of the different peoples of the lands of the empire. No attempt was made to impose Persian language and religion on other people. Instead, the kings emphasised a policy which was, to use a modern phrase, all-inclusive. This does not mean to say that there were no repercussions in case of rebellious activities, but in principle the political and religious tolerance of the Achaemenid kings towards their subject peoples was adhered to, and was, by all accounts, overwhelmingly successful.

Being at the forefront of architectural and technological innovations meant that Persian kings prided themselves on employing the best architects and engineers at their courts. The creation of an extensive imperial road network in the Achaemenid empire not only established an unprecedented and unique infrastructure, but also led to the installation of the first known postal service in history. It provided a basis for the network of international routes, known collectively as the Silk Road, opened in the Parthian period, which linked Persia and the West with Central Asia and China. The architectural innovations of Persia include the vast columned halls of the royal palaces of Achaemenid Persia; the creation of round cities, an innovation of the Parthians and adapted by their successors, the Sasanians; the change from using columns to support a roof to the construction of barrel-vaulted structures called *ivans*, which characterise Parthian and Sasanian palace architecture; as well as the introduction of the squinch, an architectural feature which allowed the Sasanians to build a domed roof over a square space.

The Persian courts, especially those of the Parthians and Sasanians, took pride in an oral literary tradition which created the romances of Vis and Ramin and Khosrow and Shirin, stories which can be compared to, and may even have influenced, European literary tradition in stories such as Tristan and Isolde and Romeo and Juliet. Banqueting and hunting were recognised pastimes of the Persian kings and their courts, and found their way to the medieval courts of Europe. Chess and polo were amongst the games Khosrow I introduced to the Sasanian court from India, and Persian and foreign philosophers, astrologers and physicians were welcomed at the royal court to exchange knowledge and expertise.

Yet the high civilisation that was ancient Persia has been overshadowed by an overwhelmingly hostile press which is embedded in the European tradition, but which ultimately originates in antiquity. Europe's first hostile encounters with the Persian world were the Persian Wars of 490 and 480/79 BC. These wars became an event of world-historical importance, shaping European historical tradition and Europe's view of Persia, and indeed the Near (Middle) East. The Greek victories at Marathon (490 BC) and at Salamis and Plataea (480/79 BC) led to their transformation into mythical events, even gaining a religious dimension. These events triggered the creation of a Hellenic identity, in which the Greeks identified themselves in contrast to the 'Barbarian'. Used initially as a reference to the Persians, it soon became a term for any non-Greek. The Greek–Barbarian antithesis dominated Greek politics throughout the fifth and fourth centuries BC, and stood for an ideology in which Greek freedom was contrasted with Asian despotism and decadence. The Romans took up the baton from the Greeks, and as their political successors continued the propaganda of the western defence against the despotic East, be they Parthians or Sasanians. While the Greeks never distinguished between Medes and Persians, the Romans made no attempts to differentiate between Persians, Parthians and Sasanians. In their centuries-long wars against the empires of Parthia and Sasanian Persia, the Romans emphasised the weakness, effeminacy and the political and military decadence of 'the Persians', making little or no attempt to present a balanced view. It is the view of the Greek and Roman sources which has exerted considerable influence on the way we look at ancient Persia today.

So, who were the Persians? The Persians were an Iranian people who migrated from the east to the Iranian plateau in c.1000 BC. When they arrived in the region that is equivalent to modern-day Iran, they settled in different areas of the country alongside the indigenous population, the Elamites. Persians are attested in northwestern Iran, in the Zagros mountains and in Persis, modern Fars, in southwestern Iran. Another Iranian group were the Medes, who settled in the northwest of Iran, around the city of Ecbatana, modern Hamadan, and further north, in the area of Iranian Azerbaijan.

Elamite civilisation dates back to the third millennium BC. The Elamites were ruled by kings whose power was centred on two royal cities, Susa in Khuzestan, and Anshan in Persis. The Elamites were renowned as great warriors and appear in the Near Eastern sources as fervent enemies of the Assyrians. In the mid-seventh century BC the Assyrian king Assurbanipal defeated the Elamite army and sacked the city of Susa, which was destroyed and the surrounding land devastated to render it unsuitable for agriculture. Despite these events a new Elamite dynasty emerged, if only for a brief period of time, centred on Susa in the western part of the Elamite kingdom, while the area east of the Zagros mountains, including the city of Anshan, appears to have been deserted.

Elamite culture possessed a distinctive art and architecture, especially with regard to its religious architecture, exemplified in the ziggurat of Choga Zanbil, the temple constructed by the Elamite king Untash-Naprisha in the thirteenth century BC. Elamite rock reliefs attest to the importance of the celebration of religious rituals of the kings and queens of Elam.

No documents survive from Elam which would allow us to reconstruct the history of this kingdom, but building inscriptions and administrative documents attest to the fact that Elam possessed a long written tradition. Writing on clay, the Elamites used a cuneiform script which was distinct from Akkadian, though it did employ Sumerian logograms as word indicators. When the Persians settled in Elam, they adapted the Elamite script to conduct their administration. As far as can be deduced from the available evidence, the early Persian kings also adapted Elamite art and culture.

Median influence on Persia is less secure. In language and culture the Medes, an Iranian people, were related to the Persians. Yet the extent of their mutual affinity, or of Median influence on Persia, cannot be determined with any certainty. The Greek historian Herodotus, who described the political dependency of the early Persians on, and their cultural debt to, the seemingly superior Medes, presented Media as a kingdom which had been unified under Deiokes and reached its political zenith under Cyaxares and his son Astyages. But in recent studies scholars have placed serious doubt on the existence of a united Median empire.[1] From the eighth century BC onwards, Assyrian documents mention the Medes alongside several other peoples who live in the northern Zagros mountains, and frequently refer to the numerous kings who rule over them. Median sites such as Nush-e Jan, Godin Tepe and Baba Jan, which represented local centres of power, support the idea that Media was most likely a confederation of smaller states. During Assyrian expansion northward some Medes were forced to accept Assyrian suzerainty, but at the end of the seventh century the Median king Cyaxares fought a victorious battle against the Assyrians. This achievement may have led to the brief political sovereignty of Cyaxares and his son Astyages over other Median peoples, centring their power in the city of Ecbatana.

Geographically, the core region of imperial Persia is roughly equivalent to modern Iran. The Iranian plateau is situated between the Arab world in the west, India in the east and Turkoman Central Asia in the north. The plateau's altitude ranges between 1,000 and 1,500 metres. The country is dominated by the mountain ranges of the Alburz in the northwest, which has the highest mountain in Iran, the Damavand (5,610 m), the Kopet Dağ in the northeast and the mountains of Khorasan. The Zagros mountains stretch in a north–south direction in the western part of the country, while the eastern territory is marked by two deserts, the Dasht-e Kavir and the Dasht-e Lut. The plains are ideal for pastoral agriculture, while the lands of Khuzestan and of the region along the Caspian Sea are suitable for arable agriculture. The climate of Iran changes dramatically across its north–south extent, with cold, harsh conditions in the north and excessive heat in the south. It was the southwestern province of Persis which witnessed the birth of the first Persian empire under its king Cyrus II.

2

THE ACHAEMENIDS

HISTORICAL SURVEY

The early Persian kings

In the second half of the seventh century BC a Persian, named Cyrus I (Elam. *Kurush*; c.620–c.590), inherited the title of 'King of Anshan' from his father Teispes. They ruled over a principality located in southwest Iran, called Parsa, or Persis (modern Fars). This region had formerly been part of the kingdom of Elam, which had stretched across the Zagros mountains from Khuzestan to Persis, and was controlled by two respective capitals, Susa and Anshan. But the defeat of the Elamites by the Assyrian king Assurbanipal and the destruction of the western capital Susa in 646 BC had created a power vacuum in Persis. The Persians, who had lived peacefully alongside the indigenous Elamite population for several centuries, had established themselves sufficiently to create a noble class, out of which Teispes emerged as the principal leader who filled the political vacuum. In recognition of the former Elamite power Teispes and his immediate successors adapted the Elamite royal title, 'King of Susa and Anshan', to the title 'King of Anshan'. This was an act of political symbolism with which the Persians gave weight to their role as successors of the Elamite kings. In using this title they also acknowledged the eastern Elamite capital, Anshan, which had ceased to function as a major city in the mid-seventh century BC.

The inscription on his personal seal refers to Cyrus I simply as 'Cyrus of Anshan, son of Teispes', alongside an image which shows the king on horseback pursuing his enemies, some of whom are already lying slain on the ground (see Fig. 1). His affinity with

Elamite culture was expressed in the adaptation of the artistic style of the Neo-Elamite period, as well as in the use of the Elamite cuneiform script for the inscription. His grandson, Cyrus II, expressed more confidence in his written testimonies, claiming the royal title for himself and his ancestors back to his great-grandfather Teispes.

It is possible that a certain Kurash of Parsumash mentioned in a Neo-Assyrian text of Assurbanipal (668–631/27?) is identical with Cyrus I. In recognition of Assurbanipal's superiority over Elam after the fall of Susa in 646 BC, this Kurash sent a son, Arukku, with tribute to the Assyrian king. While the different rendering of the name Cyrus does not present a difficulty, the location of Parsumash is disputed and its identification with Persis uncertain. Yet there remains a possibility that the Assyrian record attests to Persian power in the eastern part of Elam.

Greek sources provide us with some information about Cyrus' son and successor Cambyses I (c.590–559 BC). They tell us that Cambyses entered an alliance with the neighbouring kingdom of Media. The Medes had settled in northwest Iran, with Ecbatana emerging as a major centre of this region. Both the Babylonians and the Persians might well have regarded the Medes as a worthy ally against the dominant power in Mesopotamia, the Assyrians. The Median kings Phraortes (647–625) and Cyaxares (625–585) both launched attacks against Assyria and its capital Nineveh. Cambyses I may have sealed the political alliance with Cyaxares' successor Astyages (585–550) with a dynastic marriage to his daughter Mandane. What is not certain is whether the alliance between the Median and the Persian king was one between equal partners, or one

Figure 1   Seal of Cyrus I with Elamite inscription (drawing by Marion Cox)

7

in which the Persians were regarded as inferior to the Medes, as was claimed by the Greek historian Herodotus. In any case, it appears that the Persian dynasts were still at a very early stage of royal power. Their main aim was the defence of their kingdom, as no source records any expansionist activity during that period.

The founder of the empire: Cyrus II the Great

This changed dramatically with the succession of Cambyses' son Cyrus II (559–530), who is rightly regarded as the founder of the Persian empire. Within the space of about twenty years Cyrus II led a series of military campaigns in which he subjected the existing kingdoms of the known world, Media, Lydia and Babylonia, as well as territories east of Parsa, controlling an area roughly equivalent to the geographical territory of the modern Middle East, reaching from Turkey and the Levantine coast to the borders of India, and from the Russian steppes to the Indian Ocean. This was a phenomenal and outstanding achievement for a single ruler, whose charisma and military skill allowed him to command a vast, multi-ethnic army, and who enforced a political organisation of empire which remained an effective tool of imperial government for over 200 years.

Media was the first kingdom to succumb to Cyrus' army in 550/49. Greek sources would have us believe that Cyrus attacked the Median king Astyages in a bid for political independence from Media. The familial element of this story, according to which this was a rebellion of Astyages' grandson, added a particular poignancy. Whether this is a case of romantic fiction will remain a question of much debate, but the fact that not all Greek sources agree on this version should alert us to the possibility that the familial link could have been a fictional addition to the story of conquest in order to legitimate Cyrus' rule in Media. Thus, in contrast, the fourth-century BC Greek doctor and writer Ctesias explicitly states that no familial relationship existed between Cyrus and Astyages. This view corresponds to the Near Eastern sources which make no mention of a political or familial link between the ruling houses of Media and Persis. Furthermore, these sources claim that Astyages took the offensive in battle, leaving Cyrus to take a defensive position to his attack. According to the Babylonian Nabonidus Chronicle Astyages intended to conquer Persis and therefore mustered an army. But when part of his army deserted from the king and sided with Cyrus, the outcome of the battle was decided and Astyages' fate was sealed. Cyrus immediately took control of the Median capital Ecbatana, confiscating the treasury and transferring its wealth to Persis.

[1] (Astyages) mustered (his army) and marched against Cyrus (Bab. *Kurash*), king of Anshan, for conquest [. . .]. [2] The army mutinied against Astyages (Bab. *Ishtumegu*) and he was taken prisoner. Th[ey handed him over?] to Cyrus [. . .]. [3] Cyrus marched to Ecbatana, the royal city. Silver, gold, goods, property, [. . .], [4] which he carried off as booty (from) Ecbatana, he took to Anshan. The goods (and) treasures of the army of [. . .]. (. . .)

(Nabonidus Chronicle col. II: 1–4)

Following Near Eastern tradition, Cyrus probably married a daughter of Astyages called Amytis (Ctesias FGrH 688 F1), thereby affirming his victory over the Medes.

Reasons why Astyages wanted to attack Persia in the first place remain obscure. It may have been due to his ambition to expand the Median realm, but he also could have recognised the growing power of Cyrus and was compelled to react before his power could pose a political threat.

Cyrus' military triumph was marked by the foundation of the first Persian royal centre, Pasargadae (Elam. *Batrakatash*), in the plain of Marv Dasht in eastern Persis. The site was dominated by Cyrus' palace and audience hall, as well as his tomb, placed on a six-stepped platform. In front of his residential palace Cyrus II built the first structured garden, a *paradeisos* (Elam. *partetash*), with irrigation channels dividing four rectangular spaces (see Fig. 2).

In a next step, Cyrus II conquered the regions north of Media, including Urartu, which was located around Lake Van, and the Lydian kingdom. Lydia was one of the most powerful and wealthiest kingdoms of the sixth century BC. King Croesus (c.560–c.547) had subjected the Ionian cities of the coastal area, and made them tributaries. An alliance with the Assyrian king, which extended the Neo-Assyrian system of overland routes from Mesopotamia to the Lydian capital Sardis, brought further prosperity. His fame in the Greek world was due to the fact that he was accredited as being one of the first rulers to mint coins. But militarily Croesus

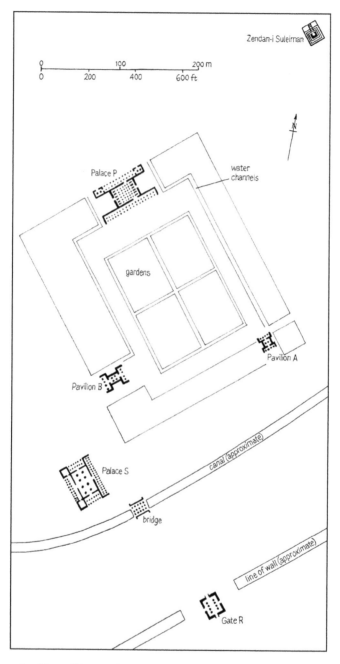

Figure 2 Plan of Pasargadae (drawing by Marion Cox)

was in a weak position since he failed to secure military support from Greece and Egypt for his fight against Cyrus. Taking the offensive, Croesus crossed the River Halys and attacked the city of Pteria, traditionally identified with the ancient Hittite capital Hattusa, modern Boğazköy.[1] In reaction to this attack, Cyrus moved his army towards Cappadocia, confronting Croesus' army, and forcing its retreat to Sardis after an indecisive battle. Back in Sardis Croesus hoped to get support from Egypt and Babylon, but Cyrus had pursued Croesus at great speed and the Lydian king was forced to face him in battle outside the capital before any reinforcements could arrive. Croesus was defeated, and Lydia became a satrapy of Cyrus' realm. Cyrus appointed a Persian, Tabalus, as satrap, or governor, of Lydia, and the Lydian Pactyes as treasurer. This choice proved to be a mistake, since it allowed opportunity for rebellion, and eventually a new satrap, Harpagus, was appointed to office.

The Ionians used the moment of political upheaval to liberate themselves from foreign control. But, unable to oppose the forces of the Median army under the command of Harpagus, the Ionian cities surrendered to Persian power. Their subjection was followed by that of the islands off the Ionian coast. When the cities of the Phoenician coast also submitted to Persian power, Cyrus possessed not only the largest army on land, but also a naval force. In addition, his control of the eastern Mediterranean meant that his empire profited from the maritime commerce of the Ionian and Phoenician cities.

We possess no records about Cyrus' campaigns over the following years until his conquest of Babylonia in 539, but it appears that he took his army eastward, intending to conquer the territories east of Persis, including Carmania, Gedrosia and Sistan in the south, and Drangiana, Arachosia, Sattagydia and Gandara in the east. In 540 he was ready to turn his army westward against Babylon. In the autumn of 539 Cyrus' army took the city of Opis on the Tigris. He made an example of a city trying to resist the Persian army, and its inhabitants were brutally killed and the city plundered. As a result, Sippar, a city located on the banks of the River Euphrates, en route to the capital Babylon, opened its gates without offering resistance to this seemingly invincible power.

[12–13] In the month Tashritu (*September/October*) when Cyrus did battle at Opis on the (bank of?) the Tigris against the

army of Akkad, the people of Akkad [14] retreated. He
carried off the plunder (and) slaughtered the people. On
the fourteenth day Sippar was captured without a battle.
[15] Nabonidus fled. On the sixteenth day (*12 October 539*)
Ugbaru, governor of the Guti, and the army of Cyrus
[16–17] entered Babylon without a battle.

(Nabonidus Chronicle col. III: 12–17)

Faced with such a display of force, King Nabonidus fled to Babylon,
where he was captured and taken prisoner. Like Sippar, Babylon surrendered to Cyrus. On 29 October 539 Cyrus made his official entry
into Babylon in a ceremonial procession, presenting himself as their
new king who assumed power with the support of the city-god
Marduk. The Babylonian Ugbaru was appointed governor of the city
and head of the administration, and ordered to select other city officials. Cyrus' son Cambyses II was officially recognised as Cyrus' heir
to the throne, and was installed as regent of Babylon. With Babylonia
the last Near Eastern power had fallen. Cyrus had now incorporated
the kingdoms of the ancient Near East and the principalities of the
eastern Iranian plateau into a world empire. In his famous inscription found in Babylon, the Cyrus Cylinder, Cyrus proudly recalled
his conquest of Babylon, and made it known that he now was a true
master of the world. In adaptation of the Babylonian royal title he
now called himself 'Cyrus, king of the world, great king, mighty
king, king of Babylon, king of Sumer and Akkad, king of the four
quarters (of the world)' (Cyrus Cylinder l.20).

Cyrus' quest for military conquest continued. His next campaigns
took him to the borders of the known world, to the northern and
northeastern border regions of Persia and to the people of the
steppes. It was probably between 538 and 530 that he took control
of Parthia, Aria and Margiana, as well as Bactria, Sogdiana and
Ferghana in the northeast, and fought against the Massagetae, probably one of the Scythian tribes who occupied the territory east of
the River Jaxartes (mod. Syr Darya). Here a city called Cyropolis,
conquered two centuries later by Alexander the Great, bore witness
to Cyrus' eastern conquests. When Cyrus died in a battle against
the Massagetae in 530 BC, his son Cambyses II ordered his body to
be returned to Persis, to be buried in Pasargadae. Cyrus' legacy was
a remarkable phenomenon. Under the leadership of a single king

the Persians had become the dominant power of the known world. No force was in a position to challenge their claim to rule and their military power. Cambyses II (530–522) acceded to the throne in a smooth succession. A Babylonian text dated to 31 August 530 noted this year as the accession year of Cambyses, 'king of Babylon, king of lands' (Brosius 2000: no. 18).

Cambyses had a younger brother, known in Old Persian inscriptions as Bardiya, but called Smerdis or Tanaoxares/Tanyoxarkes by Greek writers. According to one source this brother was appointed satrap of Media, Armenia, and of the Cadusians (Xen.Cyr.8.7.11), while another located his satrapies further east, in Bactria, Chorasmia, Parthia and Carmania (Ctesias FGrH 688 F9.8). Cambyses continued his father's expansion of the empire. During his reign Cyprus came under Persian control and in 525 he conquered Egypt. Cambyses was proclaimed pharaoh and was given the name Mesuti-Re, 'Son of (the god) Re'. These conquests, as well as the Persian control over the Phoenician cities, provided the Persian king with a substantial naval force, which he continued to enlarge. The cost of expanding and maintaining these naval armaments weighed heavily on his subjects.

Memphis became the capital and seat of the Persian satrap Aryandes. In response to the Persian takeover of Egypt, neighbouring Cyrene and Libya also offered their submission to Persian domination. Cambyses himself continued to campaign southward, reaching the First Cataract of the Nile and the island of Elephantine, where a Jewish garrison was stationed to safeguard the Persian interests in this part of the empire. Cambyses' army marched even further south and took control of at least part of Nubia. While Herodotus describes this campaign as a complete failure in which Cambyses' army suffered heavy losses in the desert (Hdt.3.25), his version is contradicted by the fact that the Nubians were recorded as one of the peoples of the empire by the beginning of the reign of Cambyses' successor Darius I in 522.

To this day Cambyses' death remains a mystery. We know that he died in the summer of 522, sometime between July and August, but there are different accounts of how he met his death. According to the account of Darius I, Cambyses 'died his own death' (DB §11), an ambiguous phrase which leaves it open whether he died a natural death or whether he killed himself. According to Herodotus and Ctesias he died after accidentally wounding himself in the thigh,

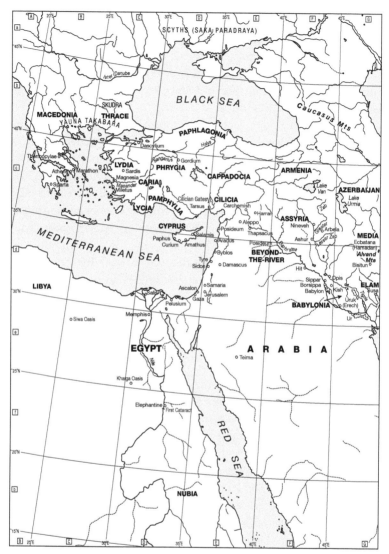

Map 1   The Achaemenid empire

while a late source, the Demotic Chronicle, simply states that he 'died on a mat' (Brosius 2000: no. 48).[2] The reason why his death has attracted so much attention is part of a complex story of fratricide, now impossible to disentangle, since each account follows its own agenda in its version of events.

14

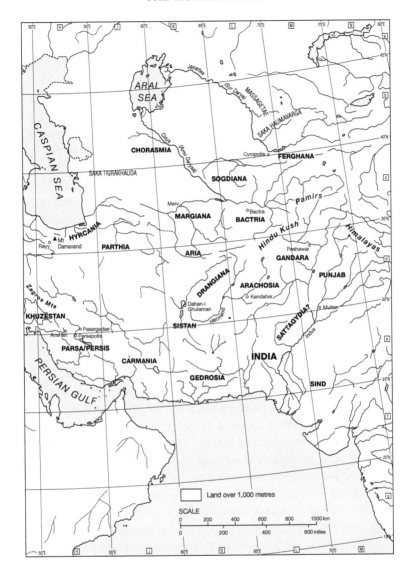

The Achaemenids: Darius I and his successors

Darius I succeeded to the throne in September 522. In his view Cambyses killed his brother Bardiya and was then confronted with an impostor called Gaumata who pretended to be Bardiya. This 'false Bardiya' ruled successfully for a period of six months, from March/

15

April until September 522, before Darius and six other noble Persians overthrew him in a palace coup and restored Persian power to the rightful successor, Darius I.

> Darius the king says: 'Afterwards there was one man, a *magus*, Gaumata by name. He rose up from Paishiyauvada – from a mountain called Arakadri. In the month Viyaxna (Bab. *Addaru*) fourteen days had passed when he rose up (*11 March 522*). He lied to the people thus: 'I am Bardiya the son of Cyrus, the brother of Cambyses.' (. . .) No one dared say anything about Gaumata the *magus* until I came. Afterwards I prayed to Ahuramazda. Ahuramazda brought me aid. In the month Bagayadish (Bab. *Tashritu*) ten days had passed (*29 September 522*), then I with a few men slew Gaumata the *magus* and the men who were his foremost followers. A fortress Sikayuvatish by name and a district Nisaya by name, in Media – there I slew him. I took the kingship from him. By the favour of Ahuramazda I became king. Ahuramazda bestowed the kingship upon me.
>
> (DB §11–13)

Herodotus provides us with a variant of Darius' account. According to his version of events Cambyses ordered the killing of his brother, whom he suspected of aspiring to the throne. Bardiya had campaigned with Cambyses in Egypt, but Cambyses, jealous of Bardiya's superior military skills, had ordered his return to Persia. Cambyses suspected his brother, once in Persis, of plotting to seize the throne, and he ordered one of his courtiers, Prexaspes, to kill him. After learning that an impostor who called himself Bardiya had assumed kingship in Persis, Cambyses recognised his brother's innocence and his own tragic error. En route to Persis to confront the impostor, he accidentally stabbed himself in the thigh and died from his injury. The 'false Bardiya' continued to reign for several more weeks before being overthrown by seven Persian nobles, including Darius, who then succeeded to the kingship. Yet the question is whether Darius' version of events, on which Herodotus' story is based, can be trusted since he had a primary interest in presenting the facts in a – for him – favourable light in order to deflect any doubts as to the legitimacy of his succession.

The crucial detail is the fact that, although he undoubtedly belonged to the Persian nobility, Darius was not an immediate member of the royal family. His father Hystaspes had been satrap of Parthia under Cyrus II and Cambyses II; Darius himself had been in Egypt with Cambyses serving as his spear-bearer. The succession of the royal dynasty was threatened because Cambyses II had left no sons. This meant that his brother Bardiya would be next in line to the throne in the event of Cambyses' death. But Bardiya, too, died without leaving any male issue, and thus, the Persian throne could be contested by a member of the extended royal family, or indeed of the Persian nobility. There is, therefore, room to speculate that Darius had a key interest in gaining the throne and that he took the necessary steps to eliminate any opposition. It is quite possible that, following the (accidental) death of Cambyses in July/August 522, his brother Bardiya succeeded to the kingship, and that it was he who was killed in a palace coup by a group of nobles headed by Darius. Bardiya's murder was then concealed behind the story of Cambyses' fratricide and the appearance of a 'false Bardiya', who was claimed by Darius and the nobles to have been a *magus* called Gaumata. The issue which makes this version of events highly dubious is the fact that Darius claimed that this impostor looked exactly like Bardiya, and thus succeeded in deceiving the entire court, including his wife, for six months. If Darius indeed succeeded to the throne through a palace coup he created an ingenious piece of propaganda which was circulated so successfully that it remained within the oral tradition until almost 100 years later, when Herodotus heard the story and recorded it.

Doubts about Darius' genuine right to succeed to the throne are also raised in the very problematic genealogy he produced in his first public declaration, the Inscription of Bisitun, carved in the rock face of Mt Bisitun in Media (see Fig. 3a and b). Darius claims in this inscription to descend from a line of kings, but he fails to list any of the known Persian kings, including Cyrus II and Cambyses II. Instead he traces his ancestral line back to a Persian called Achaemenes, whom he presents as the father of Teispes, thereby creating a familial link between his family and that of Cyrus II. But we only have Darius' word for the claim that Achaemenes was the father of Teispes. None of the earliest records, including the Cyrus Cylinder, mentions Achaemenes. Thus, consideration has to be given to the possibility that Darius 'created' this familial link in order to legitimise his succession to the throne. Furthermore, in order to prevent any future contestants to the throne who could rightfully claim a direct descent from Cyrus II, Darius I concluded a series of marriage alliances with all surviving royal daughters, Atossa and Artystone, the daughters of Cyrus, and Parmys, the daughter of Bardiya. The nobles who had assisted him in gaining the throne were honoured with lifelong privileges. Two of them, Gobryas and Otanes, were particularly honoured in that they were married to sisters of Darius, while Darius himself was married to daughters of both these nobles. The exalted position of the two families was confirmed in the next generation, when their offspring also inter-married, with Gobryas' son Mardonius marrying a daughter of Darius, Artazostre, and Otanes' daughter Amestris marrying Darius' son and heir Xerxes.

Darius' usurpation of the Persian throne was not uncontested. The first year of his reign was marked by nine rebellions, mainly in the central satrapies of the empire, Media, Elam, Babylon and Bactria, where (legitimate) claimants to the throne attempted to revive the former kingdoms. Yet in nineteen battles fought over the next thirteen months he brought the Persian empire back under his

Figure 3a Mount Bisitun (photo: MB)

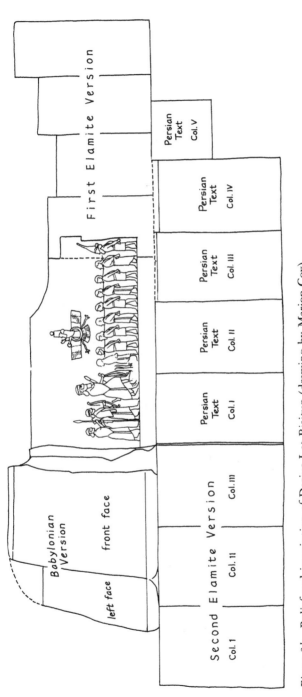

Figure 3b Relief and inscription of Darius I at Bisitun (drawing by Marion Cox)

control. His successful accession to the Persian throne was recorded in his *res gestae*, the Bisitun Inscription. An accompanying relief depicts Darius standing victoriously in front of the captured rebels, the 'false Bardiya' lying on the ground.

Darius then set out to manifest his power by laying claim to the former western Elamite capital of Susa, starting a major rebuilding of the royal residence there. He also completed building work in Cyrus' palaces at Pasargadae, perhaps a surprising act considering that he had avoided any reference to the founder of the empire in the Bisitun Inscription. Yet it was most likely a political move which was to demonstrate the continuity of Persian kingship and to emphasise the legitimacy of his reign. Pasargadae even became the ceremonial centre for the royal investiture of the Persian kings (Plut.*Art*.3.1–2). Darius' main building project, however, was the foundation of his own royal city, Persepolis (Elam. *Parsa*), situated c.80 km west of Pasargadae. Persepolis, with its royal terrace housing the palaces and audience halls of the Achaemenid kings, was to remain the centre of Persian power for the next two hundred years (see Fig. 4). The nearby rock formation of Naqsh-i Rustam became the site of the royal tombs of Darius I and three of his successors.[3]

But it was not sufficient to manifest his grip on Persian power through a major building programme. It had to be established on a more substantial basis, which would affect the peoples of the empire directly. Darius reassessed the tribute payments of his subject peoples and set a fixed tribute, possibly differing from the fiscal arrangements of Cyrus II.[4] Gold and silver coinage was introduced and minted according to a Persian standard.[5] The division of the empire into satrapies, which had been introduced by Cyrus II, remained in place, but we can assume that under Darius the satrapal and central administration was revised and improved. To foster communication between the lands of the empire, and in order to benefit imperial trade, Darius was eager to maintain and expand the Royal Roads, the imperial road system which connected the provinces of the empire from Babylon to Bactra, and from Susa to Sardis. He also was responsible for the improvements of maritime routes, building a canal which connected the Red Sea with the Nile Delta.

Darius undertook further territorial expansion, though on a smaller scale than his predecessors, on the borders of the empire. In c.518 he undertook a campaign to India in order to advance the

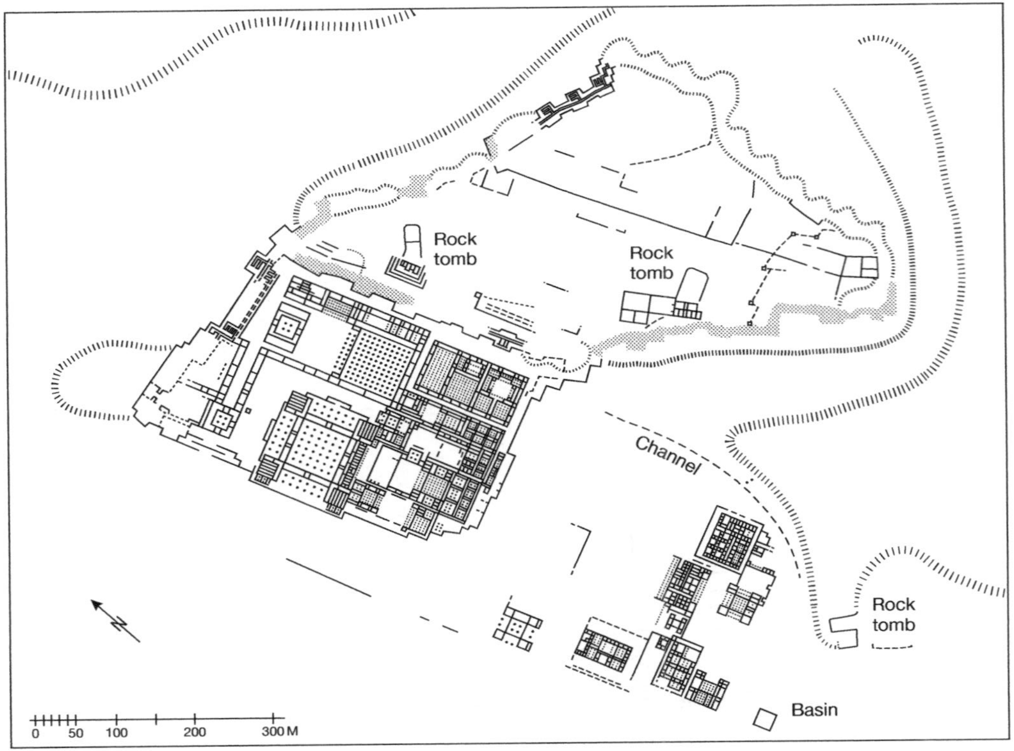

Figure 4
Plan of Persepolis
(after W. Kleiss)

Rock tomb

Rock tomb

Channel

Rock tomb

Basin

N

0 50 100   200   300 M

eastern border established by Cyrus, and in c.513 he led a campaign against the European Scythians who lived a nomadic life moving along the northern coast of the Black Sea. At the same time a contingent under the command of Megabazus was sent to Thrace and Macedon, regions which were not politically powerful at the time, but which were rich in natural resources like silver and timber. Their alliance with Persia led to a general economic prosperity of these regions because they benefited from a new infrastructure which connected the coastal area with the hinterland.

In 499 a revolt broke out amongst some of the Ionian cities, instigated by the tyrant of Miletus, Aristagoras. He had persuaded Darius to undertake an expedition against Naxos and conquer it for the empire. When the attempt failed, Aristagoras, afraid of personal punishment, rose in rebellion. He tried in vain to get military support from Sparta, renowned at the time for its excellent hoplite army, but was able to persuade Athens and Eretria to send a naval contingent to Ionia. The satrapal centre of Lydia and the Ionian cities, Sardis, was Aristagoras' first aim. With the exception of the citadel, which was defended by Persians and Lydians, the city was taken. An accidental fire destroyed the entire city, including the temple of Cybele. Persian forces pursued the Ionians to Ephesus where they defeated them in battle. As a consequence most of the rebelling Ionians dispersed and returned to their cities. Likewise the Athenian and Eretrian ships abandoned the revolt and returned to Greece. On Cyprus the city-king Onesilus of Salamis used the revolt in an attempt to gain independence from Persia, but within a year Cyprus was back under Persian control. Three Persian commanders, Daurises, Hymaees and Otanes, led campaigns to quash the rebellion, which had now spread to three different parts of the coast of Asia Minor, the Hellespont, the Propontis coast, and to the Ionian and Aeolian cities. By 493 these rebellions were quashed, culminating in the recovery of Miletus, which fell in a land and sea battle. Part of the city's population was deported to Persian territory on the Red Sea. In 492 Mardonius, Darius' son-in-law, was sent to Ionia to restore order, and Artaphernes began the reorganisation of Ionia.

But not only Miletus suffered the consequences of rebelling against the king. As a result of these events Darius set out to punish those who had caused and supported the revolt. Datis and Artaphernes, the son of the satrap of Sardis, were sent with a small force to punish Naxos, Eretria and Athens for their role in the rebellion. Athens' involvement in particular was seen as a provocation, since it constituted a violation of the Persian-Athenian treaty of 507/6. Even though their navy had not actively participated in the revolt, they had demonstrated that they were willing, if necessary, to cross the Aegean Sea and interfere in Persian politics, thereby contesting the king's sovereignty over Ionia. From the Persian perspective, the Great King controlled the Aegean coast from Rhodes to the Hellespont and along the Thracian and Macedonian coast, and therefore the appearance of Greek warships in these waters had been a direct form of aggression, challenging the king's supremacy. In the punitive campaign the Persian fleet sailed via Rhodes, where sacrifices were made to the local goddess Athena, and from there proceeded to Naxos. The city and its temples were destroyed. On Delos Datis offered further sacrifices and then sailed to Euboea. After a seven-day siege Eretria was taken, the temples destroyed and the population deported. On the advice of Hippias, the former Athenian tyrant who now lived in Persian exile, the Persian fleet landed in the Bay of Marathon in preparation for the attack on the Athenians. The Athenians met the Persians in the plain of Marathon, and, following a surprise attack, in which the Persians were unable to use their cavalry, the Persians were forced to retreat, but then suffered heavy losses in the marshy waters, where many of them perished. Those who reached their ships tried to sail around Sunion and attack Athens from the western coast, but they had to abort this plan when they realised that the Greek land forces had hurried back to Athens at great speed and posed too strong an opposition.

Despite the Persian defeat at Marathon, Darius was determined to punish Athens for its involvement in Persian affairs. He intended to prepare a renewed attack on Athens, but this time with a considerably larger land and naval force. But his plans had to be postponed when a revolt in Egypt required more immediate attention. Darius, however, died in the winter of 486, and it was left to his son and heir to the throne, Xerxes, to crush the Egyptian revolt. Before turning his attention to Athens, however, Xerxes was delayed further by a rebellion in Babylon, which erupted in the autumn of 482, led by Bel-shimani. In 481 Xerxes sent messengers to the Greek cities demanding earth and water as tokens of acceptance of Persian supremacy. Many complied with this demand, including Thrace,

Macedon and Thessaly. The Persian army gathered at Sardis and from there took the land route to the Hellespont, crossing at Abydos and then continued through allied territory, finally reaching Boeotia and the borders of Attica. At the same time the Persian navy, consisting of Phoenician, Cypriote and Ionian ships, sailed along the Ionian and Thracian coast, cutting through a newly built channel at Mt Athos, and continued along the Greek coast to Artemisium. In September 480 Xerxes' army utterly defeated a Greek force of 300 Spartiates and Thebans, led by the Spartan king Leonidas, at the pass of Thermopylae, which gave access to the plains of Attica. At sea, Persian and Greek naval forces fought an indecisive three-day battle off Artemisium before disengaging. But Persian success at Thermopylae meant that the path now lay open for an attack on Athens. Here, the leading general Themistocles had already ordered the evacuation of its citizens, and the city was taken without resistance on 27 September 480. The acropolis was seized and the temples destroyed. In the eyes of Xerxes the Persian objective of the campaign, the punishment of Athens, had been achieved. However, a subsequent sea-battle at Salamis ended in disaster for the Persian ships which were trapped in the narrow straits. Xerxes made preparations for another naval battle but then aborted this plan and ordered the fleet to return to Asia Minor. He himself returned with most of the infantry overland. Contrary to Herodotus' description of Xerxes' return as a hasty and cowardly escape from battle, Xerxes took a strategic decision not to employ the navy in another battle, since the Phoenician ships had proved to be unsuitable for naval manoeuvre in Greek waters. As it was now September and the end of the sailing season was approaching, he also wanted to ensure the safe return of the vessels to the Ionian coast. There is a further possibility that he returned because he had received the news of a renewed revolt in Babylon in 479, led by Shamash-eriba, which required the king to be closer to events in the empire. Mardonius was left in charge with an elite contingent of 10,000 men. After wintering in Thessaly Mardonius employed the diplomatic services of King Alexander I of Macedon to negotiate a peace agreement with the Athenians, including the rebuilding of the temples. The Athenians refused the offer and Mardonius occupied the city for a second time in the spring of 479. After the refusal of a second peace offer a battle was unavoidable and the Persian army met a panhellenic force on the plain outside Plataea. When Mardonius was killed during the battle, the Persian forces were left in disarray and routed. The survivors returned to Persia under the command of Artabazus. The Athenian fleet now pursued the Persians by sea and attacked their ships again off the island of Mycale in Ionia. In the following years the Persians lost their control over the Hellespont, ceding Byzantium, and over Thrace and Macedon.

Xerxes reigned for another fourteen years. He implemented further political reforms to the satrapal organisation, including the division of the vast satrapy of Babylon and Beyond-the-River into two separate provinces. The creation of the satrapy of Hellespontine Phrygia in a split from Lydia probably also has to be attributed to his reign. In Persepolis he completed the palace and throne hall begun by Darius I and began the construction of his own palace on the royal terrace. In the absence of any mention of unrest or rebellion in the empire, it appears that the Persian defeat and territorial losses in Greece had no repercussions for the stability of the empire. Then, in 465, together with the designated heir to the throne, Darius, Xerxes was killed in a palace coup, and his son Artaxerxes I (465–424/3) succeeded to the throne. The succession crisis triggered a short-lived rebellion in Bactria, and a revolt in Egypt led by the Libyan Inaros. This revolt began in 464, and in 460 received the support of Athens, which sent a 200-strong navy from Cyprus. Athens, itself now in control of an empire of allied Greek city-states, had defeated a Persian force in Lycia near the River Eurymedon in c.464. Athens' attempt to gain Cyprus may reflect the ambition to increase its control of the eastern Mediterranean, since Cyprus was a strategically important island on the sea route to Egypt and the Levantine coast. Support for Egypt also offered the opportunity for an Athenian–Egyptian alliance which would benefit trade and secure the corn supply for mainland Greece. With the exception of the citadel the rebelling forces were able to take Memphis, but when the Persian satrap Achaemenes was killed at Papremis, Artaxerxes ordered Megabyxus, satrap of Beyond-the-River, to continue the battle against the rebels. Megabyxus regained control of Memphis and blockaded Inaros' fleet on the island of Prosopitis. Disaster for Athens began when an additional contingent of fifty Athenian ships was destroyed on entering the Nile Delta via Mendes, and was complete when the remaining ships, anchored off Prosopitis, were left stranded when the Persians channelled off the water. Rather than make the Athenians prisoners of war, Megabyxus ordered them to abandon their ships, and allowed them to return to Athens by land, along the Libyan coast – a humiliating measure for both the sailors and for Athens itself. Inaros was taken prisoner and sent to Persia, where he was killed. The Persian Arsames succeeded Achaemenes in office as satrap of Egypt.

Despite the debacle, however, Athens undertook yet another attempt to interfere with Persian politics and in 450 tried to get control of Cyprus. In a battle against Phoenician, Cilician and Cypriote forces, the Athenian commander Cimon took Salamis, which was but a short-lived victory. Cimon died during the siege of Citium, and the Athenian navy withdrew from the island. Then, thirty years after the Greek–Persian wars the Athenians reached an agreement with the Persian king which officially ended the hostilities. According to a contested ancient Greek tradition, in the Peace of Callias of 450/49 both parties consented on their respective access to the eastern Aegean and Mediterranean coast (Diod.Sic.12.4.5). Persian warships were not allowed to navigate between Phaselis in Lycia and the Cynaean Islands at the entrance of the Black Sea, while Athens withdrew from Cyprus. Persia also conceded the independence of the Ionian cities from Persian rule, but maintained control of the land.

It was not until 432 that Persia re-entered Greek politics, being courted by both Sparta and Athens in their build-up to the Peloponnesian War. But at this stage Artaxerxes I saw no reason to interfere in Greek politics, since there was no obvious gain for Persia's involvement in the Greek conflict. Technically Persia was still at war with Sparta, and there was not enough pressure on Athens to enforce any significant trade-offs. This changed, however, with Sparta's occupation of Decelea and the Athenian defeat in Sicily in 413. Furthermore, Athens had provoked the Persian king with its support of the rebelling Egyptian satrap Amorges. Sparta now pursued a pro-Persian policy, seeking naval and financial support in order to fight the Athenian navy, in return for conceding the Ionian cities once again to Persian control. Athens made a vain attempt to interfere with these negotiations, being prepared to revoke the freedom of the Ionian cities, but it was not prepared to give up its dominance of the Aegean, and negotiations collapsed. The satrap of

Sardis, Tissaphernes, who led the negotiations, came to an agreement with Sparta in the spring of 411 BC, thereby sealing Athens' fate. By 404 the Athenians had to concede defeat and acknowledge the collapse of their empire. The Ionian cities once again came under Persian control, and Sparta emerged as the new power in Greece.

The Persian–Spartan alliance had been concluded under the auspices of Darius II, who had succeeded Artaxerxes I in February/March 424/3 BC. A son of Artaxerxes I and a Babylonian woman named Cosmartidene, Darius II had not been the designated heir to the throne, but had been appointed satrap of Hyrcania. His accession to the throne was the result of a succession struggle, in which Xerxes II, the designated heir, was killed after a reign of merely 45 days, and Darius II himself fought off attempts of his half-brother, Sogdianus, to succeed to the throne. The beginning of the reign of his son and successor Artaxerxes II (404–359), who succeeded Darius after his death sometime between 17 September 405 and 10 April 404, was similarly troubled. His reign was marred by numerous rebellions, mainly in the western part of the empire. The most significant loss was that of Egypt which broke free in 404 when Amyrtaeus led a rebellion in the Nile Delta, and by 400 had succeeded in bringing the whole of Egypt into open revolt. Artaxerxes' succession was further contested by his brother Cyrus the Younger. Supported by a mercenary force of 10,000 Greek soldiers, Cyrus marched through Beyond-the-River to Babylonia to confront Artaxerxes' forces near Kunaxa, where he was killed in battle in 401. This fraternal war was possibly the most serious threat to a Persian king during the period of Achaemenid rule until the invasion of Alexander the Great.

Spartan victory over Athens spurred the ambitions of King Agesilaus to appear as liberator of the Greek cities of Asia and to launch a campaign against Persian territory in Asia Minor. Between 396 and 394 Agesilaus devastated territory in Phrygia but failed to entice the local population into the revolt. Yet he was able to get support from Egypt which supplied him with 100 triremes and 500 measures of grain. With this a political pattern emerged which overshadowed Persian policy in the west throughout the reign of Artaxerxes II and through part of his successor's, Artaxerxes III (359–338). Egypt was an eager ally of any party rebelling from the Persian king, and indeed fostered rebellion in the empire wherever possible because it prevented the Persian king from focusing his military forces on Egypt itself. But the Spartan–Egyptian alliance of 396 did not meet with success, when Pharnabazus, satrap of Dascyleium, and the Athenian naval commander Conon defeated the Spartan fleet at Knidos in 394. This triggered rebellions against Sparta by Chios, Mytilene, Ephesus and Erythrae. In 393 Persian forces advanced deep into the Aegean and were able to take Melos and Cythera. For the first time since 479 Persian ships had entered Greek waters close to the Greek mainland. The Spartans immediately sued for peace, sending an embassy under Antalcidas to Persia. Other Greek states, Athens, Corinth and Argos, aware of the political significance of such a peace agreement, likewise sent delegations. When no agreement could be reached, since Greek states feared to lose power and influence in their realm, the Persian negotiator, Tiribazus, was replaced by the more pro-Athenian Strouthas. But then Athens made a political error: it entered an alliance with the Egyptian rebel Acoris in the spring of 388. Artaxerxes realised that a pro-Athenian stance on these negotiations would be damaging, too, and Tiribazus was reinstated in office. At the same time the pro-Athenian Pharnabazus was replaced by Ariobarzanes. When Sparta attempted to gain control of Rhodes, while Athens made yet another attempt for control of Cyprus, supporting Evagoras' attempt to gain control of the whole island, Artaxerxes reopened negotiations with Sparta, which resulted in the conclusion of the King's Peace of 386, in which Sparta declared Persia once again master of the Greek cities of Asia Minor. Artaxerxes could now focus on his war against Egypt, and a campaign was mounted in 385–383, which, however, was unsuccessful. At the same time Artaxerxes was forced to conduct a campaign against the Cadusians in the north of the empire. In 375 the Greek peace was reaffirmed, and following that, Persian forces were once again sent against Egypt under the command of Pharnabazus in 374/3.

The last decade of Artaxerxes' reign was dominated by four rebellions led by different satraps of Asia Minor. Datames, who had inherited the satrapy of southern Cappadocia from his father Kamisares after 384, rebelled in c.372. Neighbouring armies of the satraps of Lydia and Lycia, Autophradates and Artumpara, were commanded to quash his rebellion, but it took until 362 when Datames, betrayed by his in-law Mitrobarzanes, was killed.

A second rebellion followed, led by Ariobarzanes, son of the ruler of Pontus, who had been acting satrap of Dascyleium until the legitimate heir Artabazus could take office. Yet when Ariobarzanes refused to relinquish his post in 366, he allied himself with the Athenian commander Timotheus and the Spartan king Agesilaus. Together they withstood a naval blockade by Mausolus, dynast of Caria, and Autophradates, but Ariobarzanes' rebellion was finally quashed in 363 when he was betrayed by his son Mithradates.

In the third rebellion, which occurred between 363 and 360, Orontes, satrap of Mysia, took advantage of a succession crisis in Egypt which had put Tachos on the throne after the death of Nectanebo. While Orontes collected mercenaries for his planned revolt, a collaborator, Rheomitres, was sent to Egypt to secure the support of Tachos. Greek reports that Mausolus of Caria joined the rebellion do not seem to be borne out, since nothing further is known about Mausolus' activities, and, on the contrary, he appeared again as the king's satrap. Orontes himself was betrayed by his own supporters, and, surrendering to the king, once again swore allegiance.

Tachos tried to stir further rebellion in Persia, when, in 359, he led a campaign of 80,000 Egyptians and 10,000 Greek mercenaries against the empire, alongside Spartan support. But while Tachos was outside Egypt, Nectanebo II proclaimed himself pharaoh. Tachos swiftly changed sides and now offered his services to Artaxerxes III, who had succeeded Artaxerxes II. Artaxerxes' first action was to disband the Greek mercenary forces to curb the military power of the satraps. Despite this effort Artabazus managed to conscript an Athenian commander, Chares, and some of the released mercenaries who had placed themselves under Chares' command, to rebel against the king. Thebes, likewise, offered its support to Artabazus, but eventually the revolt had to be abandoned and Artabazus was forced to flee the empire and find exile in Macedon.

Artaxerxes III's real concern, however, was Egypt. Further campaigns were conducted in 354 and 351, but without success. To maintain the unstable situation at the Persian coast, Nectanebo supported a rebellion of the Phoenician cites in 345/4 led by the king of Sidon, Tennes, but within a year the revolt was suppressed by the forces of the satraps Mazaios of Cilicia and Belesys of Beyond-the-River. Before Egypt could do any more damage, Artaxerxes himself led a campaign against Nectanebo immediately after the recapture of the Phoenician cites. In the summer of 342 Artaxerxes entered Memphis and defeated Nectanebo in battle. Egypt was back under Persian control (see Fig. 5).

It was then that Artaxerxes III could focus his attention on a different part of the ancient world, Macedon. Following the accession of Philip II in 360 Macedon had grown into a strong military power which now, in the late 340s, emerged as a real threat to the Greek world in Philip's quest for the hegemony of Greece. In 341 Athens dispatched an embassy to Persia in an attempt to negotiate Persian aid against Macedon. When Philip attacked Perinthus at the Hellespont in 340, Artaxerxes III ordered the satraps of Asia Minor to send mercenary troops and supplies for the city. The Macedonians were forced to withdraw, but then moved to attack Byzantium. In October 340 Athens declared war on Philip, having secured the support of the islands of Chios, Rhodes and Cos, and, most importantly, of Persia. The Persian–Athenian alliance effectively meant that Philip's ambitions of a Macedonian hegemony over Greece could not be fulfilled. After his successes in Phoenicia and especially in Egypt, Artaxerxes had proved himself an able military leader. Persian resources, military and financial, were unlimited. Artaxerxes himself would not avoid a confrontation with Macedon, if necessary.

Figure 5   Seal of Artaxerxes III (with kind permission of The Hermitage Museum, St Petersburg)

If Philip wanted to keep Persia out of Greek politics, he had to prevent the interference of the western Asiatic satraps and therefore he decided to order a campaign to Asia Minor. In 337/6 Attalus and Parmenion were sent across the Hellespont to Asia on a first mission, but further operations were halted when Philip was killed in 336. It was left to his son Alexander III to continue his father's plans.

Artaxerxes III had died in 338, and Arses succeeded to the kingship, taking the throne name Artaxerxes IV. While Greek sources describe Artaxerxes III as a victim of a palace coup who was murdered with the aid of the chiliarch Bagoas, a Babylonian document simply states 'Month Ulul (*August/September*), Umakush (*Artaxerxes III*) (went to his) fate; his son Arshu sat on the throne' (BM 71537; Walker 1997: 22). The expression 'to go to one's fate' is a known Babylonian phrase to express a person's death, and is meant to refer to a death by natural causes. If so, then Greek descriptions of a court intrigue surrounding the death of Artaxerxes III have to be regarded with scepticism. Arses, however, does seem to have fallen victim to a coup two years later. It paved the way for a cousin of Artaxerxes III, Darius III Ochus (336–330), to succeed to the throne. Much has been made of the classical accounts that their accession to kingship was due to Bagoas, whom the sources pejoratively identify as a eunuch. But in fact Bagoas was a high-ranking official, a chiliarch. Perhaps more weight should be given to a Babylonian text, the *Dynastic Prophecy* (Grayson 35), according to which a reference is made to Bagoas as a *ša rēš šarri*. This term literally means 'he who is stationed at the head of the king'. It is well attested in Akkadian and Babylonian texts, and it appears that the office of the *ša rēš šarri* was adapted at the Persian court. It is rendered *saris* in Egyptian documents referring to Persian officials in Egypt, and equally is used in Hebrew texts as a reference to high officials, but was understood to mean 'eunuch' in the Greek sources.

After reaffirming Macedonian power in Greece Alexander defeated Persian forces in a first battle at the River Granicus in northern Asia Minor, and continued to move his army further into Persian territory. Yet his victory triggered the resolve of his enemies to launch counterattacks. Before the battle at Issus in 333 Memnon commanded a naval force supported by Chios, Lesbos and Mytilene to carry the war into Macedon. Even after the Persian defeat at Issus, King Agis of Sparta gathered a mercenary force of 8,000 ready to start a war in Greece with support from Darius III. But at Gaugamela the king's army once again suffered defeat. Darius III withdrew to the east, intent on mustering a new army to continue the fight against Alexander, while the Greeks still counted on his support against the Macedonian king. Darius' death in June 330 ended these plans. The death of the king and the capture of his son and his brother Oxyathres meant that no Achaemenid could challenge Alexander's power in Persia. One, the Achaemenid Bessus, satrap of Bactria, tried. He placed the royal *tiara* on his head, took a throne name, Artaxerxes, and proclaimed himself Great King (Arr.*an*.3.25.3), but he soon was captured by Alexander and killed.

The next seven years, until Alexander's death in 323, brought considerable unrest to the lands of the empire. Stability was only partially restored under Alexander's successors in the former Persian empire, the Seleucids. The Seleucid empire lasted for almost 100 years before they were challenged by a new Persian power, the Arsacids, in 247.

KING AND COURT

The Achaemenid king was the absolute ruler of the empire. He was the head of the political, judicial and military power. He claimed his right to rule through succession to the throne as a royal son of the dynastic line of the Achaemenids. To secure a peaceful transition of power the reigning king appointed the designated heir to the throne. Rules for the selection of the royal successor may have included the prince's birth 'in the purple', i.e., after his father's accession to the throne, and the mother's descent from a member of the Persian nobility, but other objectives, such as suitability to office, may also have influenced the king's decision. In practice, however, royal succession was often determined by factors such as the survival of court conspiracies staged by ambitious princes who did not refrain from assassinating the royal heir in order to secure the Achaemenid throne for themselves.

The Persian king was not a god-king, but he ruled with the support of the god Ahuramazda, the 'Wise Lord'. Ahuramazda was an Iranian deity whose cult was elevated to a royal religious cult at the time of Darius I. As the god's representative on earth, the Persian king ruled under his divine guidance, enabling him to act correctly in moral terms and representing the Good and the Truth (OP *arta*) against the Evil and the Lie (OP *drauga*). In this dualism we find the beginnings of the monotheistic religion which later became known as Zoroastrianism, but which at the time of the Achaemenids may more aptly be referred to as Mazdaism (see below, pp. 66–70). The early Persian kings as well as the Achaemenids were careful to accept the gods of other religions as well, recognising their importance for the subject peoples, and the political value the acceptance of other religions had for their own rule. Thus, the early Persian kings worshipped their own god(s), while also respecting Median, Lydian and Ionian gods, as well as the gods of Babylonia and of the conquered territories in the eastern part of the empire. *In extremis*, and (what must have been) in contrast to their own beliefs, they even adopted divine kingship in Egypt, where the pharaoh by the authority of office was a god. Cambyses II was noted as the restorer of the temple of the Egyptian goddess Neith in the city of Sais, and likewise Darius I was commemorated as the restorer of the temple of Hibis in Khargeh. In Asia Minor he demonstrated his respect for the Greek god Apollo by reprimanding his Magnesian satrap Gadatas for collecting taxes from the sacred land belonging to the temple.

> The King of Kings, Darius, son of Hystaspes, to Gadatas, his slave, thus speaks: I find that you are not completely obedient concerning my orders. Because you are cultivating my land, transplanting fruit trees from the province Beyond-the-Euphrates to the western Asiatic regions, I praise your purpose, and in consequence there will be laid up in store for you great favour in the royal house. But because my religious dispositions are nullified by you, I shall give you, unless you make a change, proof of a wronged (king's) anger. For the gardeners sacred to Apollo have been made to pay tribute to you; and land which is profane they have dug up at your command. You are ignorant of my ancestors' attitude to the god, who told the Persians all of the truth and [. . .].
>
> (Meiggs, Lewis no. 12; Fornara no. 35)

Under Xerxes' reign Mardonius offered to rebuild the Athenian temples destroyed during the sack of Athens, and in the reign of

Darius II delegates from Jerusalem reminded the king of the promise given by Cyrus II to finance the rebuilding of their temple after its destruction by the Babylonians. The cult of Ahuramazda was observed by the king and a selection of Persian nobles, but at the same time, the kings accepted other gods worshipped in Persis, as well as in the lands of the empire.

To secure the kingship, the Achaemenid king needed to produce numerous male offspring. In time, one of his sons was appointed heir to the throne, possibly in an official ceremony during which the heir received appropriate insignia which marked his new status, including his official royal throne name. The first duty of the heir to the throne was to conduct the funerary rites for the deceased king and to proclaim the official mourning period. The king's body was returned to Persis and was buried in a rock-cut tomb at Naqsh-i Rustam; later kings, probably due to space shortage, were buried at Persepolis. Royal fires which burnt for the king across the empire had to be extinguished, and the mourning period had to be observed.

The funerary ceremony was followed by the official investiture of the new king. From the accession of Darius I onwards this meant a royal procession of the king and his court from Persepolis to Pasargadae, where the king celebrated a ceremony before the court and delegates from the lands of the empire. He dressed in the clothes Cyrus II had worn, ate terebinth, a kind of pistachio nut, and drank sour milk in memory of the humble beginnings of the Persians, and possibly their original nomadic or semi-nomadic lifestyle (Plut.*Art.*3.1–2). As king, he then dressed in a Persian royal robe, a many-folded, long-sleeved garment held by a belt, and took the insignia of kingship, the *kitaris* (the royal headdress), his staff, the lotus flower, and a special pair of shoes (which made him look taller). Finally, the fires in the empire were relit to mark the accession of the new king.

Among the virtues of kingship counted the desire to act well morally and to prevent evil, to follow the Truth, produce multiple offspring, and demonstrate military prowess in horsemanship, archery and in using the spear. As was noted above, Cyrus I depicted himself as a soldier on horseback in victorious pursuit of his enemies. No image has yet been recovered which depicts Cyrus II, but we may assume that he would have followed the tradition of the early Persian kings. Display of excellence in military skills, including the use of bow and arrow, the use of a spear, and horse-riding, remained part of the palette of royal virtues which were upheld during the entire period of Achaemenid rule. However, the depiction of the soldiering achievements of the Persian king seems to be less significant than the visual presentation of the king as a peaceful ruler, which became a potent image of the empire at peace, the *pax persica*. In a deliberate break from Near Eastern tradition, the palace reliefs of the Achaemenid kings from Darius I onwards were characterised by the image of the king as a peaceful sovereign. In contrast to the palace decorations of the Assyrian and Babylonian kings who commemorated their victory in battle and their success in hunting, Darius I and his successors selected the image of the king seated on a throne supported by his peoples. The image which emerged as the embodiment of Persian kingship was that of the king in audience. The audience reliefs of Persepolis, originally the centrepieces of the staircase reliefs of the Apadana, depicted the king seated on a throne, his feet resting on a footstool, and bearing the royal insignia, staff and lotus flower (see Fig. 6).

The king is accompanied by the heir to the throne who takes his place behind the king, but sharing the same raised platform. Behind the king and heir two members of the royal court stand in

Figure 6   The audience relief originally from the Apadana staircase, Persepolis (photo: MB)

attendance. The king is approached by a man in Median dress, wearing trousers, a tunic and a rounded felt cap, who greets the king in the typical gesture of respect and deference, slightly bowed and holding his right hand before his mouth. This gesture was referred to by the Greeks as *proskynesis*. The scene, set under a richly embroidered baldachine, is framed by Persian guards. Very possibly this image was repeated on the palace reliefs of other royal cities, but this is only a surmise. Nevertheless, other evidence allows the conclusion that this image was widely distributed across the empire and thus easily recognised as a royal image. The audience scene can be found as seal impressions on clay tablets and *bullae* (sealed lumps of clay which were attached to documents), and was an artistic motif adapted on sarcophagi to depict local rulers.[6] Most intriguing perhaps is the rendering of this scene on the inside of a soldier's shield depicted in relief on a fourth-century sarcophagus from Sidon, the so-called Alexander sarcophagus (see Fig. 7).

Figure 7 The inside of a Persian shield depicted on the Alexander sarcophagus (drawing by Marion Cox)

The royal audience scene conveys the image of the king at peace, while at the same time expressing his willingness to be approached by his subjects. The audience scene is as important as the context within which it was set, i.e. the gift-bearing peoples of the lands ascending the staircase together with the royal bodyguards and royal servants (see Fig. 8).

But the approachability of the king was not limited to those who found their way to Persepolis and were admitted to a royal audience. To ensure that his presence was felt across the empire, the king maintained several royal residences in the capitals of conquered kingdoms, Ecbatana, Babylon and Susa. These residences were visited at regular intervals, allowing the fourth-century Greek writer Xenophon to remark that the king spent the winter in Babylon, the spring in Susa, and the summer in Ecbatana (Xen.Cyr.8.6.22) in order to enjoy the most pleasant season of each region. To visit his royal cities the king travelled with his court which formed a large entourage in the king's train. It included the royal bodyguard, the 10,000 Immortals, courtiers and court officials and their families, the king's family, including the king's mother, the royal wives and the women of the king, the children, members of the Persian nobility and their families, attendants, cooks, bakers, wine-bearers, etc. The entourage would travel on foot, on horseback, and in carriages along the Royal Road to their destination. Passing through villages and towns along the route the royal entourage provided a most spectacular sight. The sheer size of the king's entourage must have been overwhelming, but it was further enhanced by the opulence and splendour of the court. The message conveyed in this spectacle was, however, more than just the display of royalty; it demonstrated the king's presence in the empire, and showed him as the surveyor of his realm and as a king in control.

The king's men

The immediate loyal supporters of the king were members of the Persian nobility. Essentially these were formed by the male members of seven Persian households, of which that of Darius I was one. At the time of his reign they were headed by the Persians Gobryas, Otanes, Intaphernes, Hydarnes, Megabyxus and Ardumanish. These men, who had helped Darius to overthrow Bardiya and to succeed

Figure 8 North staircase of the Apadana, Persepolis (after F. Krefter)

to the throne, their descendants, and their extended families formed the Persian nobility. They had access to the court and enjoyed the right to approach the king. Their privileged status could probably be recognised by their appearance, i.e. through a particular piece of jewellery worked in Achaemenid court style, or an item of clothing dyed in a particular colour, and perhaps adorned with gold appliqués, which would identify it as a royal gift. More important, however, were the extensive links which were created between the royal family and members of the nobility by the intricate network of marriage alliances which bound the nobility even closer to the king. A royal sister or daughter in marriage counted amongst the most prestigious royal gifts. In granting such a marriage the king bestowed honour and privilege upon the nobleman, while at the same time securing his support and loyalty.

Yet the Persian nobility also identified itself through other means. With the establishment of a royal religious cult of Ahuramazda the Persian nobility was most likely privy to the religious rites and ceremonies connected with the cult. Rituals were performed by priests of Ahuramazda, but also involved the king and were witnessed by members of the nobility. Furthermore it has been suggested that the nobles were united by the common use of Old Persian. Old Persian was never regarded as a common script, either for administrative purposes or in everyday correspondence. As an exclusive script it was solely used in royal inscriptions, and it is therefore reasonable to suggest that it functioned as a 'court script', the use of which would have been limited to the noble class.

According to Darius he was the first man who ordered the Persian language to be written down. For this purpose, a new script was invented, modelled on the predominant form of writing in the Near East, cuneiform:

> Darius the king says: 'By the favour of Ahuramazda this (is) the inscription which I have made besides in Aryan. It has been written both on clay tablets and on parchment. I also wrote down my name and my lineage, and it was written down and was read (aloud) before me. Afterwards I have sent this inscription in all directions among the lands. The people strove (to use it).'
>
> (DB col. IV: §70)

Members of the nobility acted as councillors to the king. It is not known how many members formed the royal council, or indeed whether it met at regular intervals, but it is thought that it included members of the Persian nobility who had supported Darius I's succession to the throne. Existing laws were adhered to at regional level by the judges, lawyers and bailiffs of each satrapy, though the kings could implement legal reforms. Darius ordered a revision of the Egyptian laws, while Babylonian laws may have provided a model for Persian laws. At court level a group of royal judges, possibly not more than three (Diod.Sic.15.10.1), acted as legal counsellors of the king. Though it is difficult to comprehend the status of the royal judges in relation to the legal power of the king, it seems that they were empowered to proclaim a judicial verdict in cases brought forward in the royal court, but that the king had the right to overrule their judgement, as happened in the case of the trial of Parysatis for the murder of her daughter-in-law Stateira. Acquitted by the judges, Artaxerxes II found her guilty and sent her into Babylonian exile (Plut.Art.19.6).

One particular group around the king was the King's Friends and Benefactors. This group was made up of individuals or groups of peoples who were personally distinguished by the king for a particular service of loyalty or military achievement. Persians as well as non-Persians could be awarded the status of a King's Friend or a King's Benefactor. The Persians, so Herodotus, called Benefactors 'orosangae', possibly deriving from an Old Iranian term *varu sanha-, which means 'whose praise is widespread'. One group of Benefactors was the Ariaspians whom Cyrus II honoured for their support in his Scythian campaign. They were still known as Benefactors in the time of Alexander III (Arr.an.3.27.4). The King's Friends were individuals honoured by the king with royal gifts and special privileges, and could be invited to dine at the King's Table.

Without doubt a hierarchical structure existed among the Persian nobility. They were ranked according to a system of meritocracy, which meant that individuals received rewards from the king which distinguished them from one another. These rewards were given in the form of gifts. The process of gift-giving counted among the most important procedures at the royal court, and was of vital political importance in the establishment of an ever expanding network of royal supporters. Among the gifts were jewellery, such as necklaces and bracelets, adornment for horses, and bridles made of precious metal. Rarer gifts were the Median robe, such as Otanes received from Darius in recognition for his loyalty in the Bardiya affair, and a royal marriage alliance to a king's daughter, a gesture which signified reward for successful political acts of loyalty.

Royal women

Women belonging to the immediate royal family were known as *duk-shish*, 'princess', including the king's daughters, the mother of the king, and the king's wife. The latter two women took the highest ranks among the women at the royal court. Persian kings probably were polygamous, mainly in order to produce multiple offspring to secure the succession. Wives were selected from among the nobility, though marriage to half-siblings was also permitted. In addition to wives the king had a number of concubines who lived in the royal household and were part of the king's entourage. These women were of high rank, but their non-Persian origin meant that they could not be married to the king. Only in times of crisis did sons of these women succeed in securing the kingship, as happened in the case of Darius II, the son of Artaxerxes I and a Babylonian woman.

The king's wife, i.e. the wife whose son was the designated heir to the throne, as well as the king's mother, held very privileged positions at court. They enjoyed immediate access to the king, were able to join the king at public appearances, such as audiences, and were permitted to dine with the king, an extremely private occasion which few were allowed to witness. Though little archaeological evidence has survived which would demonstrate that royal women were depicted in art, Herodotus' statement that Darius had ordered a statue of his wife Artystone made of gold (Hdt.7.69.2) supports this assumption. The fact that women were depicted on seals, and are represented on a range of archaeological evidence recovered from different Persian satrapies, provides further evidence. The subject of the female audience scene is found on a Neo-Elamite seal from Persepolis (PFS 77*; see Fig. 9), and on a seal, now in the Louvre, carved in Achaemenid style (AO 22359; cf. Spycket 1980: Fig. 7).

The women's main responsibility was the welfare and security of the royal family. If the safety of a member of the royal family had been jeopardised, they pursued a harsh judgement on the responsible

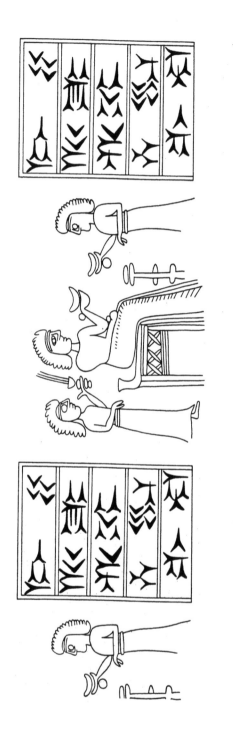

1 cm

Figure 9 Audience scene of a high-ranking woman carved in Neo-Elamite style (Composite drawing of PFS 77* courtesy of M.B. Garrison, M.C. Root, and the Persepolis Seal Project)

party with equal vigour. By the same token, if there was a dispute between the king and a member of the Persian court, leading to severe punishment of the courtier, both the king's mother and the king's wife could intervene on behalf of the noble and his family and request a more lenient punishment.

As owners of large estates, orchards and centres of manufacture for which they employed their own work forces, royal women enjoyed considerable economic independence. Irdabama, a royal woman at the court of Darius I, employed a force of almost 500 workers at Tirazzish (probably modern Shiraz), while being personally attended by just three people, who not only were referred to as 'workers of Irdabama' (Elam. *kurtash Irdabamana*), but who also bore their own title, *matishtukkashp*.

Royal women also owned properties across the empire, which are attested in Persis as well as in Egypt, Babylonia, and in Beyond-the-River. They employed their own officials who managed their estates, while bailiffs were in charge of the administrative and legal side of their businesses. To authorise their orders regarding the payment of their workers and the distribution of the produce from their estates, royal women used their own seals. Apart from land, they also owned villages; according to Herodotus (2.98.1) the king's wife owned a village in Egypt which was responsible for manufacturing the queen's shoes, and Parysatis, the wife of Darius II, was known to have owned villages in Media (Xen.*an*.2.4.27). Royal women travelled across the empire, not only as part of the king's entourage, but also in their own right, visiting their estates and private residences, accompanied by their personal attendants and servants. They travelled in their own carriages, providing a comfortable space for long overland journeys and protecting them from heat and dust. Their ability to travel and their economic independence are a far cry from the Greek notion that Persian women lived in the seclusion of the palace, hidden away from the outside world.

The status of noble women reflected that of royal women, even if on a smaller scale. As members of the Persian nobility, or indeed as descendants of the royal family, they, too, were members of the royal court and could hold high positions at the satrapal court. They participated in the satrapal entourage, and indeed travelled in the king's entourage. Like the royal court, the satrapal court included married wives as well as concubines (cf. Polyaenus 7.18.1).

Royal pursuits

Hunting was a royal pursuit of the king and members of his court. Hunts were staged in vast royal enclosures in which wild animals, such as leopards, lions and boars, as well as deer, gazelles and ostriches, were chased across the enclosure for the hunt (see Figs. 10 and 11). They not only served to exercise one's hunting skills, but also served to practise military skills in using different weapons, spears, daggers, and bows and arrows. But hunting was also conducted in the wild, outside the 'organised hunt', offering a challenge to the hunters' stamina and endurance. In addition, hunts fostered a sense of identity amongst the nobility. While it was important for the king to demonstrate his hunting abilities, military skills, courage and physical fitness to his court, the social aspect of the hunt will have been at least of equal importance. A hunt provided an opportunity for the nobleman to ingratiate himself with the king, affirm, if not improve, his status among his peers. It was not always easy to find the right balance between demonstrating one's skill and at the same time adhering to court etiquette, which prescribed that no one was to surpass the king. This, however, happened in the case

Figure 10   Seal of Darius I from Egypt (drawing by Marion Cox)

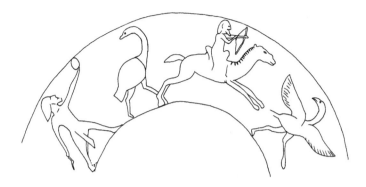

Figure 11   Persian seal depicting an ostrich hunt (drawing by Marion Cox)

of Megabyxus, who, when trying to save the king from the attack of a lion, took the first shot at the animal, but thereby violated the king's privilege to shoot an animal before anyone else. There is some indication that women were able to join the hunt, for Amestris, the daughter of Artaxerxes II, was said to be very skilful with bow and arrow. Other royal women may simply have participated in the hunt as part of the king's entourage, while female musicians joined the hunt as part of the court's entertainment.

Apart from hunting, banqueting was one of the most important court activities. Banquets have a long tradition in the civilisations of the ancient Near East, and the Persian kings continued this custom. The banquets were political as well as social occasions; their duration and their opulence, the number of the guests as well as the variety of the foodstuffs served, were a demonstration of the king's power, and equally, if held at local level, a demonstration of the satraps' power (see Fig. 12). Royal official banquets were held on special feast days celebrated by the king, such as the king's birthday, the royal investiture, the anniversary of the beginning of the king's reign, and possibly the Persian New Year, which began in March.

Private royal banquets included selected members of the court who were invited to dine with the king. The king's wife and sons were particularly privileged on occasion by being allowed to dine together with the king. To be invited to sit at the King's Table was an extraordinary honour, because it signalled a special closeness of the member of the nobility to the king. The extraordinary occasion of the banquet is described by Heracleides of Cumae:

Figure 12 Persian banquet scene on an ivory from Demetrias, Greece
(with kind permission of Sir John Boardman)

All who attend upon the Persian kings when they dine first
bathe themselves and then serve in white clothes, and spend
nearly half a day on the preparations for the dinner. Of those
who are invited to eat with the king, some dine outdoors,
in full sight of anyone who wishes to look on; others
dine indoors in the king's company. Yet even these do not
eat in his presence for there are two rooms opposite each
other, in one of which the king has his meal, in the other
his invited guests. The king can see them through the
curtain at the door, but they cannot see him. Sometimes,
however, on the occasion of a public holiday, all dine in a
single room with the king in the great hall.

(Heracleides FGrH 96, Athenaeus 4.145b)

For the King's Dinner the meat of several hundred large cattle was
served, as well as lamb, gazelle, and birds such as geese and turtle-
doves. Different kinds of wheat and barley were prepared to bake

46

breads and cakes, and a variety of oils, spices and herbs were ordered for cooking. Wine was the main drink at a banquet, though beer may also have been served. It is quite possible that royal women held their own banquets, as is indicated in the case of Artystone, the wife of Darius I, who, on one occasion, received 2,000 quarts of wine ($\approx$ 2,000 litres) and 100 sheep from the king's estate, which may have been used for a special celebration. In another instance, recorded in the Book of Esther, the king's wife celebrated a feast for the women while at the same time the king held a banquet for the male members of the court.

ORGANISATION AND ADMINISTRATION OF THE EMPIRE

In order to control the vast Achaemenid empire it was essential to operate a highly sophisticated and efficient organisation. This was a world empire, of hitherto unprecedented geographical dimensions, political power and economic resources. The conquered kingdoms and principalities had to be governed as one entity, requiring a political organisation on a scale for which there was no precedent or model. What was in place, however, in the highly developed societies of Egypt, Mesopotamia, the Levant and Asia Minor, was an administrative tradition which had already been developed over several millennia, and it was one of Cyrus the Great's most ingenious decisions to leave the existing administration of the conquered lands in place, rather than imposing a Persian model on them. However, one innovation made by Cyrus was the introduction of a governor to head each conquered land. This governor was called a 'satrap' (OP *xshaçapāvan*) which means 'protector of the realm'. In the very early phase of conquest the satraps and other high officials could be recruited at local level. Thus, the Lydian Pactyes was placed alongside the Persian satrap Tabalus as treasurer, but when he rose in revolt against his new overlords, Cyrus ordered a Persian contingent to fight his rebel supporters and capture Pactyes alive. Despite the risk involved in appointing non-Persians to high office, Cyrus was not deterred by the Lydian episode and appointed the Babylonian Ugbaru as satrap after the conquest of Babylon in 539. But, following the accession of Darius I, the satrapal office was given

to members of the royal family. A number of cases point to a preference for brothers of the king being appointed to the office, but
other relatives, like the king's cousins and nephews, as well as sons-
in-law, could be selected. In some cases the satrapal office passed on
to the satrap's son, and even developed into a dynastic position, but
this was always subject to the king's approval and not a sign of
satrapal independence.

The satrap ruled the province, or satrapy, as the king's representative. He resided in his own satrapal palace set amidst a park. He
maintained his own court and entourage, and enjoyed the same royal
activities, i.e. banqueting and hunting, for which he kept his own
enclosures or paradises. He enjoyed the privileges of being the royal
representative of the king, albeit on a smaller scale. His duties
included the managing of the satrapal administration, collection of
taxes, overseeing the satrapy's commerce and trade, and mustering
military forces if and when required. In the event of political unrest
in a province, the king ordered the governors of the neighbouring
satrapies to levy troops and quash the rebellion. A satrap was able
to make political decisions at regional level, but had to consult the
king on any major issues. Thus, Artaphernes, the satrap of Sardis,
consulted Darius I on the question of a campaign against Naxos.
Other responsibilities will have included the observation of royal
court duties, such as celebrating royal feast days, maintaining the
royal fire, and observing the royal religious cult. Like the king, the
satrap may have held audiences for delegations from his satrapy or
for foreign ambassadors seeking his support in political or military
matters.

Satraps were not the only governors in the empire. City-kings or
tyrants ruled in the coastal cities of Asia Minor and in the city-states
of Cyprus and Phoenicia. They exercised their power within the
walls of their city, while pledging allegiance to the Persian king,
and offering the same services as the satraps, including the collection of taxes and the mustering of military forces.

High officials working under a satrap could be recruited at local
level, enjoying considerable status within the administration. One
of the best examples of the co-operation between Persians and non-
Persians is the Egyptian Udjahorresnet, who had already served
under the pharaohs, but continued to hold high office under
Cambyses II and Darius I:

(. . .) The one honoured by Neith the Great One, the mother of the god, and by the gods of Saïs, the prince, count, royal seal-bearer, sole companion, true king's acquaintance, his beloved, the scribe, inspector in the assembly, overseer of scribes, great leader, administrator of the palace, commander of the king's navy under the King of Upper and Lower Egypt Ankhkare (*Psammetichus III*), Udjahorresnet; engendered by the administrator of the castles (of the red crown), chief-of-Pe priest, *rnp*-priest, he who embraces the Eye of Horus, priest of Neith who presides over the Nome of Saïs, Peftuaneith. He says: 'The Great King of all foreign Lands, Cambyses, came to Egypt, and the foreigners of all foreign lands were with him. He rules the entire land. They made their dwellings therein, and he was the Great King of Egypt, the Great King of all foreign Lands. His Majesty assigned to me the office of chief physician. He caused me to be beside him as a companion administrator of the palace. I made his royal titulary, his name being the King of Upper Egypt and Lower Egypt Mesuti-Re (*Cambyses*).

(Brosius 2000: no. 20)

The peoples of the empire

The Achaemenid empire comprised about thirty lands. In addition to the Persian heartland, Darius I listed the following lands in an inscription from Susa:

Darius the king says: 'By the favour of Ahuramazda these are the countries which I seized outside Persia: I ruled over them, they brought me tribute. They did what I told them. My law held them firm. Media, Elam, Parthia, Aria, Bactria, Sogdiana, Chorasmia, Drangiana, Arachosia, Sattagydia, Gandara, Sind, Amyrgian Scythians, Scythians with pointed caps, Babylonia, Assyria, Arabia, Egypt, Armenia, Cappadocia, Sardis, Ionia, Scythians from Across-the-Sea (*Black Sea*), Skudra, *petasos*-wearing Ionians, Libyans, Ethiopians, men from Maka, Carians.'

(DSe §3)

These lands were populated by different ethnic groups of peoples and tribes, each of which spoke a different language or dialect, with each group pursuing its own culture and religion. Not all of these peoples were settled in urbanised centres; some were pastoralists or migrating peoples living a nomadic or semi-nomadic lifestyle. Owing to the lack of written evidence recovered from the eastern part of the empire it is assumed that its society was still predominantly based on oral tradition, in contrast to the literary traditions of Mesopotamia and Asia Minor. While this may have been the case it must be taken into account that the satrapal organisation would have made an impact on the eastern provinces of the empire, and that Persian administrative record-keeping practice was introduced at least in the satrapal centres.

The Persians had no wish to impose their language, culture and religion on their subjects, and instead allowed each ethnic group to retain its cultural identity and heritage. The reason for this attitude was political expediency. It was a way of integrating the different peoples by not appearing as an oppressing power, and instead recognising the value of ethnic identity. It was also an effective way of limiting regional opposition and rebellion against the king. It meant that multilingualism formed a vital part of Persian administration, with official documents being copied in bi- or trilingual scripts. Satrapies like Egypt and Babylon continued to conduct their administration in the same way as they had done before the Persian conquest, possibly with gradual adjustments. This had the effect of continuity within the administration since bureaucratic procedures were not disrupted and the scribes, one of the most important classes in ancient society, had no reason to feel resentment against the new government. Our best example for the continuity of the administrative routine comes from Babylon, where administrative texts continued to be written in Babylonian cuneiform script in both the public and the private sphere. Babylonian scribes are even attested in Persepolis where, presumably, they were in charge of the Babylonian section of the royal archives.

Aramaic, a Semitic script, was used in the western part of the empire, but because it was predominantly written on parchment, only a few documents have survived. It has been suggested that Aramaic became the official imperial language in the later period of the Achaemenid empire, an assumption which has been made on the basis of the apparent absence of cuneiform tablets dated later than the reign of Artaxerxes I (465–424/3). However, this is an argument *ex silentio*; bearing in mind the limited extent of excavations in royal and satrapal centres, and the even more limited finds of archival material for the Achaemenid period, it seems more appropriate to keep an open mind on the issue of bureaucratic change.

Administration of Persis

The administrative centre for Persis was the royal capital Persepolis. Here, during Darius I's reign, Parnaka, the king's uncle, headed the administration, supported by a core of assistants, amongst them a man called Zishshawish, and a battalion of lower administrators and scribes. Parnaka controlled all incoming and outgoing goods, grains, wine, beer and livestock for Persepolis and the royal storerooms across the region. His control also extended over the workforce of Persepolis, officials travelling on official business from all parts of the empire to the king, expenses for the celebration of religious rites and foodstuffs for animals. Cylinder and stamp seals were impressed on administrative documents to serve as official signatures authorising food transactions and distributions. Few seals have survived, but they were usually made of semi-precious stone such as carnelian, agate, lapis lazuli and rock crystal. Cylinder seals had a long, rounded shape through which a hole was drilled to secure the seal on a string or chain, which would be worn around the neck, while stamp seals were encased in a fastener made of gold or silver, terminating in a ring. The stone was engraved with an image, predominantly depicting a Persian motif, i.e. the royal hero in combat with wild or mythical beasts, and sometimes bore an additional inscription identifying the owner of the seal.

While Parnaka and Zishshawish authorised the distribution of materials and foodstuffs, countless scribes and low-level administrators recorded the processes involved in the documentation. An order from Parnaka to provide certain foodstuffs from a royal storehouse to an individual, a group of workers or animals meant that the store manager needed a copy of the order while keeping one copy to file for his own records.

Tell Harrena, the cattle chief, Parnaka spoke as follows: '75 sheep (are) to be issued to Appizaknush and his companion(s), (who are) *tidda* makers. Let them give it as *sat* (*an extra ration*) to workers subsisting on rations (at) Urandush. In the 20th year (*of Darius*), for a period of 3 months. 544 *pasha* women whose apportionments are set by Shuddayauda; 176 workers whose apportionments are set by Marduka; 30 workers, makers of *W.GIR.lg* whose apportionments are set by Shashadu. Total 751 workers. Mushka wrote the text. He received the *dumme* (*copy?*) from Nanitin. There is 1 sheep for each 30 (workers).'

(PF 1794; PFS 9)

Monthly accounts were made on the basis of the individual receipts and were eventually checked by royal accountants. These administrative processes reflect a sophisticated system of record-keeping which ultimately derived from a centuries-old archival tradition of the Near East, which to this day is testimony to a highly developed society. Of course, errors were made, scribal as well as accounting errors, but they do not diminish the achievement of such a complex administrative system.

Among the recipients of foodstuffs were the workers of Persepolis who were involved in the construction of the royal terrace and the surrounding city. The workers included whole families, men, women and children, who lived in nearby villages, and who received monthly food rations as payment for their work. By all accounts the workers of Persepolis, called *kurtash*, were free labourers. They were drawn from different ethnic backgrounds, including Egyptians, Babylonians, Greeks and Persians. Their work ranged from unqualified labour to highly specialised craftsmanship including stone-masons, workers in precious stone, gold- and silversmiths. A refined system of ration scales reflects the fact that workers were paid according to their level of qualification within their profession, distinguishing the workforce between male and female workers, and boys and girls. Children were probably paid according to their age and their ability to contribute to the workload. A typical document recording a monthly payment would read:

5,280 quarts of grain supplied by Manukka, *abbakkanaš* workers, Irmyziyans, of Irdabama, whose apportionments are set by Rašda, subsisting on rations, received as rations,

for a period of 6 months. Year 22 (*of Darius*). 10 men each
30, 2 boys each 25, 3 boys each 20, 3 boys each 15, 1 boy
10, 1 boy 5. 18 women each 20. 1 girl 15, 3 girls each 10,
1 girl 5, total 43 workers. For 1 month they receive 880
quarts of grain.

(PF 849; PFS 36)

Two issues are especially noteworthy when looking at the ration
payments for workers. A female chief of workers, the so-called
arashshara, seems to have headed work groups across the villages in
Persis. Her extraordinary position was reflected in the highest
monthly ration of 50 quarts of grain, 30 quarts of wine and ⅓ of a
sheep given to a labourer. Women also seem to have received particular attention with regard to motherhood. Female labourers who
gave birth were entitled to receive a special ration for one month,
consisting of flour and wine. What is intriguing is that mothers of
sons received twice the ration amount of mothers of girls, reflecting
not necessarily a preference for boys, but the idea that mothers of
male offspring needed more nourishment.

Royal Roads

After administration the most crucial factor assuring the smooth
running of the empire was a good infrastructure. The Achaemenids
drew on an already existing road system which had connected Asia
Minor and Assyria as early as the second millennium BC. They
extended this system to connect the main cities, the satrapal and
royal centres across the empire. The most important of these Royal
Roads was the one which led from Persepolis via Susa to Babylon
and from there to northern Iran, where the route split into a northern
route leading through Cappadocia and a southern route through
Cilicia to Lydia and its capital Sardis. In its eastern extension, one
route led from Persepolis to Ecbatana in Media, and from there went
around the Caspian Sea eastward towards Bactra and then further
east into Central Asia, while another route led south via Arachosia
towards the River Indus and the satrapies of the southeast. A further
road connected Egypt with the centre via Jerusalem and Damascus,
from where one route led north towards Asia Minor, and another
east to Media.

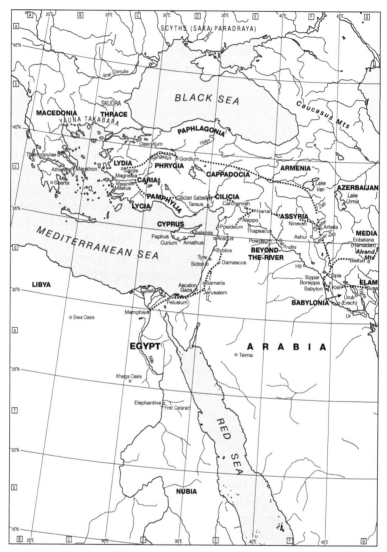

Map 2 The Royal Roads of Achaemenid Persia

Distances were measured in a Persian unit called a *parasang* which was 5–6 km. At intervals of 25–30 km the Achaemenids maintained road-stations which provided food and shelter. The Greek historian Herodotus provides us with a description of the Royal Road leading from Susa to Sardis:

54

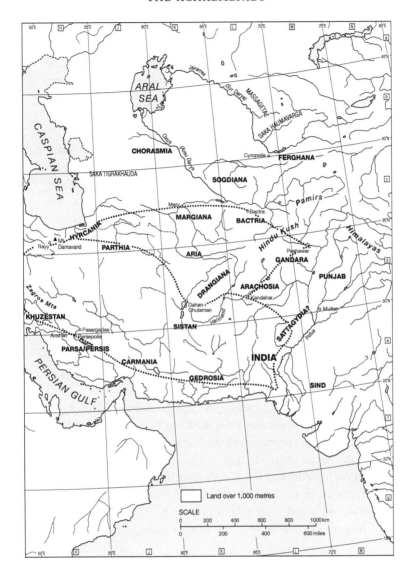

The nature of this road is as I shall show. All along it are the king's stages and very good hostelries and the whole of it passes through country that is inhabited and safe. Its course through Lydia and Phrygia is of the length of 20 stages and 94½ parasangs. Next after Phrygia it comes to the River Halys where there is a defile, which must be passed before the river can be crossed, and a great fortress to guard it. After the passage into Cappadocia the road in that land as far as the borders of Cilicia is of 28 stages and 104 parasangs. On this frontier you must ride through two defiles and pass two fortresses; ride past these and you will have a journey through Cilicia of 3 stages and 15½ parasangs. The boundary of Cilicia and Armenia is a navigable river the name of which is Euphrates. In Armenia there are 15 resting stages and 56½ parasangs, and there is a fortress there. From Armenia the road enters the Matienian land where there are 34 stages and 137 parasangs. Through this land flow four navigable rivers, that must be crossed by ferries, first the Tigris, then a second and a third by the same name, yet not the same stream nor flowing from the same source; for the first mentioned of them flows from the Armenians and the second from the Matieni; and the fourth river is called Gyndes, that Gyndes which Cyrus once parted into 360 channels. When this country is passed the road is in the Cissian land, where are 11 stages and 42½ parasangs as far as yet another navigable river, the Choaspes, whereon stands the city of Susa.

Thus there are 111 stages in total. So many resting stages there are on the journey from Sardis to Susa. If I have rightly numbered the parasangs of the Royal Road and the parasang is of 50 furlongs' length (which assuredly it is), then between Sardis and the King's residence called Memnonian (*Susa*), there are 13,500 furlongs, the number of parasangs being 450; and if each day's journey be 150 furlongs, then the sum of days spent is 90, neither more nor less.

(Hdt.5.52–53)

Economic texts from Persepolis record that messengers and their transport animals were in the service of the king and his officials to carry messages to and from the king. The messengers were called *pirradazzish*, which means 'fast messenger', and their horses were express horses (Elam. *ANSHE.KURRA pirradazzish*). The messenger was entitled to a daily ration of flour and wine from the royal storehouses along the Royal Road. Other travellers were delegates and the satraps themselves, who journeyed from the satrapies to the king. One of them was Abbatema, probably the satrap of India, who received a daily ration of 70 litres of flour, while his twenty attendants each got 20 litres per day for a journey from India to Susa in the spring of 499.

> 110 quarts (of) flour Abbatema received. (For) his own rations daily he receives 70 quarts. 20 men receive each 20 quarts. He carried a sealed document of the king. They travelled from India. They went to Susa. Month 2, Year 23 (*of Darius*). Ishbaramishtima is his elite guide. The seal (of) Ishbaramishtima was applied (to this tablet.).
>
> (PF 1318; PFS 49)

This unique system created by the Achaemenid kings was effectively the first postal system known in history, and as such evoked the admiration of the Greeks:

> Now nothing mortal travels faster than these couriers, by the Persians' skilful contrivance. It is said that the number of men and horses stationed along the road equals the number of days the whole journey takes – a man and a horse for each day's journey; and these are stopped neither by snow nor rain nor heat nor darkness from accomplishing their appointed course with all speed.
>
> (Hdt.8.98)

The Achaemenid empire was first and foremost a land empire, and most traffic will have passed overland via the Royal Roads. Yet naval routes also existed, particularly off the eastern Mediterranean coast where Phoenician and Cilician trade ships were docked. Another route went from the Red Sea to the Gulf of Oman and from there via the Indian Ocean to the mouth of the River Indus. It was Darius I who furthered naval progress by completing the construction of a canal linking the Red Sea with the Nile, a construction which had begun under the Egyptian Pharaoh Necho (610–595) but had remained incomplete. Twelve stelae were set up along the 84 km-long canal to commemorate its construction. In the inscriptions, written in four languages, including Egyptian, Darius proudly declared: 'I ordered the digging of the canal from a river called Nile which flows in Egypt, to the sea which begins in Persia. Afterwards this canal was dug just as I ordered, and ships passed through this canal from Egypt to Persia, as I had wished' (DZc §3).

The army

The first Persian empire was based on the military strength of the army of Cyrus II, yet very little is known about its size and make-up, though it can be safely assumed that the strength of the army was the cavalry, which allowed it to cover vast distances quickly. How did Cyrus gather enough forces behind him to fight the Median king Astyages? How did he control the Lydian and Babylonian forces? How strong was the cavalry, how strong the infantry? It is difficult to provide answers to these questions. Yet clearly Cyrus commanded a considerable force when he confronted the army of Astyages. He himself must have commanded the respect of his soldiers and exercised charismatic leadership in order to pursue twenty years of almost continuous conquest with an army which increasingly incorporated contingents from the conquered lands. Presumably, with the fall of the greatest military power of the time, Assyria, Cyrus and his army stepped into a military vacuum.

It is probably fair to say that the cavalry formed the backbone of the early Persian army. The Persians, like other Iranian peoples, had a long tradition of horse-breeding, and possession of horses was one way of evaluating their social status and worth. Horse riding counted among the virtues of a good Persian. The rider fought on horseback equipped with a short dagger, bow and arrows, and javelins or spears. The riding costume, trousers and tunic, was complemented by a soft felt cap, with flaps which allowed him to cover his mouth protecting him from dust and sandstorms, and a sleeved coat worn as a mantle, the *kandys*. In addition to the cavalry, soldiers fought riding on camels, while elephants were used to frighten the enemy's horses.

The army was headed by a *karanos* who had overall command, and a *hazarapatish* (Gr. *chiliarch*) who commanded one division of 1,000 men, which again was divided into 10 battalions. Each battalion was subdivided into 10 companies of 10 soldiers each. The soldiers fought with weapons similar to those of the riders, but in addition carried wicker shields as a defence weapon. The infantry was probably divided into units of spearmen and archers.

The most famous unit in the Persian army was the Ten Thousand. They were known as the 'Immortals' because their number never diminished; if they suffered any losses, the soldiers were immediately replaced to complete the unit. Of the Immortals one division served as the king's bodyguard, and was distinguished by its members carrying spears with apple-shaped ends of gold. The spears of the remaining 9,000 Immortals were decorated with silver pomegranates.

The core of the army consisted of Persians, with ethnic units added as necessary. The king, and later on the satraps also, employed Greek mercenaries. Apart from the 10,000 Immortals in the immediate vicinity of the king, there was a royal cavalry of equal size. Garrisons were stationed across the empire to protect the cities, the roads and the borders of the empire. The most famous of these garrisons is probably the Jewish garrison at Elephantine. Jewish mercenaries had been in Egypt since c.650 and had served under Egyptian pharaohs in their battle against the Assyrians. Following the Persian conquest of Egypt in 525 the Jewish soldiers came under the command of the Persian king. At Elephantine they protected the borders of the Achaemenid world. No records attest to their presence beyond 399, a year after Egypt was in full revolt against the Persian empire.

In addition to the military core centred on the king, the army also included ethnic units comprising men from different lands of the empire. They were led by Persian commanders, but they were organised in ethnic groups, fighting with the weapons they were best able to use. Thus we find the famous Scythian chariots, and the Scythian horsemen and bowmen, the Bactrian cavalry and camel-riders, and even Greek soldiers fighting as hoplites. The use of Greek mercenaries in the Persian army has often been remarked upon as a sign of military weakness and dependence on foreign soldiers. This seems to be emphasised by the fact that the use of Greek merce-naries seemingly increased in the fourth century. Yet this practice must be put in perspective. Mercenaries from Caria and Ionia had been used as early as the archaic period, when they hired their ser-vices to the pharaohs of Egypt. With the development of the hoplite army this became the most effective form of infantry and brought

Sparta to the forefront of military repute. Arguably the increased use of mercenaries has less to do with a weakening Persian army, than with the economic situation in Greece which had been ravaged by the cost of the Peloponnesian War (431–404) and the continued fighting between the Greek city-states throughout the fourth century. If the Persian kings and their commanders employed Greek mercenaries, it was because of their reputation as an effective infantry force, and they were used as one among many other units. The use of mercenaries itself does not necessarily point to the military decline of the employing state, although it certainly demonstrates a state's preference for 'imported' troops, instead of using its own people, as well as its ability to pay for them.

While the Achaemenid kings emphasised the image of the Persian empire at peace, underlying this image was a military capability which at no point was to be doubted. Of the king's virtues his ability to fight as a soldier was most important:

> This indeed is my courage as far as my body possesses the strength; as a commander I am a good commander; immediately, the right decision is taken according to my understanding when I meet a rebel, and when I meet (someone who is) not a rebel, at this moment, due to my understanding and judgement, I know that I am above panic when I see a rebel as well as when I see (someone who is) not a rebel. I am trained in my hands and in my feet; as a horseman, I am a good horseman; as a bowman, I am a good bowman, both on foot and on horseback; as a spearman, I am a good spearman, both on foot and on horseback.
>
> (DNb §8–9)

The king was a good king because he was a soldier who could fight in battles, defeat his enemies and win victory for the empire. The imagery on the Achaemenid coinage shows a royal archer, a Persian man in a half-kneeling, half-running position shooting his arrow. The only violent depiction seen in Persepolis is that of the royal hero in combat with a wild beast, but the royal hero is already victorious, because the beast has been mortally wounded by his dagger (see Fig. 13).

The king also took central position in the battle line. He stood in a chariot, dressed in a purple-coloured *chiton*, trousers and *kandys*,

Figure 13   The royal hero on a palace doorway at Persepolis (photo: MB)

wearing the upright *tiara* on his head. On each side the king was surrounded by 1,000 spearbearers, the 10,000 Immortals and 10,000 cavalry. In front of the king's battle line were the scythed chariots; he was followed by the rest of the army.

The king's presence in battle was, however, not required in every military conflict. While the foundations of the empire undoubtedly lay in the military prowess of Cyrus II and Cambyses II, the military involvement of the Achaemenid kings ceased with the consolidation of empire and the absence of an outside threat. Darius I still led the campaigns against the European Scythians and India, but internal conflict within the empire was left to his commanders. Thus the Ionian rebellion of 498–492 BC was quashed by Artaphernes, son of the satrap of Sardis, and Datis, a Median commander. They were even put in charge of the punitive campaign against Naxos, Eretria and Athens. Xerxes may have been involved in the quashing of the Egyptian rebellion of 487/6 and the Babylonian rebellion of 482, before embarking on the march on Greece and the attack on Athens, but we do not know for certain. The satraps of adjacent satrapies and their commanders were usually ordered to fight neighbouring rebels. Only a few internal conflicts were considered sufficiently crucial for the security of the empire that they demanded the king's involvement. One frequent centre of conflict was the tribe of the Cadusians in northern Iran, which resented Persian supremacy. The most disturbing conflict threatening Achaemenid kingship was undoubtedly Artaxerxes II's fight against his younger brother Cyrus, who gathered an army of his own to challenge the king. It was an extreme measure, far more threatening than previous palace intrigues, since it involved the recruitment of an army. It is the first known instance since Darius' accession to the throne in 522 BC of an individual in a position of power and able to finance an army, using his power against an Achaemenid king.

But despite further rebellions, the involvement of the king in battle was not considered necessary until Artaxerxes III decided to lead the army against the rebellious Egyptians in 342. Both cases were of grave concern for the monarchy. In the first case, the fraternal struggle posed an immediate threat to the stability of the empire, and Artaxerxes II could not be seen as failing to defeat his rebelling brother. In the second case Egypt had been in rebellion from Persia since 404/400 despite a series of Persian military campaigns to quash the revolt. It was only when Artaxerxes III decided to take matters into his own hands that Egypt came once again under Persian domination. The Macedonian invasion under Philip's commanders Parmenion and Attalus into Persian territory, as well as Alexander's first attack on Persia at the River Granicus, was opposed by local satraps and their forces, but once the imminent threat was recognised, Darius III led his army at Issus and at Gaugamela.

It also needs to be emphasised that the Achaemenid empire had not been faced with any external threat until the Macedonian invasion. For 230 years no power had existed which could challenge the empire. Upheavals came from within, through rebellions in individual satrapies. In the case of Egypt this was probably caused by the fact that it had once been a mighty kingdom in its own right but lost its independence to foreign rule. In most cases, however, rebellion was stirred by the accession of a new king, the weakest period of power, after the old king had died and when the new king was not yet established, or, as happened in the fourth century, when individual satraps attempted to create their own power base in their satrapy, not directly contesting Achaemenid kingship, but making a bid for personal power in their region.

This was possible in part because satraps had the responsibility to recruit an army from their province on the king's request. They therefore had the resources, rations and/or money to pay the soldiers, a power which gave them a degree of independence from the king. Satraps could be, but were not necessarily, the head of their army section. Quite often we find that the military commanders of ethnic units were different from the local satraps, although they, too, were members of the immediate or extended family of the king.

RELIGION

The Persians regarded the natural elements, earth and sky, water and fire, as well as rivers and mountains, as sacred, a belief shared with other Iranian peoples like the Medes, as well as with the Elamites. Sacrifices were made by pouring libations before sacred fires which burnt on an altar, or by offering animal sacrifice (see Fig. 14). The most precious animal which could be offered was a horse. No temples have been found which can be dated to the Achaemenid period, and we must assume that Persian rituals were conducted in sacred precincts, such as can be found in Pasargadae and Persepolis.

The early Persians worshipped many gods. On his campaign to Media Cyrus II first sacrificed to the Persians gods, and, after crossing the border, performed another sacrifice for the gods of the Medes. In Babylon he claimed the support of the city-god Marduk, restored his cult and performed the appropriate rituals. Similar celebrations may have been performed for the city-gods of other Babylonian cities

Figure 14   Seal from Persepolis (PFS 75) (drawing by Marion Cox)

during the Babylonian conquest. We can assume that the gods of the Lydians and Ionians were similarly respected by Cyrus II.

With respect to Egypt the Persians kings assumed the title of pharaoh and, in accordance with Egyptian cultural and religious belief, were regarded as gods. As pharaohs Cambyses II and Darius I bore the epithet Mesuti-Re, 'Son of Re' (the Egyptian sun god). Udjahorresnet, the chief physician and administrator of Cambyses II, turned the king's attention to the re-establishment of the temple of the goddess Neith at Saïs, which had been neglected:

> His Majesty commanded to purify the temple of Neith and to return all its personnel, the [. . .] and the hour-priests of the temple. His Majesty commanded that offerings should be given to Neith the Great, the mother of the god, and to the great gods who are in Sais, as it was before. His Majesty commanded (to perform) all their festivals and all their processions, as had been done since antiquity.
>
> (Brosius 2000: no. 20)

In the same way that Cyrus II had reinstated the cult of Marduk in Babylon, his son wanted to be seen as a restorer and preserver of religious cults. This is a far cry from the image given in the Greek sources, an image dominated by Cambyses' disrespect for foreign cults. Here he is being accused of sacrilege, killing the sacred Apis bull in a deliberate act of wilfulness and contempt for other religions. The facts, however, were different. Cambyses buried the Apis bull which had died in 524 with all appropriate honours in the necropolis, the Serapeum. He commemorated the bull with an epitaph inscribed on a stele in Egyptian hieroglyphs:

[Year] 6, third month of the season of Shemu, day 10(?)
(*November 524*), under the Majesty of the King of Upper and
Lower Egypt, Mesuti-Re, given life forever. The god was
taken up [in peace towards the perfect West and was laid to
rest in his place in the necropolis], in the place which His
Majesty has made for him, [after] all [the ceremonies had
been performed for him] in the Hall of Embalming. Sets of
linen were made for him [. . .], there were brought [to him
his amulets and all his ornaments in gold] and in all precious materials [. . .] temple of Ptah, which is within Hemag
[. . .] ordered [. . .] towards Memphis, saying: 'You may lead
[. . .].' All was done that His Majesty had ordered [. . .] in
year 27 [. . .] (of Apis) in year [. . .] of Cambyses [. . .].

(Brosius 2000: no. 21)

The policy of accepting and supporting foreign cults and religions
continued under the Achaemenid kings, beginning with Darius I.
In the satrapies other religions flourished, while in Persis itself a
whole variety of gods were worshipped. In Egypt, Darius performed
the necessary official duties for the burial of the Apis bull that died
in 514. At el-Khargeh Darius rebuilt the temple of Amun-Re, and
in Saïs he restored the House of Life:

His Majesty did this because he knew the worth of his craft,
in making all that are sick live, in making the names of all
the gods, their temples, their offerings, and the conduct of
their festivals endure forever.

(Brosius 2000: no. 54).

Xerxes continued Darius' policy of demonstrating respect for
other religions across the empire. In Athens, Mardonius had the
authority to propose the rebuilding of the temples which had been
destroyed in the sacking of the city in 480, while in Babylon the
cult of Marduk continued to be upheld since Cyrus' days. Herodotus'
claim that Xerxes committed a sacrilege by removing the statue of
Marduk from the temple has been revealed to be a misinterpreta-
tion, since only the statue of a man was removed from outside the
temple. However, as a result of the rebellions in Babylonia, Xerxes
seems to have exerted a much tighter control on the country, which
might also have affected Babylonian temples.

The Achaemenids and the cult of Ahuramazda

While there is no concrete evidence for the celebration of the cult of Ahuramazda at the time of the early Persian kings, it rose to prominence following the accession of Darius I. Here we find our first evidence, mainly in the royal inscriptions, that Ahuramazda was the principal god of the Achaemenid royal dynasty: 'Ahuramazda is a great god, who created this earth, who created the sky, who created man, who created happiness for men, who made Darius king, one king among many, one lord among many' (DSf §1). Ahuramazda, the 'Wise Lord', was the god who installed the king in power, who guided him, and who made him act in a truthful and moral way. Though the king was not a god himself, he was no less than Ahuramazda's representative on earth. The forces opposing Ahuramazda and the king were the Lie and acting in a morally wrong way. Though Ahuramazda was the principal god of the Achaemenids, he was not the only god. Inscriptions of Darius also include references to 'the other gods', though these are not specifically mentioned. The reference is too ambiguous to determine whether these include only other Iranian gods or the gods of the peoples of the empire. We do know, however, that in Persepolis itself other gods were worshipped. In addition to the worship of mountains, rivers and lakes, we find references to the cult of Elamite gods like Humban, and Babylonian gods like Adad. The gods were served by two different groups of priests, *shatins* and *magi*, who conducted the ritual and performed sacrifices.

It seems that at a later stage, probably during the reign of Artaxerxes II, two further Iranian gods were elevated to the royal religious cult alongside Ahuramazda, Mithra, the sun-god and god of treaties, and Anahita, the goddess of water and fertility. We know very little about the cult ritual for any of these gods, i.e. how they were worshipped and who their followers were. Artaxerxes is also said to have set up statues of the goddess in the royal cities of the empire, Babylon, Susa and Ecbatana, as well as in Persis, Bactria, Damascus and Sardis (Berossus FGrH 680 F11). This is not an unproblematic reference, since its author, Berossus, does not actually name Anahita, but refers to the Greek goddess Aphrodite, with whom Anahita may or may not have been identified in the Hellenistic period. This particular reference is furthermore problematic in that it claims that the Persian king set up statues of divinities. The difficulty is that so far excavations have yielded no statues of any Persian deity. Rather, on the basis of other evidence referring to religious rituals of the Persians, it seems that they did not make images of their gods. Having said this, the figure in the winged disc featuring so prominently on the reliefs of Achaemenid monumental architecture, including the royal tombs at Naqsh-i Rustam, has been identified as Ahuramazda, but another interpretation suggests that the figure represents Achaemenes, the eponymous founder of the empire. Most likely, however, is the suggestion that the image of the figure in the winged disc represented the 'good fortune', *khvarrah*, which symbolised the special status of the Achaemenid dynasty on which Ahuramazda had bestowed the kingship (see Fig. 15).

The worship of a sun-god and a goddess of water comes as no surprise in a country where both elements are held in high regard, as they dominate agricultural life and determine the well-being of its people. Water and water supply were crucial in the hot and dry regions of Persis, and indeed in the whole empire. The establishment and development of water channels, drainage systems and irrigation channels was essential for the preservation of human and animal welfare. The Persians' creation of extensive gardens was the epitome of their ability to defy nature and to create sources of water even in dry areas, allowing the cultivation of seemingly non-arable land.

Figure 15   The royal *khvarrah* in the winged disc, Persepolis (drawing by Marion Cox)

Two important questions surround the cult of Ahuramazda: first, were the Achaemenids, if not Cyrus II and Cambyses II, already followers of Zoroastrianism, and second, who were the followers of the royal cult? Zoroastrianism, the religion preached by the prophet Zoroaster, is a religion characterised by the dualism between Good and Evil, Truth and Lie, presented in the good god, Ahuramazda, and Ahriman, the evil god. Men's lives are a struggle between these two powers, but they hope to achieve redemption and enter paradise after death. The sayings of the prophet were collected in the Avesta, the Holy Scriptures, a collection of different texts used in Zoroastrian ritual. The earliest manuscripts are based on a text which cannot be dated before the ninth/tenth century AD, though historical evidence attests to the fact that the Zoroastrian religion was practised at the time of the Sasanians. There can be no doubt that elements of Zoroastrian beliefs are included in the Achaemenid cult of Ahuramazda, but it was probably far removed from the pure religion established in later centuries.

The Persians, like the Elamites, believed in many divinities, represented in the natural elements and celestial constellations. These were combined with a pantheon of Iranian deities, whose cults had been introduced to Persia over the long period of migration from the east and northeast. Ahuramazda, like Mithra and Anahita, was one such deity, whose cult probably originated in the eastern part of the Persian empire, but only received an exalted status under the Achaemenid kings beginning with Darius I. This religion is probably best described as Mazdaism, the belief in Mazda, the Lord.

Throughout Achaemenid rule the cult of Ahuramazda remained the principal royal cult of the Persian kings. As Greek writers tell us, the spiritual presence of the god was symbolised in an empty chariot, driven alongside the king's chariot in the battle line of the armies of Xerxes and Darius III. This image was to signify that the god was the protector of the king and guarantor of peace or victory in battle. But it is important to note that the god was the god of kings; never, it seems, did his cult become a common cult celebrated by the peoples of the empire, either through imposition from above or through its adaptation from below. The cult of Ahuramazda was a cult celebrated by the kings, and therefore practised in the royal cities, with a group of priests in charge of upholding its rituals. A different question is whether, in addition to the king, the cult was observed by the Persian noble class. This means not only the immediate members of the royal court who travelled in the king's entourage, but the Persian nobility in the satrapal centres of the empire. Were they bound to uphold the royal cult as part of their duties at their satrapal court? Were they privy to attend, if not conduct, the ritual for the cult of Ahuramazda? Their access to the royal cult would confirm their status as the king's representatives in the satrapy, while at the same time it would signify their closeness to the king, which in turn would enhance their exalted status.

The Achaemenids did not impose their religious royal cult of Ahuramazda on other peoples. Instead, the cults and religions of other peoples, however diverse, were accepted. Having said that, there was, however, a limit to this seeming 'religious tolerance', and it was linked with political issues. While the Achaemenids followed the policy that the loyalty of their subjects was best procured if their cultural and religious environment was left undisturbed, things changed drastically when this loyalty was not given. A case of revolt or uprising of a people against Achaemenid rule was not only answered with military force, but its effects rippled into people's lives as well. Short of resettling the populace, an attack on people's religious cults was regarded as an appropriate measure of punishment. As has been noted above (p. 23) this punishment was exacted on Naxos, which had resisted Persian attempts to be incorporated into the empire, as well as on Eretria and, in 480/79, on Athens.

Rebelling satrapies like Egypt and Babylon may well have felt religious repercussions too, after trying to resist Persian supremacy in the 480s. Maybe this is where we can place Xerxes' *daiva*-inscription:

> Among these countries there was a place where previously demons (OP *daivas*) had been worshipped. Afterwards, by the favour of Ahuramazda, I destroyed that sanctuary of demons, and I made a proclamation: 'The demons had been worshipped.' Where previously the demons had been worshipped, there I worshipped Ahuramazda in accordance with Truth reverently.
>
> (XPh §5.)

Here Xerxes refers to a country in rebellion which had worshipped demons. He destroyed their sanctuaries and proudly announced that he now worshipped Ahuramazda in this country instead. This is a difficult inscription to understand, not only because we do not know which country Xerxes is actually referring to, but also because of the difficulty of determining which tense is being used in the inscription. Therefore it is possible that Xerxes speaks only in general terms: *if* a country follows a religion (which turns the country against the Persian king), *then* I will eliminate that religion and establish my power (i.e. worship Ahuramazda) in its place. Yet in any case, it is important to note that the cult of Ahuramazda will not be imposed on the people, but that Xerxes will worship Ahuramazda there – a significant distinction.

The Jews in the Achaemenid empire

In the Books of the Old Testament the Persian conquest of Babylon was seen as a blessing. In his campaigns against Jerusalem the Babylonian king Nebuchadnezzar (Bab. *Nabu-kudurri-usur*) had deported Jewish prisoners of war to Babylon where they had lived in exile since 598/7. When Cyrus conquered the kingdom, he ordained that the Jews be allowed to return to their homeland and gave them permission to rebuild the Temple in Jerusalem which had been destroyed in the Babylonian raid. This political decision has always been regarded as a particularly generous act of the Persian king which signalled the special status of the Jews and the high regard in which they were held by the Persians. Yet Cyrus' treatment of the Jewish exiles in Babylon has nothing to do with a particular concern for the Jewish religion. Rather, their case is an example of the Persian policy of controlling resistance against Persian rule through acceptance of local religions and cults. His attitude towards them was in no way different from his attitude towards other peoples and religions. The permission to allow the rebuilding of the Temple in Jerusalem has to be seen in the same light as his care for the restoration of the cult of Marduk in Babylon or Darius' rebuilding of the Hibis temple at el-Khargeh. Care for the restoration of public buildings was one of the virtues of a king. Royal duty prescribed that the king needed to be seen to improve a city, enhance its splendour and increase its welfare. The rebuilding of the Jewish temple was nothing more or less than that. What makes this case interesting is the fact that the rebuilding took a number of years and was still ongoing at the time of Darius II, for Cyrus' decree regarding the temple building had to be retrieved after construction had come to a temporary halt under Artaxerxes I and a letter was sent to the king requesting further funds for the building work, claiming that this was what Cyrus had promised the Jews. A copy of the decree was eventually found in Ecbatana and construction commenced once again.

In 410 the Jews stationed in the Persian garrison at Elephantine in Egypt were confronted with a different problem. Widranga, the governor of Syene, the city on the shore opposite Elephantine, had been bribed by the priests of the temple of Hnum, adjacent to the Jewish temple, to disrupt their rituals and damage the temple. In the absence of the Persian satrap Arsames, the Jews wrote to the governor of Judah, Bagohi, to report on the atrocities and demand the reinstatement of their temple so that their religious services could be continued. But three years later, in 407, the temple had still not been rebuilt, and once again they wrote to Darius II to ask for help. This episode reveals an interesting issue. While the Egyptian priests may have been intolerant towards the Jews and their religion, it is perhaps more likely that they resented the presence of the Jewish garrison in Elephantine and sought to disrupt their lives as much as possible.

Funerary customs

Though it should be noted that the funerary architecture of the early Persian kings was different from that of the Achaemenid kings, it was always important that the king's body was returned to the homeland, to Persis. Cyrus' tomb was erected in his city of Pasargadae. Its distinctive architecture appears to reflect an indigenous Iranian design, but there is a possibility that it may have been influenced by Lydian tombs, such as the so-called tomb of Alyattes from Sardis. Majestic in its simplicity, his tomb is a single-chambered building with a gabled roof which is placed on a six-stepped platform hewn out of huge blocks of stone (see Fig. 16). Its total height is 11 m, achieving perfect proportions through an equal height between the height of the steps and that of the tomb chamber

Figure 16   The tomb of Cyrus II at Pasargadae (photo: MB)

itself. The king's body was probably embalmed and then clothed in royal splendour, and adorned with the king's crown and royal insignia, before being laid in a coffin placed on a couch. He was provided with vessels and other objects to equip the body for a funerary symposium in the afterlife. Similar examples of such single-chamber tombs exist in Iran; but perhaps most intriguing is the unfinished tomb near Persepolis, of which only the raised platform is preserved. This may have been the tomb-site Cambyses had intended for his own burial, but the succession troubles following his early death could have altered any such arrangement.

The distinctive architecture of the early Persian kings changed with Darius I. His tomb, and those of his successors, established a new form, the rock-cut tombs, designed in a cross shape, which were set up in the rock façade of a mountain face close to Persepolis (see Fig. 17).

ART AND ARCHITECTURE

Persian art of the sixth to the fourth centuries BC is defined by the art of the early Persian kings, best exemplified in the site of Pasargadae, and the art of the Achaemenid kings, beginning with

Figure 17   Achaemenid royal tomb at Naqsh-i Rustam (photo: MB)

Darius I. While the architecture and the decorative reliefs at
Pasargadae reflect more explicitly Cyrus' attempt to incorporate
different elements from the conquered lands into the artistic design,
Persepolis takes this a step further, and in synthesising artistic
elements from Egypt, Babylon, Elam, Media, Urartu and Ionia/
Lydia, the Achaemenids created a unique court style. An innovation

of Darius I, it was adhered to by his successors until the end of Achaemenid rule, and while Persepolis epitomises Achaemenid royal art, this new style was also applied to the palace architecture of the royal residences at Susa, Ecbatana and Babylon.

The most stunning building on the royal terrace of Persepolis is undoubtedly the Apadana, the Throne Hall, of Darius I. Columned halls, known from the Median sites such as Nush-e Jan and Godin Tepe, were the basis of Achaemenid palace architecture, in which audience halls and private palaces, as well as treasuries, were laid out in a square or rectangular plan with columns reaching 20 m high. The fluted columns were Greek in style, but their bases, resembling lotus flowers turned upside down, followed Egyptian influence. These columns were topped with stone capitals which were completely Iranian in design. They were carved in the shape of bull-heads or the heads of griffins. Set inside these capitals were wooden planks which supported ceilings made of cedar wood.

The staircases leading to the Throne Hall are decorated with reliefs showing the delegations of the peoples of the empire bringing gifts to the king: textiles, weapons, such as daggers, jewellery, objects made of precious metal, such as cups and vessels, and animals, such as horses, lions, zebus and onagers. These delegations are joined by Persian palace guards and the courtiers of the king (see above Fig. 8). The Persian nobles, who are also depicted on the inside of the staircase, appear at ease, not at all apprehensive of meeting the king, but seemingly looking forward to the occasion (see Fig. 18).

The calmness of the Persian nobles and the ordered but relaxed appearance of the delegations of the peoples are part of the image of an empire at peace. The doorways of the palaces and other royal buildings show scenes of the king walking in procession through the palace, accompanied by parasol bearers, or with personal attendants carrying perfume bottles and towels. Others show the king seated on his throne, which itself rests on a huge throne supported by the peoples of the empire. The image is repeated in the reliefs of the Achaemenid tombs at Naqsh-i Rustam and at Persepolis itself. It is a figurative expression which declares that the king enjoys the support of the people, that his kingship is being upheld by his subjects. It is, in short, the image of 'pax persica'.

To this day the function of Persepolis remains a mystery. While some scholars have defended the argument that it was a purely

Figure 18 Persian nobles ascending the staircase at Persepolis (photo: MB)

religious site, this is not borne out by the evidence on the ground. No building or space can be identified on the terrace which would allow the conclusion that the terrace had a religious function. Instead, the gift-bearers, the royal audience scene and the profane motifs depicted in the doorways, showing the king seated on his throne or in procession, are far removed from any religious context. Besides, the archive of Persepolis attests to the everyday activities of a regional centre, in which the emphasis is being placed on tax-collection and administrative organisation rather than religious activities. By all accounts the royal terrace of Persepolis had a cere-monial function, and the gift-bearing peoples of the empire may provide the best clue for the function of the city. Whether they depict a real or an ideal situation is indeed immaterial. But what they do show is the fact that this was a place where the king received the subjects of his empire, where the royal bodyguard stood to atten-tion, and royal courtiers ascended the steps to join the king, while servants, dressed in Median dress, prepared food for a vast feast, car-rying sheep and goats, wineskins and vessels filled with foodstuffs.[7]

Though the monumental Achaemenid art seems dominant, Achaemenid court style was also apparent elsewhere, most promi-nently in vessels, vases, cups and bowls made of precious metal or stone. While the king controlled the gold and silver mines, and thus controlled the workshops which were allowed to produce objects worked in the Achaemenid court style, these were used as models for the production of luxury objects at local level in the satrapies of the empire. Ample finds from Egypt, the Levantine coast, Asia Minor and the Caucasus region testify to the fact that the vessels, cups, weapons and jewellery were crafted regionally following the Achaemenid court style. Owing to the looting of the royal treasuries during the conquest of Alexander III, few objects have been recovered from the Achaemenid centres themselves. Most of the extant examples, therefore, come from the satrapies of the empire, including finds such as the Oxus Treasure and those from Pazyryk in Siberia,[8] as well as from the border regions of the empire in the sub-Caucasus.

These finds still inspire awe and admiration for their aesthetic beauty, the quality of the design and their exceptional craftsmanship. Vessels were made in gold and/or silver, with handles crafted in an anthropomorphic design, featuring ibexes, lions, winged griffins. Objects were often inlaid with precious stone, turquoise, lapis lazuli and carnelian, brought from all corners of the empire to be used by the artists.

EXCURSUS I: THE CREATION OF 'THE OTHER': THE PERSIANS AND THE GREEK–PERSIAN WARS

Few historical events can be recalled which shaped historical views and historical tradition over the centuries in such a profound manner as the Persian Wars. The history of these wars was written by the victors, the Greeks. In doing so, they created not only a sense of 'the Other', but also a collective identity of the Greeks as 'Hellenes'. The Greek–barbarian antithesis became more pronounced by singling out Persia as the epitome of the barbarian, and, by the second half of the fifth century BC, the enemy *par excellence* (Wiesehöfer 2002: 213). The conflicts of 490 and 480/79 then became a historical symbol for the fight of democracy versus monarchy, freedom versus despotism, and beyond that, of Europe versus Asia, and, ultimately, of the West versus the East. How did this come to be?

For the Greeks the battle of Marathon soon became engulfed in myth, while the victories at Salamis and Plataea received a religious dimension. According to Herodotus Themistocles proclaimed the historic triumph to have been achieved not by men, but by gods and heroes (Hdt.8.109.3). The poet Simonides invoked the tomb of the men who fell at Thermopylae as an 'altar' (Simonides, frg.531 PMG), while Pericles placed the men who fell for the city on a level with the immortal gods (Plut.*Per*.8.9). Cults were instituted to keep the memory of the victories alive, including the cult of Pan the goat-god, who had appeared to the runner Philippides on his way to summon Spartan help at the time of Marathon (Hdt.6.105), the cult of Boreas, the north wind which had damaged the Persian fleet (Hdt.7.189), and, later on, the cult of 'Pheme', rumour, which miraculously spread announcing the victory of the Greeks at Eurymedon (Aesch.1.128; 2.145).

Monuments were erected in commemoration of the wars, including the *stoa poikile*, an open gallery, with paintings featuring the battle of Marathon, the fight between Theseus and the Amazons, the capture of Troy, and a contemporary battle at Oenoe between Athens and Sparta (Paus.1.15).[9] When Aeschylus' tragedy *The Persians* was performed in 472, the Persian king was depicted as a weak and decadent despot, a notion which was soon transferred to describe the empire as a whole.

But it is at the time of the Athenian empire and the growing conflict with Sparta that the image of Persia as the enemy became most strongly expressed. Internal conflicts are often dealt with by focusing on the foreign threat. Within a deeply divided Greek world, first through the Peloponnesian War, and then through the strife for hegemony which characterised much of fourth-century Greece, political unity was to be achieved under the slogan of the 'freedom of the Greeks of Asia', which was appropriated first by the Spartans, and later on by Philip of Macedon and Alexander the Great. In this way the image of Persia as the enemy was fostered until the end of the empire in 330 BC, and the Persian Wars provided the vital event on which to hinge Greek unity, Greek civilisation and superiority against the barbarian, despotic Persians.

As Anthony Spawforth has discussed in a highly illuminating article, the theme of the Persian Wars was adapted by the Romans, who saw themselves as the heirs of the Greeks and the Macedonians, who had taken up the baton to defend the West from eastern despotism.[10] For the Romans the Greek–Persian Wars became a means of propaganda to justify Roman campaigns against the East. The terms 'Persians', 'Parthians' and Sasanians' were used indiscriminately by the Romans to refer to their eastern 'enemy' (see also below, pp. 136–138). But what truly turned Marathon, Salamis and Plataea into world-historical events was the philosophy and historiography of the nineteenth and twentieth centuries.[11] Hegel introduced the notion of the moral and intellectual triumph of the individuals of the Greek city-states over the unfree mass of Asiatic peoples ruled by a single despot, the only free person of his state. Greek triumph over Persia thus embodied the triumph of the 'free world' over the enslaved East. This notion became the standard view of nineteenth-century accounts of Greek history, and shaped much of the classical scholarship of the twentieth century. It is explicit in statements such as the following, made by the eminent historian Barthold Georg Niebuhr:

> One of the particular traits of the Persians of ancient times is their highly unruffled servitude and subservience; a Persian man has never been a free and proud man, but it is the greatest difference between Persians and Arabs, and even between Persians and Kurds, who are related. (. . .) At the same time the Persians are exceptionally cruel. (. . .) The orientals are an evil and morally corrupt people through and through . . .[12]
>
> (transl. after Niebuhr 1847: 155)

3

THE PARTHIANS
(ARSACIDS)

PRELIMINARY REMARKS

An unwarrantedly negative and suspicious attitude towards
the Parthians appears strangely widespread among scholars,
with whom Parthians, at bottom, have never been popular:
in the case of Iranists, because of the absence, perhaps, of
adequate historical sources originating from the Parthian
empire that might have engaged their attention by providing sound evidence of the specifically Iranian cultural
conceptions of the Arsacids and of the continuity of these
conceptions between the Achæmenids and the Sasanids, in
the case of the archaeologists, because of the heterogeneity,
perhaps, of the culture of the countries of the Parthian
empire, though such a view overlooks the fact that precisely
this heterogeneity is one of the reasons for the cultural
greatness and vitality of this empire.

(Invernizzi 1998a: 47)

The observation made by Antonio Invernizzi pointedly sums up the
problems we face when trying to understand the history and culture
of the Parthian empire. Despite the fact that this empire existed for
almost 500 years, from the mid-third century BC to AD 224, our
knowledge about its history and its peoples is far from complete.
To a large extent this is because of a lack of historical texts from
Parthia itself, which would allow us to reconstruct a historical narra-
tive from primary sources. Archaeological evidence sheds some light

on Parthian royal capitals and other sites of the empire, but – partly because of present-day political circumstances – excavations have been carried out to a limited degree only. Above all, we are to an extreme degree dependent on external – and overwhelmingly hostile – sources to provide us with an outline of Parthian political events. Further difficulties arise from the fact that some of the places mentioned in the Greek and Roman sources have not yet been identified with certainty. Available ancient reports often mention the royal cities and other important sites of the empire only in passing and do not provide extensive descriptions of the places themselves, or of the events with which they were connected. The best primary source we possess for the Parthian empire is coins, which allow us, often in the absence of any other data, to establish a chronology for the kings of Parthia, and to deduce some information about them through the images and legends used on their individual coins. Their findspots as far away as India and Russia furthermore provide some indication of the extent of the economic exchange between Parthia and its neighbouring countries.

The consequence of having to rely mostly on Greek and Roman sources is that we look at the history of the Parthian empire from the outside and through the eyes of its most fervent enemies, the Seleucids and the Romans. Over a period of time the Seleucids lost considerable domains in the eastern part of their empire to the Parthians, while at a later stage the Romans, in their relentless pursuit of expansion and world domination, repeatedly invaded Parthian territory east of the River Euphrates, which came to be officially acknowledged as the natural border between the two realms. Yet with the Parthians the Romans were faced with an opponent whose power and military strength were those of a world empire at least equal to Rome, and for two and a half centuries they resisted Rome's attempt to move the borders between the two realms. However much contempt Rome displayed for its Asian enemy, as an empire Parthia constituted a political power with a determination to rule and preserve its existence which was comparable to that of Rome. Only the Chinese sources, which for the first time record contact with the western world, provide less opinionated observations on Parthia (Chin. *An-hsi*) and her peoples.

HISTORICAL SURVEY

Introduction

When the Parthians emerged as a new political power in the second half of the third century BC they did so in a world which had undergone considerable changes in the political make-up of the ancient Near East since the end of the Achaemenid empire. The changed political landscape had been brought about by the Macedonian conquest of the Achaemenid empire between 336 and 323, and the dissolution of Macedonian power under the Successors of Alexander, which led to the foundation of the Seleucid empire in the former Persian territories in western Asia, from Asia Minor to Syria and the Iranian plateau. The easternmost provinces of Achaemenid Persia came under the control of the Mauryan empire which controlled the territories of the Indus basin. The administration of the Achaemenid empire provided a model for the Seleucids who maintained the satrapal organisation of the provinces. However, the Seleucids' ability to consolidate their government and maintain control over the satrapies was impeded by the constant rivalry with the Ptolemies, as well as by fraternal wars among the Seleucids themselves. These upheavals eroded the foundations of empire and resulted in increasing attempts by local satraps and dynasts to strive for independence. In particular this affected the western part of the Seleucid empire, Asia Minor. In the east, the Seleucids suffered their greatest losses when, in 239, the Seleucid ruler of Bactria, Diodotus, broke with the empire and founded the Greco-Bactrian kingdom which was to last for more than a century. About the same time Andragoras, satrap of Parthia, revolted from Seleucid rule, but his bid for independence was cut short by the rise of the Parthians under Arsaces.

External threats to Seleucid rule had begun with the Gaulic invasions of Asia Minor in 278/7. Further migrations of the Scythians, nomadic peoples from the Eurasian steppes, brought additional instability into the territories. Themselves forced to find new pastures due to the occupation of their border territory by a people called the Tocharians, Scythian tribes invaded Seleucid territory from the north and northeast. Finally, Roman intervention in Asia Minor, which began in the second century BC, further added to the political and military pressure on the Seleucids. The coinciding events of the migrations of nomadic or semi-nomadic peoples and the political instability, caused largely by individual ambition for power, which obscured the vision for long-term strategies and political alliances, had a profoundly destabilising effect on the world of the Successor kingdoms in the third and second centuries BC.

Parthia's rise to power was intrinsically linked with the Seleucids, but as an empire it met an even more determined enemy in the Romans. From the early first century BC until the beginning of the third century AD Parthia remained a constant enemy of Rome. Unable to accept an empire as powerful as itself, and myopically treating Parthia as yet another barbarian region which had to be conquered, over the next centuries first Roman Republican generals and then Roman emperors led campaigns against the East, at overwhelmingly great cost in human life, in return for, if any, short-lived territorial gain. Most of the campaigns were led in the region of the Euphrates, the river which formed a natural border between the two empires, but control of Armenia, a crucial buffer state, became a constant cause of strife and war. Armenia was to remain the political punchbag between Rome and Persia throughout the Parthian and the Sasanian periods.

Yet unlike the Roman empire, for which Parthia was the only political opponent of comparable status amongst its barbarian enemies, the Parthian empire was aware of its position amongst other great powers. Apart from the Greco-Bactrian kingdom, China emerged as an empire when it united under the Han Dynasty (206 BC–AD 220). For the first time in its history, it initiated contact with the outside world, leading to the establishment of diplomatic and commercial relationships with Parthia, and through Parthia with Rome. Both China and Parthia were at one stage or another threatened by invading hordes, the Huns. These Huns had forced other nomadic tribes westward into the Greco-Bactrian kingdom, where some of them settled and even founded a new realm, the Kushan empire (c.128 BC–AD 99). The fact that Parthia was set amidst these different powers inevitably affected its foreign policy, and indeed will have shaped Parthia's own identification as an empire set amidst other major powers.

The beginnings

The empire of the Parthians stretched from the Euphrates in the west to Central Asia and the borders of Bactria in the east. It possessed a rich and varied culture, which, at its centre, revealed distinctive Iranian influences deriving from the former Achaemenid empire and from the peoples of Central Asia, as well as Hellenistic and Seleucid influences. The political, social, administrative, cultural and religious outlook of the empire was multicultural, combining the imperial heritage of the Achaemenids and the Seleucids with the cultural tradition of the Iranian peoples of the steppes.

The Parthians based their own identity on these foundations, expressed in a gradual change of a linguistic preference from Greek to their own language, an increasingly explicit Iranian identity in kingship, as well as in art and literature, and in their economy and military power. They were innovators in architectural design, and their technical and military advancement was unrivalled in the contemporary world. The Chinese emperor sought their military alliance in his battle against invading hordes, and Parthian horses were one of the most important export goods to China. Although the basis of Parthian economy was agriculture, they also developed an excellent sense for commerce and trade, especially for luxury goods. It made them one of the leading countries responsible for a worldwide market, created through the opening of the Silk Road, which connected the world from China to Rome and from Turkmenistan to the Arab peninsula.

Parthia had been a satrapy of the Achaemenid empire, and, after its collapse, became a Seleucid province with the city of Shar-e Qumis/Hekatompylos (Chin. *Ho-tu* or *Fan-tou*) as its capital. Other cities, like Asaak, were located across the mountain ranges of the Kopet Dağ and Binalut. Parthia bordered on Hyrcania on the southeastern shore of the Caspian Sea and the desert Dasht-e Kavir in the south, while the River Oxus probably formed a natural border in the northeast. In the third century BC, more than 700 years after the migration of the first Persian peoples to the Iranian plateau, a nomadic tribe called the Parni, or Aparni, crossed into the northern border of Parthia. The Parni were an Iranian-speaking people who belonged to a larger confederation known as the Dahae. After a period of an apparently peaceful settlement in Parthia the Parni adopted the name of the province, and became subsequently known to the outside world as Parthians. With their establishment as a political power the term 'Parthia' became a generic term for their empire as a whole, and the term 'Parthians' for the many different peoples which inhabited it.

The Parni-Parthians also adopted Parthian, a northwest Iranian language, as their official language. It was distinct from another Iranian language, Middle Persian, which was spoken by the Persians of Persis. Parthian became the official court language, and remained so well into the Sasanian period. However, it must be emphasised that the Parthian empire was multi-ethnic and multilingual, where Parthian and Middle Persian were spoken alongside Aramaic, Babylonian, Greek, Armenian, Sogdian and Chorasmian, amongst others.

The emergence of the Parthians as a new world power in the ancient Near East was a gradual process which took over 100 years. Parthian control was first limited to the region north of the mountain range of the Kopet Dağ, with Asaak as its regional centre. It was in this city that the leader of the Parthians, Arsaces, was crowned king.

> Beyond [Hyrcania] is Astauene, 60 *schoeni* (*c.630 km*), in which there are 12 villages in which there are stations; and the city of Asaak, in which Arsaces was first proclaimed king; and an everlasting fire is guarded there.
>
> (Isidore of Charax, *Parth.Stat.* 11)

In line with Achaemenid and Seleucid traditions, and as an expression of his political ambition, Arsaces introduced a new dating era, the Arsacid era, in 247. Arsaces' name became the designated title for the kings of Parthia, who referred to themselves as 'Arsaces' in preference to their personal name. As the eponymous founder of the empire, Arsaces also gave his name to the royal dynasty, and references to the 'Arsacid dynasty', or the 'Arsacids', are therefore interchangeable with the denominations 'Parthian dynasty' and 'Parthians'.

After the Parni's settlement of northern Parthia, Arsaces made a first attempt to expand southward into Margiana, a province of the Seleucid empire. In response to this military aggression the Seleucid king sent an army under the command of his general Demodamas against Arsaces and forced him to retreat. Yet some time before 246 Arsaces made a second incursion into Margiana, only to be forced out once again, this time by Diodotus, the Seleucid satrap of Bactria.

Unable to expand his power southward, Arsaces moved into central Parthia. His decision to do so may have been facilitated by several events which affected the Seleucids' ability to launch a successful counterattack. This chain of events was triggered by the death of the Seleucid king Antiochus II in 246, which prompted Ptolemy III of Egypt to challenge Antiochus' successor Seleucus II and invade Syria and Mesopotamia in the hope of expanding his power. Ptolemy III's invasion triggered the so-called Third Syrian War (246–241) which forced Seleucus II to concentrate his forces for the next five years on the western part of his realm. His preoccupation with the war provided an opportunity for two Seleucid satraps, Diodotus of Bactria and Andragoras of Parthia, to rebel against Seleucid rule and proclaim their independence. Seleucus II was unable to respond instantly to these rebellions. However, when Andragoras was faced with a rebellion within his own realm, he found himself without Seleucid alliance to provide military support. Arsaces used this vulnerable position to his advantage, and in 239/8 Andragoras was killed. Arsaces now controlled the entire province of Parthia and its capital Hekatompylos.

From Parthia Arsaces advanced west into Hyrcania. Potentially, he had to expect military opposition from Seleucus II or even Diodotus I, but once again, political events worked in his favour. Diodotus I died in 234, and his son and heir, also named Diodotus, entered an alliance with Arsaces. As defectors from the Seleucid empire they both recognised the advantage of mutual military support against a potential Seleucid attack. Yet, during the eastern campaign of Seleucus II, the king succeeded in expelling Arsaces from Parthia, who was thus forced to take refuge with the tribe of the Apasiacae to the north towards Chorasmia. But soon afterwards Arsaces led a victorious counterattack against Seleucus' army. Due to further unrest in the west Seleucus II was unable to maintain a military presence in Parthia. Seleucid power was further threatened when a civil war broke out between 222 and 220, in which Seleucus' successor, Antiochus III (223–187), was confronted with a rebellion of Molon, the governor of Media. He quashed the rebellion and brought Media back under Seleucid control. In eastern Iran the establishment of the Greco-Bactrian kingdom still rested on fragile foundations, as became apparent when, in 221, Diodotus II was killed by Euthydemus, who then assumed power.

Arsaces died – apparently a natural death – in 217 and was succeeded by his son Arsaces II (217–191). He continued his father's policy, maintaining control of Parthia and Hyrcania, while confronting military reprisals of Antiochus III. In 210/9 Antiochus III launched an extensive eastern campaign, intent on regaining control of both provinces, as well as Bactria (Justin 41.5.7; Polyb.10.28–31; 10.49; 11.34.1–11). Despite initial successes, however, Antiochus III ceased his campaign after reaching an agreement with the Parthian king. Arsaces acknowledged the supremacy of the Seleucid king, but Antiochus III recognised Arsaces' rule by bestowing on him the title of king (Gr. *basileus*) (cf. Sherwin-White, Kuhrt 1993: 199). Under Arsaces' successors Phriapatius (c.191–176) and his son Phraates I (176–171) Parthian control remained uncontested.

Establishing an empire

With the reign of Mithridates I (171–139/8), a brother of Phraates I, the history of Parthia entered a new phase of growing political power and geographical expansion. The death of Diodotus II signalled the end of the Greco-Bactrian alliance with Parthia. Indeed, it appears that the relationship between the two kingdoms deteriorated to the extent that sometime between 160 and 155 Mithridates I conducted a campaign against the Bactrian kingdom, taking control of two regions, Turiva and Asponius (Strabo 11.11.2). Westward expansion resulted in Parthian control of Media, where Mithridates I deposed the Seleucid governor Timarchos and installed a Parthian called Bacasis in the capital Ecbatana (Justin 41.6.7). From Media Mithridates I moved south towards Mesopotamia, where he took control of the neighbouring cities of Seleucia and Ctesiphon.

In the province of Elymais in Khuzestan Mithridates I found considerable opposition, however. In October/November 145 the leader of the Elymaians, Kamniskares, attacked Babylonian cities, which at that point were under Seleucid control, and was met with a counteroffensive in June/July 144. After Mithridates had taken control of Babylonia, the Elymaians attacked Apamea-Silhu in 141, demonstrating their resistance against the Parthians. This power struggle continued into the reign of Phraates II, at least until May/ June 138.

Despite the political unrest, Babylonia recognised Mithridates I as king by summer 141, and an official investiture ceremony held in Seleucia signalled the beginning of Parthia's imperial power:

> [Against him] (*the Seleucid king Demetrius Nicator*) Arsaces the king (*Mithridates I*) [went] to Seleucia. [The city of . . ., of] the land of Assur, which before the face of Arsaces the king [had bowed down], . . . [Into Seleuci]a, the royal city, he entered; that month, on the 28th day, [he sat on the throne]. Year 171 (*Seleucid era*), Arsaces the king, on the 30th of the month Du'uzu (*9 July*)(. . .).
>
> (BM SH108; Kugler 1907–35, vol. 2: 442)

Expressing the growing confidence of kingship, Mithridates' coins minted in Seleucia showed the Parthian king no longer wearing the soft cap, but the royal diadem (see Fig. 19). Ctesiphon became the royal centre of the empire, while the foundation of Mithradatkert/ Nisa in Parthia proper emphasised the province's recognition as the homeland of the Parthians.

Figure 19 Tetradrachme of Mithridates I, Seleucia (courtesy of the Bibliothèque Nationale de France, Paris)

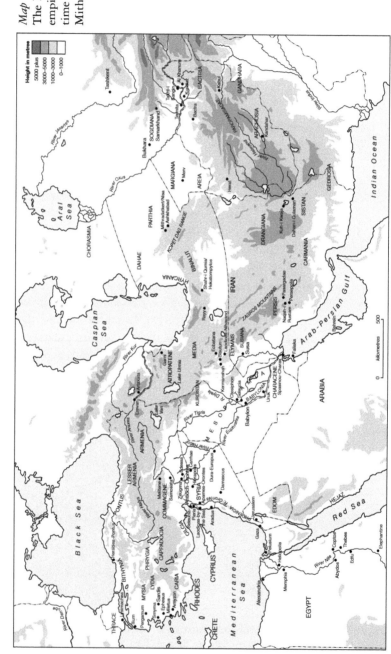

Map 3
The Parthian
empire at the
time of
Mithridates I

Shortly after the conquest of Media Mithridates I returned with his army to Hyrcania to fend off an attack by invading nomads from among the Scythian tribes. These tribes had been forced to give up their territory after attacks from the Tocharians, probably identical with the Yüeh-chih, who had emerged from the eastern steppes in search of new land. A result of these raids may have been the first measure to secure the Parthian frontier, the construction of a defence wall in Hyrcania, north of the Gurgan River, which extended eastward from the Caspian Sea over a distance of 170 km.[1]

But the withdrawal of his army from Mesopotamia created a military weakness which allowed the Seleucid king Demetrius II Nicator (145–141) to regain control of Mesopotamia. In a way, these events epitomised the conundrum Parthian kings (and the Seleucids before them) were faced with throughout their rule: the difficulty of controlling the vast borders and territories of the empire and conducting wars on two fronts. The king was the leader of the army in war, but two fronts necessitated a military commander who could be entrusted with a sizeable army to fight the king's cause, but who would not abuse his military position to obtain power. The latent threat of wars on two fronts may explain to some extent why the Parthians endeavoured to reach a diplomatic solution before resorting to military conflict. In this case, however, a Parthian force was dispatched to fight Demetrius II Nicator, who was defeated and taken prisoner. Mithridates I treated the Seleucid king with honour and even gave him his daughter Rhodogune in marriage. This may have been a symbolic gesture which served to legitimise Mithridates' political takeover of Seleucid power.

Within his thirty-year reign Mithridates I had changed the political landscape of the Near East and established Parthian imperial power. With his successful expansion of the empire, and, more importantly, his ability to maintain control over the newly gained territories, he had changed Parthia from a small kingdom east of the Caspian Sea to an imperial contender for Seleucid power. His successors, Phraates II (139/8–128) and Artabanus I (128/7–124), were able to maintain control over the empire, though they each faced threats both from the Seleucid army in the west and from nomadic invasions in the northeast. But the Seleucids finally had to acknowledge that they could not recover their former eastern provinces. Further east, the Greco-Bactrian kingdom succumbed to invading tribes, who established their power in the capital Bactra. Known as the Kushans, these tribes established an empire to the east as far as northern India and the Ganges basin. They remained a political power from 128 BC to AD 99.

Consolidation of power

Under their king Antiochus VII Sidetes (138–129) the Seleucids were able to regain temporary control of Babylonia and Media (130–129/8), but their success was undermined by internal opposition. Their own garrisons rebelled against them, forming an alliance with the Parthians. Amidst these power struggles a new local dynasty emerged in Characene in southern Mesopotamia. Some time in the 130s a certain Hyspaosines began campaigning in southern Elymais and by 133 was regarded as an enemy of the Parthians. By 130 Susa was under Parthian control, but Hyspaosines, who had proclaimed himself king of Characene, remained in control of the region until his death in 124. Despite attempts by Mithridates II (124/3–88/7) to curb Characene's independence, it remained under the rule of kings throughout the Parthian period.

Mithridates II's reign signalled a third phase of Parthian expansion and consolidation of empire. He secured Parthian control in northern Mesopotamia by curbing the power of the kingdoms of Adiabene, Gordyene and Osrhoene, and by bringing the city of Dura-Europos under Parthian control. He also regained control of Babylonia and the eastern provinces (see Map 4).

Parthia's power was recognised in the east, when China 'discovered' its western neighbours after a reconnaissance mission of Zhang Qian. He had been sent by the Chinese emperor Wu (140–87), and after a long absence, from c.138 to 126, returned, having gathered information about Parthia, known in Chinese sources as An-hsi. In 121 an embassy was sent by Wu to Mithridates II to establish formal relations between the two empires:

> When the Han envoys first reached Parthia, the king of Parthia (*Mithridates II*) ordered (a general) to take a force of 20,000 cavalry and welcome them at the eastern frontier. The eastern frontier is several thousand *li* distant from the king's capital. Along the way (to the capital) one passes

several tens of cities; settlements are continuous and the population is very numerous. Only when the Han envoys returned (to China) did (the king) send out his own envoys to accompany the Han envoys and to come and observe the size of Han territory. They brought skilful conjurers from Li-Kan (*the Seleucid Empire*) and ostrich eggs as a tribute for the Han (Emperor).

(Shih-Chih 123, 3172–3173; transl. Leslie,
Gardiner 1996: 34–35)

The initial reason for Chinese contacts with Parthia may have been military, for the Chinese empire was threatened by invading Hsiung-nu, Huns, the same people who had pushed the Tocharians into Greco-Bactria. Not only was there a Chinese demand for the famous Persian horses, but also for the trained skills of the Parthian cavalry. In the event, it was not a military alliance which was concluded between the two empires, but a trading agreement. Recognising a mutual demand for luxury goods, the Chinese opened a network of overland trade routes between China, Central Asia and the Iranian plateau, collectively known as the Silk Road (see Map 5).

The establishment of these trade routes, which connected China with the eastern Mediterranean coast and Asia Minor, was perhaps one of the reasons why Mithridates II wanted to gain more control over the northwestern border of his empire, for in 97 he subjected Armenia, an independent kingdom, to Parthian rule. He deposed the Armenian king and replaced him with his pro-Parthian son Tigranes. Through Tigranes, the Parthians began to establish contacts with other kingdoms of Asia Minor. Tigranes entered into an alliance with the king of Pontus, also called Mithridates, which was cemented by a marriage to the latter's daughter Cleopatra, and both Tigranes and the king of Pontus then led a campaign against King Ariobarzanes of Cappadocia. A year after the Parthian subjection of Armenia a Roman delegation led by Sulla met the Parthian ambassador Orobazus at the Euphrates River, to acknowledge the river formally as the border between the two powers (Plut.*Sull.* 5.3–4).

Mithridates II himself ensured his influence in the west by marrying a daughter of Tigranes, called Aryazate Automa, and by establishing an alliance with Mithridates of Pontus. Yet despite his successful foreign policy and his attempts to tie the different powers closer together, Mithridates II's reign did not remain unchallenged. A contender for the throne, Gotarzes I (91/0–81/0), assumed the kingship of parts of the Parthian empire as an independent ruler of Babylon, and gained full political power after Mithridates' death in 88/7. Before assuming the kingship Gotarzes I seems to have held a very high position in the empire, for an inscription at Bisitun refers to him as 'Satrap of Satraps', a title hitherto unknown, and clearly echoing the royal title of 'King of Kings', which Mithridates II had adopted from the Achaemenids. However, Gotarzes I, who was not a member of the Arsacid dynasty, was opposed by Tigranes of Armenia, who, on several occasions, sent forces into Parthia to contest Gotarzes' power. With the accession of Sinatruces (78/7–71/0) and his son Phraates III (71/0–58/7) power was restored to the Arsacids.

Enmity with Rome

From the mid-first century BC to the end of the second century AD Parthia's main political and military focus was turned towards the western frontier. That this focus was a 'real' one and not just one perceived through the dominant Roman sources seems to be proved by the fact that the Kushans made no attempt to expand their empire westward. The settlement of these previously nomadic tribes had temporarily calmed the migration into Parthian territory.

Rome, the new Mediterranean power in the ascent, had a political interest in the Seleucid provinces in Asia Minor and the Near East, and was able to exert its political influence in Asia Minor after the defeat of Antiochus III and the peace of Apameia in 188. Rome was a willing ally for anti-Seleucid powers as well as for anti-Parthian activities. Thus, it found eager allies in some of the Armenian kings as well as in Parthian pretenders to the throne who sought external military support. However, pro-Roman attitudes seldom penetrated deeply below the political surface. 'Romanised' Parthian kings were never able to persuade the Parthian aristocracy to give them full political support.

After the initial diplomatic exchange between Parthia and the Roman Republic in 97 in which both sides seemed to express mutual acknowledgement, tension increased over the next few decades, and Rome seemed to be increasingly determined to head for a military

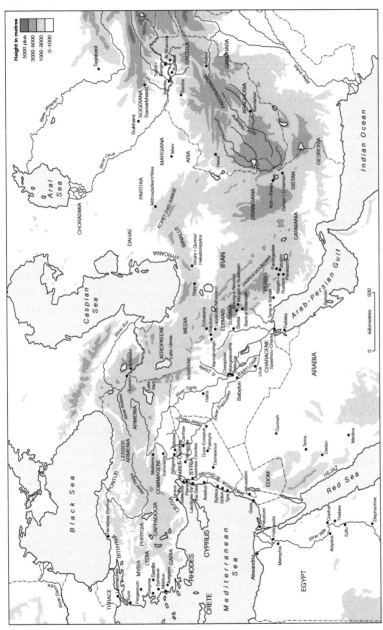

Map 4
The
Parthian
empire

Height in metres
5000 plus
3000–5000
1000–3000
0–1000

encounter with Parthia. The conflict of interest between the two empires lay in the control over Armenia and the kingdoms of Asia Minor. Syria became a further zone of conflict as the Parthians undertook campaigns into Syrian territory in retaliation for Roman aggression towards Parthia. What marked the Roman attitude towards the Parthians was a staggering lack of intelligence about the make-up of their empire in terms of geography, political set-up, resources and military strength. After 20 BC imperial Rome lost itself in propaganda and myth-making about Parthia as yet another inferior barbarian country, the Parthians themselves as a people on horseback, lacking culture, discipline, political and moral values. Rome paid for its unwillingness to understand what Parthia and the Parthian empire meant with considerable losses in return for minor and short-lived military successes, dragging itself into an unnecessary two-frontier war it could ill-afford, to the detriment of the defence of its northern frontiers where the Roman empire was increasingly threatened by rebellions.

The growing Roman aggression can be sensed in the actions of the Roman commander Lucullus and those of his successors Pompey and Crassus. Rome led several campaigns against Asia Minor. After Mithridates VI of Pontus had been defeated by Lucullus he fled to his ally, Tigranes of Armenia. In 69, without considering the political consequences, Lucullus decided to attack the Armenian city of Tigranocerta. When both kings, Mithridates and Tigranes, sought the support of their Parthian ally, Lucullus pretended to adhere to the Parthian king's reminder that the Euphrates had been recognised as the border between Rome and Parthia, but secretly prepared an attack on Parthia. He was only prevented from doing so because his own forces threatened to rebel if he carried out his plan (Plut.*Luc.*30; Cic.*Manil.*23–24). Lucullus appears to have acted on his own initiative, rather than on the orders of Rome. His campaign was a spontaneous spurt of military aggression which failed to take any account of the strength of the Parthian army and to consider the potentially disastrous situation he exposed his army to.

Under Lucullus' successor Pompey Rome actively supported a contender to the Parthian throne, thereby openly attacking the Parthian king Orodes II (58/7–38). With Crassus' appointment as commander of Syria in 55, Rome was set to go to war against Parthia. Crassus' own ambition, not only to conquer Parthia, but also take to control of Bactria and even India, expressed a fatal mixture of arrogance and ignorance about the new power structures in the Near and Further East, as well as lacking any realistic view about the logistics for such a campaign. In the event, Crassus did not advance beyond northern Babylonia. At Carrhae, ancient Harran, he was confronted by the Parthian forces and suffered a colossal defeat, losing many soldiers in battle. While Crassus advanced with his army from the south, Orodes had marched into Armenia to cut off Crassus' vital ally. Crassus reached Carrhae after a long and exhausting march along the Royal Road, but instead of resting his army he ordered them to engage immediately with the Parthian forces. Crassus had given no consideration to Parthian strategy and supplies, and he was now faced with an army which may have been smaller than the Roman forces, but which was rested and extremely well equipped. The Parthian army was led by 1,000 horsemen in full mail armour, followed by 9,000 archers on horseback who shot with composite bows. To support the archers on horseback, 1,000 camels carried further supplies of arrows to secure continuous fighting. The Roman forces were unable to withstand the storm of arrows with which they were attacked, and were furthermore deceived when the Parthians seemingly retreated only to turn their bodies backwards in their apparent flight and to shoot the pursuing enemy, a tactic which became known as the 'Parthian shot'.

> And when Crassus ordered his light-armed troops to make a charge, they did not advance far, but encountering a multitude of arrows, abandoned their undertaking and ran back for shelter among the men-at-arms, among whom they caused the beginning of disorder and fear, for these now saw the velocity and force of the arrows, which fractured armour, and tore their way through every covering alike, whether hard or soft. (. . .) At once then, the plight of the Romans was a grievous one; for if they kept their ranks, they were wounded in great numbers, and if they tried to come to close quarters with the enemy, they were just as far from effecting anything and suffered just as much. For the Parthians shot as they fled, and next to the Scythians, they do this most effectively.
>
> (Plut.*Crass.* 24.4–6).

Crassus retreated with the remaining force to Carrhae, only to be killed after failed negotiations led to an immediate attack on the Roman troops. The scale of the Roman losses was massive: of the 42,000 soldiers only 10,000 returned to safety. Of the remaining army, those who had not been killed were made prisoners of war. The Roman standards were lost to Parthia. Crassus had gone to war against Parthia lacking any profound intelligence about the empire, and Rome paid a heavy price for this folly. Parthia was now Rome's prime enemy; fighting it with, or without, cause became the greatest goal of the most ambitious generals and emperors of Rome.

Following Caesar's assassination in 44, Rome fell into civic strife between the republicans and the imperialists, culminating in the war between Caesar's successor Octavian Augustus and Antony, which ended with Antony's defeat at Philippi in 42. Supporters of the Republic including the then Roman governor of Syria, Cassius, and his envoy Labienus, found themselves seeking the support of Parthia. After Octavian's victory against Antony in 42, Parthia demonstrated its position against the new powers with invasions into Syria and Asia Minor. In the course of these campaigns Pacorus, son of Orodes and heir to the throne, was killed, as was Labienus, who had remained in Parthia to fight against Rome. Pacorus' death caused a serious succession problem for Orodes, who, in 38, selected his son Phraates IV (38–3/2) as his successor. Phraates IV failed to use Antony as a potential support against Rome, and his refusal to enter into an alliance led to Antony's attack on Parthia with the support of Armenia. Phraates IV did not wait to offer a proper battle. His forces attacked the Roman military supplies and the baggage train, destroying the siege engines, vital for any attack on cities, and diminishing the army's food supplies. At this point, the Armenian king Artavasdes deserted Antony's cause, realising that the campaign was doomed to failure. Regardless, Antony marched on as far as Phraaspa in Media, a city probably located near the modern city of Maragheh in Iranian Azerbaijan. The siege of Phraaspa soon had to be abandoned and Antony was forced to retreat to the Araxes River. His campaign cost the lives of 24,000 Roman soldiers.

In 20 BC Phraates IV came to a diplomatic agreement with the new ruler of Rome, Augustus. Rome once again confirmed the Euphrates as the border between the two empires, and Phraates IV agreed to return the Roman standards captured during the battles with Lucullus, Crassus and Antony. Ten years later, Phraates sent four of his sons, Seraspadanes, Phraates, Rhodaspes and Vonones, as well as members of their families, to Rome. This was the first of many 'evacuations' of members of the Persian court to Rome, and they occurred for different reasons. On the one hand this action could be taken in order to confirm an alliance between the kings of Rome and Parthia. On the other, it is possible that Parthian kings sent their sons to the Roman court in order to ensure their upbringing and survival away from their own court. However, in Rome this was used as a splendid piece of propaganda, presenting the members of the Parthian royal family as 'hostages'. Their presence in Rome was used as a means to demonstrate Parthia's acceptance of Rome's polit- ical supremacy, if not moral superiority. It tied in perfectly with the way Augustus had 'marketed' the return of the Roman standards in 20 BC: in word and image this event was presented as a major diplo- matic achievement on the part of Augustus, in which he had persuaded the Parthian king to accept Roman rule. The famous statue of Augustus from Prima Porta shows the emperor wearing military dress; the central motif on his breastplate is the return of the standards by a Parthian. In contrast to the erect stature of the recipient, the figure of the Parthian is curved, his hair in disarray, and his many-folded Parthian clothing untidy (see Fig. 20).

Roman coins were issued which showed a man in Parthian dress, presumably representing the king himself, in a kneeling position, offering the Roman standard with his right hand, the left hand in open submission (see Fig. 21).

A triumphal arch was built to commemorate the historic event, and by 2 BC the standards were housed in the temple of Mars Ultor, Mars the Avenger, built specifically for that purpose. For Rome, Augustus had achieved the impossible: the 'takeover' of Parthia without a war. It was the beginning of a myth created by Augustus which was to cloud the judgement of subsequent emperors with regard to Parthia, and shrouded the Parthian empire and its real political and military force in mystery. It was a brilliant piece of spin, based on no fact. Roman supremacy had to be demonstrated to the (Roman) world, and that was precisely what Augustus did.

Phraates' political connection with Rome ultimately can be seen as one of the causes of the considerable dynastic upheavals which were to plague Parthia for the next two centuries. First, in

Figure 20 Detail of the statue of Augustus from Prima Porta (with kind permission of R.M. Schneider)

Figure 21
Denarius of Augustus depicting a kneeling Parthian (with kind permission of R.M. Schneider)

the question of royal succession he gave preference to a son born not to a daughter of the Parthian aristocracy, but to a 'foreigner', a woman called Musa, whom Phraates IV had accepted as a gift from Augustus. She succeeded in securing the throne for her son, thereby elevating herself to the status of king's mother (Jos.*Ant.*18.2.4). Her ambitions went even further. She married her own son and thus became recognised as queen. But the resentment of the Parthian nobility towards the selection of a king not of full Arsacid descent was soon to be apparent. Phraates V survived only four years on the throne before he was killed, and the Parthian nobility placed Orodes III on the throne. His reign ended two years later, and was followed by a stream of successors, beginning with an Arsacid, Vonones I (AD 8/9), one of the sons of Phraates IV who had been sent to Rome. But the hopes of the Parthian nobility to get a 'pure' Arsacid back on the throne were dashed when they realised that Vonones I had adopted more Roman manners than they considered acceptable. They therefore backed another 'candidate', Artabanus II (10/11–38), who had a maternal link to the Arsacid dynasty. Eventually Artabanus II was able to defeat Vonones I and proceeded to restore Parthia's relationship with Rome. Armenia remained the bone of contention between Rome and Parthia, and while Artabanus II's diplomacy in the matter led to a renewal in AD 18/19 of the earlier agreements made between Rome and Parthia, his interference in Armenian politics in AD 35 led once again to an eruption of hostilities. The political situation was worsened by the Parthian nobility's dissatisfaction with Artabanus II, which led them to seek Roman support in order to place another of Phraates' descendants on the Parthian throne. For a brief period of time this caused some dynastic upheavals, but by the spring of 37 Artabanus could reassert his position. When he died a year later, his son Vardanes (AD 38–45) was able to secure his succession.

Politically Parthia had pushed itself into a difficult corner. This was mainly for two reasons: first, the latent hostility between Parthia and Rome over Armenia, and second, perhaps more damaging, the considerable power wielded by the Parthian nobility, whose status and influence had risen to such a degree that they could 'make or break' the king. In this power game Rome was a key player, offering itself as a potential supporter of one side or another, without losing sight of its own interests. It meant that Rome took advantage of the debacle of Parthian internal political fractions as much as it could. A temporary reprieve was achieved only in AD 63, when the Parthian king Vologeses I (51–76/80) concluded a treaty with Rome in which both sides took a share of control over Armenia – Parthia, because it secured the right to appoint the Armenian king from among the Parthian royal family, and Rome, because it maintained political supremacy over Armenia. Tiridates, an Arsacid and king of Armenia, travelled with the royal family to Rome to receive his kingship from Nero, which was publicly celebrated in a lavish ceremony. One of his daughters remained in Rome, possibly as a confirmation of the alliance (Tac.*Ann*.15.30).

In the struggle of royal succession, kings and contenders for the throne appeared on the Parthian political stage until the reign of Vologeses IV (147/8–191/2) brought a degree of political calm back to Parthian rule. All the while hostilities with Rome continued to flare up over Armenia, culminating in the great eastern campaign of Trajan between 114 and 117, in which Ctesiphon was taken, and territories east of the Euphrates River came under Roman occupation. Roman success was short-lived, however, for by the winter of 115 most of the newly conquered regions were in rebellion from their Roman oppressors and had killed or expelled their garrisons. Hadrian, who succeeded Trajan after his death in 117, immediately implemented a return to a *status ante quem*, ordering that the new territorial acquisitions be returned to Parthia. The main reason for Hadrian's decision was the fact that Rome did not possess sufficient military resources to maintain a presence east of the Euphrates.

Rome staged three further attacks on Parthia. One was led in 165 by Avidius Cassius, who was able to take Seleucia and Ctesiphon, only to retreat soon afterwards after the outbreak of an epidemic. During the reign of Vologeses V (191/2–207/8) the emperor Septimius Severus led a war against Parthia between 195 and 199. His army was able to take the cities of the western part of the Parthian empire once again: Seleucia, Babylon and Ctesiphon. Hatra, as it had done before, withstood the Roman siege.

The last Roman attacks on Parthia occurred between 216 and 218 under Caracalla and Macrinus. The whole campaign ended in disaster for the Romans and the humiliating demand to pay the Parthians a sum of money amounting to 200 million dinars and additional gifts (Dio Cassius 79 [78.27.1]). In total denial of the historical facts even this disastrous defeat was presented in Rome as a victory, and coins were minted bearing the legend 'VIC(TORIA) PART(HICA)', 'Victory over Parthia'.

The end of the Parthian empire was not, however, brought about by Rome, but by internal opposition. The king of Persis, Ardashir, son of Papak ruler of Istakhr, rose in rebellion and challenged the last Parthian king, Artabanus IV (213–224). On 28 April 224 Artabanus IV and his son were defeated and killed in battle. Ardashir's victory opened a new chapter in the history of ancient Persia, which he entered as the founder of the Sasanian dynasty.

KING AND COURT

Arsaces I, the founder of the Parthian empire, was the *primus inter pares* of the clan leaders of the Parni, a position which allowed him to claim kingship. His coronation in 247 BC in Asaak officially marked that status. If the early Arsacid coins can be dated securely to Arsaces' reign, the obverse pictured the king wearing the distinctive Iranian soft cap with cheek flaps, the *bashlyk* (Gr. *kyrbasia*). The image on the reverse shows a man seated on a backless chair wearing a soft cap and the riding costume, a tunic worn over trousers, and holding a bow in his outstretched hand. It was consistently maintained on coins throughout the Parthian period. The image is reminiscent of fourth-century Achaemenid coins representing satraps of the western Asiatic provinces, as can be seen on the coins of Datames, and may have served as a model for the early Arsacid coins. It has also been suggested that the figure depicts Arsaces I himself, wearing the traditional costume, while the bow symbolises his royal power. These two interpretations are not incompatible, however, for Arsaces may well have chosen an image whose tradition went back to Achaemenid coins, but which was given a contemporary meaning as an image of the founder of the Parthian empire. The accompanying Greek legend reading 'Arsaces *basileus*', 'Arsaces, the king', perfectly complements this combination of Achaemenid and Seleucid iconography (see Fig. 22). As successors of both empires the Parthians adopted symbols of power and iconography of kingship from both realms.

Following the reign of Mithridates I and Parthia's establishment as an empire Arsacid kingship became more pronounced and

Figure 22   Drachme of Arsaces I (courtesy of the Bibliothèque Nationale de France, Paris)

imperial sentiments more strongly expressed. The Parthian kings laid claim to their legitimate succession from the Achaemenids as well as from the Seleucids. The latter, after all, had been rulers of former Achaemenid territory for almost 100 years, and therefore, at least to some extent, had been the inheritors of Persian power, while at the same time they had introduced Hellenistic ideas of kingship to Iran. Greek epithets echoed the Seleucid royal form of address in the king's full royal title: 'Arsaces, King of Kings, the Benefactor, the Just, the Manifest, the Friend of the Greeks'. The royal diadem replaced the soft cap as one of the royal insignia. In the late Parthian period the diadem could be exchanged for or complemented by the upright *tiara*, a high, rounded headdress, richly embroidered and set with pearls and jewels.

Owing to the absence of any extensive Parthian royal inscriptions which would shed light on the importance of divine support for the Parthian kings, it is difficult to assess to what extent the Arsacids regarded their kingship as divine. The problem is enhanced further because virtually nothing is known about the religion of the Parthians. Mazdaism had developed into an early form of Zoroastrianism, but it is not clear to what extent the Arsacid kings adhered to the religion. We know that royal fires were lit for the Arsacid kings, and possibly for other members of the royal family. As was the practice during the Achaemenid period, these fires were probably extinguished at the king's death to mark the beginning of the official mourning period, and new fires were lit at the accession of the new king. Considering the special position of the Parthian dynasty we may assume that their kingship was blessed with *khvarrah*, the divine fortune: only members of their family were confirmed, or selected, as kings by the Parthian nobility. Parthian rock reliefs and coinage suggest that the practice of religious sacrifice offered before a fire altar continued to be an important form of public representation of kings and local rulers.

Elements of Seleucid kingship which were incorporated into Arsacid kingship are discernible not only in the adoption of Greek epithets of the royal title, but also in the more public presentation of the royal family in, for example, the inclusion of the names of the king's wives in official documents. The appearance of the king's family in the king's entourage, in the train of the king's migrations between royal residences and on campaigns, followed a long Near Eastern tradition.

The Arsacid kings maintained several royal capitals in the empire, concentrating on two regions, Parthia and Mesopotamia. Arsaces I built the city of Dara on Mount Apaortenon near Abivard (Justin 41.5.1–4), a site not yet discovered, while Mithridates I founded Mithradatkert/Nisa. The city was known as the burial place of the Parthian kings (Isidore of Charax, *Parth.Stat.*12). In the first century AD Vologeses I founded a further city, Vologesocerta, in Mesopotamia. Old capital centres were also maintained. Shar-e Qumis/ Hekatompylos was the centre of the early Parthian empire, and remained a royal residence even after Ctesiphon became the representational city of the Arsacids and was regarded by the Romans as the Parthian capital. Here the coronation and the official investiture ceremony were held. According to Chinese sources the Parthian capital was called Ho-tu or Fan-tou, thought to be Hekatompylos in Parthia (Leslie, Gardiner 1996: 34 n.13). Hekatompylos, Ecbatana in Media, and Seleucia were the official mint centres of the empire.

Succession to the throne

The heir to the throne was selected from among the sons of the Arsacid king, and ideally the choice would fall on the first-born son. Arsacid kings were polygamous, but it seems that an heir born to a wife belonging to the Arsacid dynasty was preferred (Herodian

4.10.5). This accounts for interfamilial marriages, i.e. the king's marriage to nieces and sisters, though it is not clear whether the latter were marriages between full siblings. Regarded as strengthening the dynastic line, brother–sister marriages were known from the Ptolemies, and are attested in the marriages between Ptolemy II and Arsinoe and between Ptolemy VIII and Cleopatra II. They are less well attested among the Seleucids for whom we only know of the brother–sister marriage between Antiochus, son of Antiochus III, and Laodice. Since hardly any details are known about the descent of the Parthian royal wives it is not possible to reach an accurate view on this issue. The case of Musa, a foreigner and a 'gift' of Augustus to Phraates IV, who was elevated to queen, and then, by marrying her son, affirmed her status as the king's wife, appears to have been an extreme case of a dynastic marriage and cannot be taken as the 'norm'.

With Parthia's rise to empire the Parthian nobility took a more prominent role in the royal succession. They had the right to approve of the chosen king and the head of one of the aristocratic families, the Suren, had the privilege of crowning the king. The Parthian aristocracy took full advantage of the right of confirmation and selected and eliminated royal successors according to their assessment of the quality and political suitability of the ruling king. While descent from the Arsacid dynasty was the principal factor for choosing a successor, individual kings could be 'dropped' when their attitude did not suit the Parthian nobility. Thus resentment was caused when a successor was considered to be 'Romanised', or simply when a king no longer suited the politics of the aristocracy. It was this power of the nobility which contributed to no small degree to the dynastic instability of the later Parthian empire, as the existence of kings and counter-kings became a frequent appearance on the Parthian political stage. The fact that investiture was a vital point of royal rule is reflected in the investiture reliefs, such as that of Orodes at Tang-e Sarvak, and of the Elymaian king Kamniskares at Khung-e Nouruzi (see below Fig. 29).

We possess barely any information about the Parthian court, its organisation, its members, court procedures and the routines of court life. It may be assumed that it was made up of members of the Parthian aristocracy, a hierarchically structured group of nobles, who included the members of the royal family and the heads of noble families and clans who belonged to the original Parni. Likewise, heads of the local dynasties and the local aristocracy belonged to the court. By building a network of political alliances with the members of the local elite the Arsacids ensured political and military support. Members of the Parthian nobility served as advisers to the king and as royal councillors, amongst whom a hierarchical order existed which was based on seniority and merit. Titles such as *batēsā* and *āzādān*, which differentiate between different groups of noble freemen, indicate that a hierarchical structure existed.

Among the duties of the court was their presence at the royal investiture, their participation in the mourning ceremonies for the deceased king and possibly other members of the royal family, and the celebration of official feasts. Hunting and banqueting had maintained their status as royal activities from the Achaemenid period, and despite the scarce evidence which has come down to us we may safely assume that these formed the most important social occasions at court. The find of the spectacular ivory *rhytha*, drinking-horns, in Nisa may give us a small but important indication of the value Parthian kings placed on ceremony and extravagantly celebrated rituals (see Fig. 23).

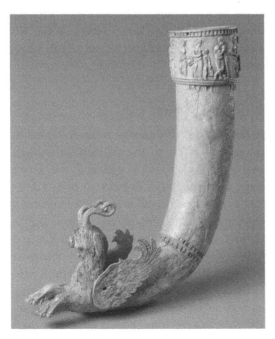

Figure 23
Rhython from Nisa (with kind permission of the Centro Ricerche Archeologiche e Scavi, Turin)

Furthermore the custom of gift-giving, the political means of creating and confirming loyalties between the king and the nobility, was practised among the Parthians.

The appearance, in the Parthian period, of the court minstrel, the so-called *gōsān*, gives some indication for the performance of storytelling, recitation of literature and poetry at the royal court, and, presumably, at the courts of the regional kings. The performance of the minstrel could be accompanied by a musical instrument; the stories were composed in verse, though it is not possible to determine whether they were written down, or whether the minstrels were trained in an oral transmission of court literature. The tradition survived down to the Sasanian period, when Persian literature was committed to book form in the fifth century, and thus found its way into the early Islamic literature, where Parthian elements of storytelling can be identified in the *Shahnameh*, the Book of Kings, of Firdowsi. One of the most compelling stories which derives from a Parthian original is that of Vis and Ramin, a complex love-story in which the two lovers have to overcome not only the differences between the two nobles houses from which they descend, but also Ramin's brother, who has been pledged in marriage to Vis. A first union is achieved with the help of a nurse, but eventually, after the death of Ramin's brother, they are free to live together. When Vis eventually dies, Ramin buries her in an underground tomb, where he joins her in her death.

Royal women

Babylonian cuneiform texts, Greek documents from Avroman in Kurdestan, and Roman sources attest to the prominence of royal Parthian women, most notably the king's wife and the king's mother. These references, however, often amount to only a brief mentioning of their existence, rather than allowing us to reconstruct a picture of their status at court, the importance of their public appearance, their activities, and their ability to act within and without the court. Archaeological material, including numismatic evidence, is limited, and we can only surmise from comparison with finds in places such as Dura-Europos and Hatra that high-ranking women held a recognised official status. Parthian royal women, especially the sisters and daughters of the king, played important parts in the conclusion of political alliances with local kings, as well as with Parthian and foreign nobles, and thus continued to be used in the creation and extension of a network which would tie powerful nobles to the Arsacid dynasty. The prominence of royal women in official documents reflects Seleucid influence, for it is here that we encounter the mentioning of the names of the king's wife in official decrees and royal correspondence. According to Babylonian texts the king's wife was referred to as *sharratu*, 'Queen', and as *beltu*, 'Lady', terms, perhaps, which differentiated between a title and a form of address for royal women.

The documents attest to the fact that the Parthian kings were polygamous. A parchment text from Avroman mentions the names of the wives of Mithridates II, referring to them as the queens 'Siace, his compaternal sister and wife, and Aryazate, surnamed Automa, daughter of the Great King Tigranes and his wife, and of Azate his compaternal sister and wife' (Avroman I: 2–5). Two wives are attested for Gotarzes I, one of whom was called Ashi'abatum (Minns 1915: 34). A further text from Avroman names the wives of Phraates IV as Olenieire, Cleopatra, Baseirta and Bistheibanaps (Avroman II: 5). We only know of one wife of Orodes I, Ispubarza, who also was his sister (cf. Strassmeier 1893: 112; Potts 1999: 392).

The status of a king's wife differed from that of those women belonging to the king's household, but who were not married to the king. These women are usually referred to as concubines, though it has to be emphasised that these women had entered the king's household as part of political alliances, as captives, or even as 'gifts'. One example of such a fate is the story of the daughter of Demetrius and niece of Antiochus, who entered the king's household after she was captured by the Parthians following the death of her uncle (Justin 38.10.10). Apart from the case of the notorious Musa there is evidence for another foreigner, a Greek concubine living at the Parthian court, who became the mother of a king, Vologeses I.

Women of the king's family played their most important part in the conclusion of political alliances. At royal level, marriages like that of Mithridates I's daughter Rhodogune to Demetrius (App.*Syr*.67) served to legitimise power, or to consolidate a political alliance, as happened in the case of the sister of Artavasdes of Armenia, who was married to Orodes' son Pacorus, thereby confirming Artavasdes' alliance with the Parthian king (Plut.*Crass*.33).

Royal women formed part of the king's entourage and their public appearance was part of the expression of kingship. They moved with the king between royal residences and even joined him on campaigns. This practice was adopted by the regional kings and the Parthian nobility, who also included women in their military entourage. Thus Suren is said to have needed 200 wagons to accommodate the women in his entourage while on campaign.

If the king failed to secure the women's safety, they often paid with their lives. Rather than allowing them to fall into enemy hands and become hostages, some of the Parthian kings resorted to killing the women, including their wives and daughters. Such actions were not just tragedies in themselves, they also bore grave consequences for the continuation of the dynastic line. Phraates IV was accompanied by his female household when he was attacked by the pretender Tiridates. Rather than letting the women fall into enemy hands, Phraates killed them. A daughter of Osroes survived an attack on Ctesiphon by Trajan in 115/16, but was taken prisoner. Twelve years later she was returned to the king by Hadrian. The fates of the royal women of the regional kingdoms could be equally harsh. When in AD 72 the women of Pacorus of Media Atropatene fell into the hands of the invading Alani, Pacorus negotiated the ransom for his wife and his concubines. Rhadamistus of Armenia, fleeing from his enemies, stabbed his pregnant wife and threw her into the River Araxes, when she was unable to continue the arduous journey on horseback. She was found alive and, after her recovery, was sent to Tiridates (Tac.*Ann*.12.51; 13.6).

Only in exceptional cases were royal women depicted on coins. Thus, the portrait of Musa appears on coins of Phraates V, and the ruler of Elymais, Kamniskares, is depicted together with his wife Anzaza on his coinage (Potts 1999: 392). Women were more commonly depicted in art. Statues and sculptures show wealthy women, wearing splendid Parthian dress, long-sleeved floating robes over a long underdress, made from textiles which were richly adorned and embroidered. They wore high headdresses, equally beautifully crafted and adorned with jewellery. High-ranking women wore several necklaces, made of pearls and precious stones, as well as earrings and bracelets. The outfits which adorn female statues in Hatra undoubtedly follow Parthian fashion dictated by the centre (see Fig. 24).

Figure 24a
Women in
Parthian dress
from Hatra
(with kind
permission of
the Centro
Ricerche
Archeologiche
e Scavi, Turin)

Figure 24b
Statue of a princess
in Parthian dress
from Hatra (copy;
with kind permission
of the Centro Ricerche
Archeologiche e
Scavi, Turin)

Thus, from the admittedly scarce evidence it appears that the position of Parthian royal (and noble) women was defined through the king. Their splendour, the number of their (male) offspring, and their public appearance all were expressions of the king's power.

Royal cities

The Parthian kings migrated between several royal residences across the empire. Shar-e Qumis/Hekatompylos, the central city of Parthia, became the first royal residence of Arsaces I. Following the conquests of Media and Mesopotamia under Mithridates I Ecbatana, the ancient Median and Achaemenid capital, and the cities of Ctesiphon and Seleucia became royal capitals. Among the royal cities Ctesiphon and Mithradatkert/Nisa took a prominent place. Ctesiphon, or Tīsfūn, became the representational capital of the Parthian kings, while neighbouring Seleucia remained the administrative centre and housed one of the royal mints. Mithridates I's foundation of Mithradatkert marked the Parthians' recognition of their homeland, to which the bodies of the deceased Parthian kings were returned. As the representational capital Ctesiphon probably was the royal centre where the Parthian kings were crowned and celebrated their investiture. According to Strabo,

> (Ctesiphon) has been equipped with buildings by the Parthians themselves; and it has been provided by the Parthians with wares for sale and with the arts that are pleasing to the Parthians; for the Parthian kings are accustomed to spent the winter there because of the salubrity of the air, but the summer in Ecbatana and in Hyrcania (Nisa?) because of the prevalence of their ancient renown.
>
> (Strabo 16.1.16)

Ctesiphon was targeted several times during campaigns of Roman emperors. It appears that the Romans equated the conquest of the city with the conquest of the empire, for in the case of Trajan, his successful attack on the city in AD 115 led to his epithet 'Parthicus' (Dio Cassius 68.30.2–3). The city was taken again in 165 under Avidius Cassius, who destroyed the palace of Vologeses, but did not occupy the city. A final attack on Ctesiphon was commanded by

Septimius Severus in 198. His troops plundered the city, but again it was not occupied by the Romans:

> Later, upon capturing Ctesiphon, he permitted the soldiers to plunder the entire city, and he slew a vast number of people, besides taking as many as a hundred thousand captives. He did not, however, pursue Vologeses, nor even occupy Ctesiphon, but, as if the sole purpose of his campaign had been to plunder this place, he was off again, owing partly to a lack of acquaintance with the country and partly to the dearth of provisions.
>
> (Dio Cassius 76.9.4–5)

But it was Mithradatkert, the city 'built by Mithridates', and known in classical sources as Nisa, which became the first genuine Parthian city, built in the homeland of the Parthians, in northern Parthia. As Invernizzi rightly observes, Nisa is in fact the first city where an Arsacid-Parthian culture can be recognised and defined (cf. Invernizzi 1994: 193).

According to Isidore of Charax, a historian of the first century AD, the Parthian capital housed the tombs of the Parthian kings. Nisa was divided into two walled complexes, the citadel of Old Nisa, and the city of Nisa. Its architecture exemplified the Parthians' ability to incorporate elements of Greek art and architectural styles with Iranian designs. Excavations at Nisa yielded not only exciting forms of architecture, including the so-called Square House and the Round Hall, but also statues made of clay or stone, the famous ivory *rhytha*, and several hundred *ostraca* documenting economic activity on the citadel.

The architecture of Nisa shows no Greek influence, but, as Invernizzi, the principal excavator of the site, suggests, it was modelled on Central Asian and Seleucid architecture, both of which, however, are scarcely known. Few features echo Achaemenid influence. In principle, the Square House could be linked to the palace architecture of the Achaemenids, yet the comparison remains superficial. Likewise, the Round Hall may be compared to round halls known from Hellenistic palaces, but it rests on a different architectural idea, namely to construct the circle and vault inside a square space (Invernizzi 1998a: 52). Elements such as these must originate from Parthian designs, but so far no archaeological data have been recovered which would confirm this assumption. Despite this lacuna, the architecture of Nisa ultimately presents a new, original style of architecture, which may have derived from local forms used in Parthia (see Fig. 25).

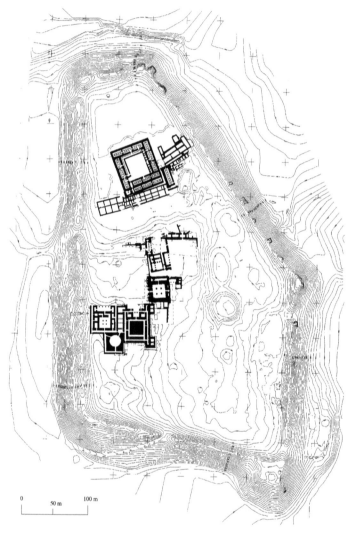

Figure 25   Plan of Old Nisa (with kind permission of the Centro Ricerche Archeologiche e Scavi, Turin)

In contrast to the architecture, artefacts which were recovered in the Square House, which for a time served as a kind of treasury, are distinctively Hellenistic. The interior and exterior of the buildings were adorned with marble sculptures crafted in Greek style. They were probably sculpted locally by Greek stonemasons. Most extraordinary are the more than fifty large drinking-horns, *rhytha*, made of expensive ivory, and with carvings depicting Hellenistic scenes, including Dionysiac scenes (see above Fig. 23).

ORGANISATION OF THE EMPIRE

According to Pliny, a Roman writer of the first century AD, Parthia was divided into a number of kingdoms (Lat. *regna*):

> The Parthians possess in all eighteen kingdoms, such being the divisions of their provinces on the coasts of two seas, as we have stated, the Red Sea on the south, and the Caspian Sea on the north. Of these provinces the eleven designated the 'Upper Kingdoms' begin at the frontiers of Armenia and the shores of the Caspian, and extend to the Scythians, with whom the Parthians live on terms of equality. The remaining seven kingdoms are called the 'Lower Kingdoms'.
> (Pliny, *nat.hist*.6.112)

The Upper Kingdoms included Parthia, Hyrcania, Margiana, Aria, Choresmia, Media Atropatene, Armenia, Hatra, Adiabene, Osrhoene, and Sittacene, the Lower Kingdoms Babylonia, Characene, Garmikan, Persis, Elymais, Kerman and Sistan.

Historians have found it difficult to explain a political system which, as an empire, was under the rule of a dynastic monarchy, but which at the same time was made up of regional kingdoms. This phenomenon has been seen as a lack of central power on the part of the dynasty and as evidence for the political independence of the regional kings. Referred to as 'client kingdoms' or 'semi-independent kingdoms', none of these terms provides an accurate description of such a system of government. Recently D. Potts suggested that the Parthian empire may not have been more 'than a very loosely knit agglomeration of provinces in which local rulers exercised considerable autonomy' (Potts 1999: 354), while Josef Wiesehöfer upholds more firmly the idea of empire. He emphasises that its kings were 'masters of an ethnically, politically and culturally heterogeneous empire and had to cope with a multiplicity of political institutions and cultural and religious traditions' (Wiesehöfer 1996: 57). In essence, this is a fair assessment, though as a definition, it would also be applicable to the empires of the Achaemenids and Seleucids. Yet the Parthian empire was different from either of these. It was a heterogeneous empire, and distinct through its political make-up of kingdoms. But their kings recognised the Parthian king as the 'king of kings'. How can this phenomenon be explained?

Principally, the existence of semi-independent kings under a central monarch was not a new occurrence. The Achaemenids had divided their empire into satrapies, but alongside these city-kings ruled in the cities of Phoenicia, Cyprus and Ionia, while some satraps and local rulers were even able to establish their own dynasties, such as in Hellespontine Phrygia and in Caria. Their rule posed no threat to the Achaemenid kings because they recognised the supremacy of the king, paid tribute and provided military support.

The Seleucids took over the satrapal administration of the Achaemenids and the system remained in place during their rule. Thus, Molon and Alexander governed the satrapies of Media and Persis at the time of Antiochus III in 223, and a Cleomenes was still attested as satrap in Media in 149/8 BC. A *pahatu*, the Babylonian term for 'satrap', was in charge of Seleucid Babylonia. Sistan/Drangiana and Karmania were still Seleucid satrapies at the time of Antiochus III. The Seleucid satraps had to collect tribute and taxes for the royal treasury and provide (and pay for) armed forces as necessary.

Yet the Seleucid empire increasingly saw the formation of local dynasties which sought independence from the supreme power. In Pontus a royal era began early in the third century BC, in 297/6, though it was not until 281 that Mithridates I was proclaimed king there. By the mid-third century BC an Iranian dynasty rose in Cappadocia, and a royal era started with their king, Ararathes, in 255. Commagene also was a kingdom which was established under Orontes in 230 BC. In 188 BC kingship was established in Armenia. For a satrap of a province like Bactria, rich in natural resources, urbanised, with excellent trade connections and well populated, it must have been more than tempting to revolt from Seleucid domination and proclaim independence, as indeed happened when Diodotus of Bactria rebelled and eventually proclaimed himself king. Similarly Andragoras, satrap of Parthia, defected from Seleucus II. By the second century BC local dynasties had become irreversible political institutions in the Near East. The political landscape of the region had also become more complex with the appearance of Greek-style city-states established by the Greeks who had settled here as citizens, administrators, traders and soldiers.

The concept of independent kingdoms which, however, recognised a supreme power first seems to appear when Antiochus III recognised the 'independence' of Parthia and Bactria, while they, in turn, recognised the supremacy of the Seleucid king. This distinction between a local king and a supreme king seems to be implied in Arsaces' coin portrait which shows him wearing the satrapal cap and diadem.

The Parthian empire inherited its basic political structure from the Seleucids. The office of satrap continued under their rule, satraps being installed in Media and Mesopotamia. But other regions which enjoyed more independence, like Persis and Elymais, were ruled by kings. Under the Seleucids dynasts called *frataraka* had governed Persis since the end of the third and the beginning of the second century BC, and by the mid-second century had become independent rulers. Elymais had been governed by kings since 147 and continued to be so after the political takeover by Mithridates I. Furthermore, in the 130s BC Hyspaosines rose as king of Characene, and by the end of the first century BC Media was ruled by a king. In the first century AD Izabates was recognised as king of Adiabene.

Obviously the establishment of Parthian kingdoms was the result of a development which occurred over several decades, and which had begun already in the Seleucid period. One can only speculate why local governors saw the need to distance themselves from the satrapal office and wanted to be regarded as kings. One possible explanation is that through the Macedonian takeover and later the Seleucid organisation, the office of satrap had suffered a loss of its former prestige and social status. Satrapies were no longer the size of the lands of the former Achaemenid empire, and had been subdivided into smaller regions, so-called *eparchies*. A satrap was also no longer the sole authority in a province, but took an administrative role while a treasurer controlled the finances. If the satrapal office had indeed suffered a loss of authority and overall control, it may explain why it was no longer a desired title for the governor of a province. A local king, a local dynasty, however, would represent that authority. And their exercising local control was compatible with their acceptance of the Parthian king as king of kings. In contrast to the development experienced by the Seleucids, the Parthian local dynasties did not strive for total independence. But their establishment was the result of the development of political institutions, in which the former office of satrap had been devalued, governing smaller territories, and lacking the close network of alliances with the king. They were not immediate members of the royal family, but local dignitaries. They were powerful in their own right and accordingly exercised considerable influence over the local aristocracy. Both sides benefited. Small kingdoms would not have been able to withstand external threat, while their economy and commerce might have been limited to regional exchange, but as part of the Parthian empire they could count on mutual military support, on central investment in the infrastructure and overland trade, as well as on a share of official recognition as members of the king's court. In return the king of kings needed their support in war, since they formed the core of the Parthian army, the heavy and light-armed cavalry.

The regional kingdoms were the result of the change of the political climate. Extensive reigns of kings which indicated peace and stability were rare, and consequently affected a king's ability to consolidate the empire. And unlike circumstances in the Achaemenid period, there now were constant threats from external political powers, the Seleucids, the Romans, and different groups of nomadic invaders. This does not mean that the Parthians did not attempt to implement a dynastic policy and establish an internal network of power, but the goalposts had shifted and conditions for maintaining a *status quo* were hardly ever given. Now the focus lay much more on military support and securing the defence of the borders of the empire. Armies were recruited and financed at local level. The most important military force, the mailed cavalry, or *cataphracts*, was formed by members of the aristocracy, who alone could afford the horses and the costly armour. In return for this military service their demand was greater independence from the Parthian king at local level, and this meant having their own king who governed their territory.

Thus, it is easy to see how the Parthian empire came to be made up of multiple kingdoms, each with a local dynast, its own administration and military resources. Their loyalty to the Parthian king was guaranteed by the fact that they would not be able to withstand the various outside threats on their own, but would risk being subjected by foreign rulers. Their existence was secured further through the trading network which benefited the kingdoms bordering on the Persian Gulf, along the Euphrates, around the Caspian and along the Royal Roads via Merv to Bactra and Samarkand. Nobody had an interest in disturbing the equilibrium established through the global market of luxury goods transported to and from the East.

Thus, the existence of these regional kingdoms should not be regarded as evidence of a weak empire which lacked centralised rule and government, and was therefore bound to collapse. These kingdoms did not exist because the Parthian kings were too weak to exercise control over the empire, but because the political conditions for maintaining power had changed and mutual military alliances between the king of kings and the local ruler determined the running of the empire.

Parthian society

Three main classes dominated Parthian society: the aristocracy, free men and a serf population. In addition there existed an unfree population made up of prisoners of war and slaves. The aristocracy was hierarchically structured, and included noble Parthians as well as members of the local nobility who took high positions at court, in the administration of the empire and in military command. The aristocracy provided the armed cavalry forces in war, and therefore were a fundamental support for the king. Quite possibly the noble families were connected to the Arsacid royal house through political alliances. The aristocracy were known as 'the Greatest' (Gr. *megistanes*). The group of the 'King's Friends' formed an intimate circle which surrounded the king, but even within this group there existed a hierarchy. Through the rank of a 'First Friend' a noble could be elevated to an 'Honoured Friend', and finally to a 'First and Most Honoured Friend'. Undoubtedly these different grades of King's Friend were expressed in the bestowing of royal privileges and were physically discernible in the Friend's appearance. Items of clothing, the quality of the fabric, its colour and design, the dress ornament,

as well as weapons and jewellery could all signify royal gifts expressing the status of the wearer. Those nobles referred to as 'kinsmen of
the king', the *syngeneis*, may indeed have been relatives of the king,
but it could also have been a figurative term for those acting in the
king's interest. These groups, together with further advisers known
as sages (Gr. *sophoi*) and *magi* (Gr. *magoi*), formed the King's Council
(Gr. *synhedrion*, Lat. *senatus*). The class of free men (Gr. *pelatai*)
was made up of farmers and peasants, manufacturers, craftsmen,
merchants and traders.

Administration

The Parthian administration used a variety of languages and scripts
written on a range of different media such as clay tablets and parchment. The latter was a phenomenon which the Chinese found most
noteworthy: 'They keep records by writing horizontally on strips of
leather' (Shih-Chih 123; transl. Leslie, Gardiner 1996: 34). The use
of parchment explains the almost complete absence of written documents from royal archives and other administrative centres, and is
the reason why it is difficult to grasp the structure and organisation
of the empire. Descriptions provided by Greek and Roman sources
tend to be of a general nature, and we cannot always be certain that
their authors understood the genuine meaning of an official title or
occupation. Sources from the Sasanian period may shed some light
on Parthian organisation, since the basic structure of the society as
well as the administrative hierarchy were adopted by the Sasanians.
The most genuine records come from Nisa, where administrative
documents were found, preserved only because they were written on
clay sherds, rather than on perishable material. These are economic
texts written in Middle Persian and recording deliveries of wine from
different estates and vineyards in the region. The following texts
provide some examples:

> (1) In this jar from Artabānukan from (2) the *uzbari* vine-
> yard called *Artaxshahrakān*, through the satrap (3) 18 *mari*
> of wine. (4) Brought by Baxtdatak, wine factor (5) deliv-
> ered for the year 176 (72 BC). (3) From the store 3k. of wine
> (added).
>
> (Diakonoff, Livshits no. 150)

(1) Chief scribe. (2) In this jar 7 *mari* of wine. (3) Brought by Rashnmihr, wine-factor who is from (the village) Kamūk. (4) For the year 220 (*28 BC*).

(Diakonoff, Livshits no. 209)

Apart from the office of satrap, the *ostraca* from Nisa also mention margraves (wardens of the marches) and commanders of fortresses, while documents from Dura-Europos mention tax collectors or commanders-in-chief of a fortress (MP *argbed*), among high administrative positions. The copy of a letter by Artabanus II, dated to AD 21 and written in Greek, addresses the citizens of Susa and their governors, who are described as archons. This rare document allows some insight into the Parthian administration. Not only does it explicitly mention royal offices such as Preferred Friend, Bodyguard and Treasurer, but it also allows us to see that while there were local jurisdictions and proceedings to appointment to high office, the king could intervene on behalf of an individual, review a case and amend the local ruling if he considered it appropriate.

> King of Kings, Arsaces (*Artabanus II*), to Antiochus and Phraates, being the two archons in Susa, and to the city. Greetings.
> [Whereas Hestiaios, son of Asios, one of] your citizens, and one of the Preferred Friends, and one of the Bodyguards, having held the office of Treasurer in [according to the former] reckoning, the 329th year, conducted himself in the best and most just manner and with all scrupulousness, having held back [no expense] on his own account towards outlay on behalf of the city; and [whereas] twice, when the city during his term of office [had need of an envoy he went out] himself, placing at nought attention to his private interests and considering the city's interests of greater consequence, (. . .) – he came forward and pleaded that he was barred according to established practice from holding the same office twice, unless a period of three years intervened; and (whereas) the city, [as it had formerly experienced] his good character and remembered the administration of the aforementioned office, decided to choose him to hold the office, upon which he was chosen for the 33[2nd]

year, in the archonship of Petasos, son of Antiochus, and Aristomenes, son of Philip; therefore, since [they unjustly charge] Hestiaios on the above grounds, we decide that his election is valid and that he is not to be ejected from office on the grounds that he has held the same office [twice] without a period of three years intervening, nor on the grounds of any other royal order whatsoever [which might be presented] concerning these matters, and that in general, setting aside any interdiction or investigation, it is necessary to discharge the [summons?] expressly mentioned, of this [investigation?] or any other(?).

(SEG 17 = RC 75)

The army

The backbone of the Parthian army was the cavalry. For the Parthians, who, as former inhabitants of the steppes, had lived a life of transhumance, horses were an essential part of their way of life. Their Persian predecessors, the Achaemenids, were renowned for their Nisaean horses, which were bred in Media. In the Parthian period, the region of Ferghana on the Jaxartes River became renowned as a further centre for horse-breeding. Horseback was also the most effective way of covering, in war, the vast distances of the Parthian territory, which featured high mountains and vast plateaux. The plains provided an ideal terrain for battle.

The strongest cavalry force was the *cataphracts* (probably identical with the later *clibanarii*) (see Fig. 26). The *cataphracts* wore fully mailed armour, and their horses were protected by a blanket of chain mail. As weapons the rider carried a lance, bows and arrows. They were equipped for a full frontal attack on the enemy lines.

The lighter cavalry was also equipped with the composite bow and arrows, but their clothing only consisted of a belted tunic and wide trousers and boots (Fig. 27). Their relatively light clothing allowed a freedom of movement needed in an attack, for their task was to deceive the enemy and encourage him to break his ranks. To do that, they attacked and then seemingly retreated from battle, giving the enemy soldiers a false sense of security which made them pursue their attackers, only for the Parthians to turn backwards on their apparently fleeing horses and shoot their arrows in mid-gallop.

Figure 26
Graffito of a
cataphractus
from Dura-
Europos
(after M.J.
Rostovtzeff,
Caravan Cities,
Oxford, 1932:
fig. 3, p. 195)

Figure 27
Parthian horseman
(courtesy of the
Pergamonmuseum –
Museum für
islamische Kunst,
Berlin)

Infantry, consisting of soldiers and mercenaries, was only employed after a cavalry attack had broken up the enemy lines, and battle was continued on the ground. The infantry probably included peasants who were obliged to do military service, as well as mercenaries and special forces like the Scythians. The fact that the Parthian army was not a standing army had no bearing on the Parthians' ability to muster an army quickly and efficiently. Forces were recruited as close to a military conflict as possible, and reinforcements would be brought in on demand.

Economy and trade

An-hsi is situated some several thousand *li* west of the Great Yüeh-Chih (*Tocharians*). It is an agricultural country, where the fields are cultivated, rice and wheat are grown, and wine is made from grapes. They have walled cities like those of Ta-yüan (*Ferghana*). Several hundred cities large and small are subject to it. It is several thousand *li* square, the largest of the states. It borders on the Kuei River (*the Oxus*). They have marketeers, and merchants who travel by cart or boat to neighbouring states, even journeying several thousand *li*.

(Shih-Chih 123, transl. Leslie,
Gardiner 1996: 33–34)

This Chinese report from the early Han period essentially sums up the characteristics of the Parthian economy. It was still largely based on agriculture, including farming and the rearing of livestock. To increase the amount of arable land, the existing systems of irrigation channels were extended. Barley and rice were grown, as were other types of grain. Wine was produced on large estates, and orchards allowed the cultivation of different kinds of fruits and nuts.

Much of the prosperity of the Parthian empire came from the opening of the caravan routes which led from Mesopotamia through Central Asia to China. This network of roads had partially been provided by the Royal Roads which had been established by the Assyrians, and especially the Achaemenid Persians. But contact between the Parthian empire and China was only established at the end of the second century BC, following the visit of the Chinese general of the emperor Wu. For both empires, the desire for luxury goods proved an expanding basis for commercial exchange, and even included Parthia's enemy Rome in commercial exchanges. The most important items were steel (seric iron) and silk, the production of which remained a secret that only became known in the West after AD 551. Silk was the most luxurious textile and in strong demand by kings and the aristocracy of both Parthia and Rome.

A caravan could include up to 1,000 Bactrian double-humped camels, each of which was able to carry 400 to 500 pounds of goods and merchandise. The animals did not necessarily travel the entire distance from China to Parthia, but were exchanged at post-stations along the routes of the Silk Road. The caravans traversed the mountainous regions of China across the Great Wall to Xian accompanied by Chinese guards. From Xian they could move via three different routes towards Central Asia. A southern route went via Dunhuang along the southern border of the Taklamakan desert, towards the Pamir mountains to Kashgar. There were two northern routes, either via the 'Heavenly Mountains' (Tian Shan) to Tashkent, or via Turfan, connecting with the southern route at Kashgar. Goods going further west were then taken on the old route along the Royal Road, passing through Samarkand, Bukhara and Merv, and then proceeded to Hekatompylos, south of the Alburz mountains past Rayy, and on to Ecbatana. From Media the caravan route then continued southward towards Seleucia and Ctesiphon, and at Charax connected with the Persian Gulf. A route along the Euphrates from Charax went up to Dura-Europos and Palmyra, from where routes branched southward towards Petra, and northward towards Antakya and Damascus. Further east and in Central Asia, Indians, Kushans and Sogdians profited as middlemen from the taxation of the merchandise, but Parthian traders took the bulk of the profit to safeguard the caravan across the Parthian empire from Merv to Charax (see Map 5).

In addition to the network of overland routes the Parthians also profited from the maritime routes which passed from the Persian Gulf, via Bahrain and Oman into the Indian Ocean, made possible through the discovery of the monsoon winds which had given the Indians and Arabs a hold over maritime trade until the first century BC.

Another significant commodity exchanged between China and Parthia was pearls, which enjoyed a huge market among the Parthian nobility. Pearls were valued as jewellery, but they were also used for

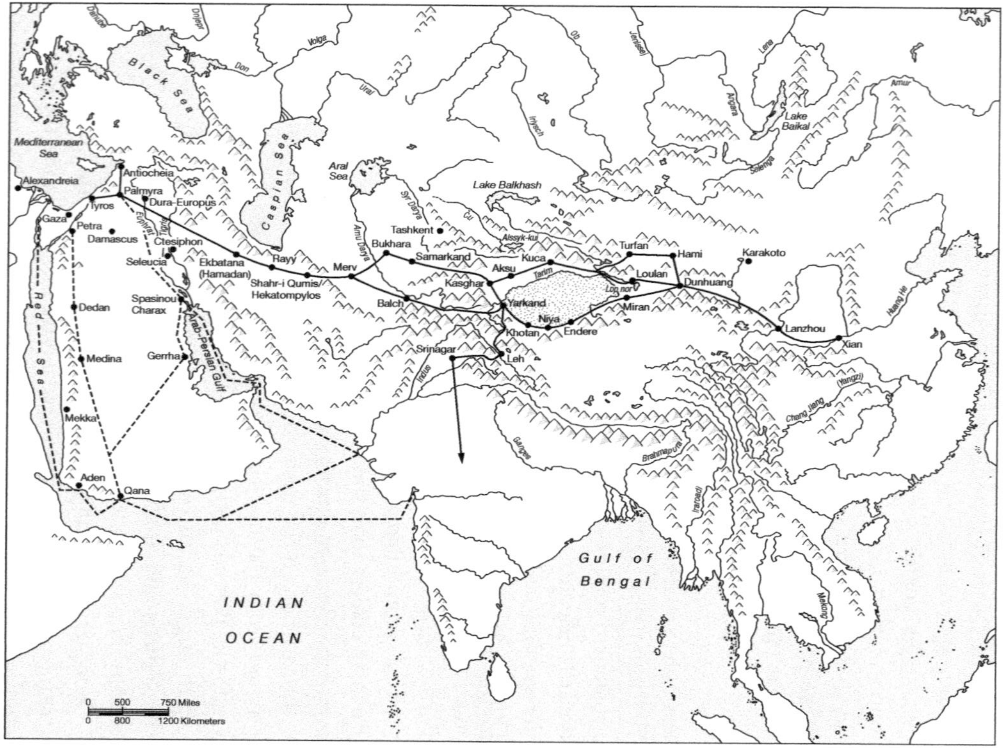

Map 5
The Silk Road

richly embroidered textiles worn by the Parthian nobility and the noble classes of the empire. Pearl-encrusted Parthian costumes have been identified on Parthian sculpture, and were a sign of wealth and status. Furthermore there were furs, gold, precious metals and stones, ivory, textiles such as linen, spices, aromatics and perfumes. In return, China had a great demand for horses, but also for Persian fruits like apricots, peaches, dates and pomegranates, which were aptly known as 'Parthian fruit' in the ancient world. Wine, lucerne and storax, a drug made from lion's dung(!), were goods imported from Parthia as well as Rome. 'Arsacid aromatic', which was a name given to several substances, such as bdellium or gum guggul, was used as an adulterant of frankincense, and, together with frankincense and myrrh, was among the precious goods exported to China.

RELIGION

The Parthians and the peoples of the Parthian empire were polytheistic. Each ethnic group, each city, and each land or kingdom was able to adhere to its own gods, their respective cults and religious rituals. In Babylon the city-god Marduk continued to be the main deity alongside the goddesses Ishtar and Nanai, while Hatra's main god, the sun-god Shamash, was revered alongside a multiplicity of other gods. The Jews practised their religion without restriction from the Parthian rulers, a tolerance which repeatedly led to Jewish support for the Parthians or their use of Parthian territory as refuge from the Romans. Perhaps most interesting is the syncretism between Greek and Iranian gods which occurred during the Hellenistic period and continued throughout the Parthian empire. Thus Greek Zeus was equated with Iranian Ahuramazda, Helios with Mithra, and Heracles with Verethragna.

As far as the Arsacids themselves are concerned it can be assumed that they, too, were polytheistic, but they were followers of Mazdaism, the religion which placed Ahuramazda at the head of a pantheon, accompanied by other gods, including Mithra and Anahita. Religious rituals celebrated for the gods included fire altars and the services of priests, referred to as *magi*.

Burial customs dictated that direct contact of the body with the earth had to be avoided. Therefore, the body was buried in a sarcophagus made of stone, and sometimes formed in the shape of a large slipper. *Astodans*, or ossuaries, in which the bones of the dead were placed, point to a different kind of burial, i.e. the exposure of the body to the sky, allowing birds of prey to pick the body clean, before placing the bones in a casket or in a rock-cut niche.

ART AND ARCHITECTURE

How is Parthian art best described? We are faced here with two fundamental problems: the state of excavation of Parthian sites, and the classification of Parthian art throughout the Parthian empire, which may have been modelled on 'royal' or 'court' art, but which was subject to local adaptation and taste outside the centre. Art and architecture are never static entities; there may be a continuation of artistic tradition and convention, but we need to take account of innovations, modifications and external influences which occur over long periods of time. Likewise they are dependent on geographical location and the adaptation of local art forms.

The difficulty of defining 'Parthian art' stems from the disparate finds, the state of excavation of Parthian levels on many sites in Iran and Iraq, as well as from a scholarship which in the past measured and assessed the quality of Parthian art by the degree of Hellenistic influence. At its extreme this led to the denial of the existence of an indigenous Parthian art, claiming a lack of originality in Parthian designs, crafts and craftsmanship. The import or local manufacture of Greek art and architecture, evident in sculptures and statues worked in the Hellenistic style in body posture, dress, hairstyles, the use of Hellenistic motifs on small objects, as well as the Greek influence on decorative designs of public and private buildings, all were used to demonstrate that the Parthians lacked originality and needed to borrow heavily from Greek culture. These Greco-centric views dominated scholarship for most of the twentieth century. Only in the past two decades have attempts been made to assess Parthian art on its own merits and to recognise its heterogeneity. While it is the case that the manufacture of Greek art occurred in the early Parthian period, an artistic movement, which included the assimilation of other cultural elements as well as the development of indigenous Iranian art, led to new developments and independent art forms which were distinctively Parthian. Thus, while there is no

question that Parthian art incorporated Iranian and Hellenistic–
Seleucid artistic elements in architecture as well as in decorative
art and sculpture, it can be established that in the course of its
almost 500-year history the art of the Parthians underwent notice-
able changes. These, according to Hubertus von Gall, belong to
three geo-historical phases: (1) the art of Parthia proper, (2) the art
of the Parthians on the Iranian plateau, and (3) the art of the
Parthians in Mesopotamia (von Gall 1998: 78). This presentation
of Parthian art in a historical-geographical context seems to be
preferable to an attempt at one definition which claims to cover the
entire period.

In figurative art certain themes were prevalent within the corpus,
including the royal hunt and the investiture of the Parthian king.
The latter motif was extended to include the depiction of the investiture of local kings. New scenes included the depiction of chivalrous
combat and sacrifices at altars. Both motifs are found on rock reliefs,
on seals, on frescos, and as graffiti. The most remarkable innovation
within these depictions is the appearance of frontality. Until then
figures in reliefs or in paintings were shown in profile, but the
Parthians introduced the depiction of individuals in frontal positions, either fully frontal or with the head turned in profile.

The first phase is characterised by the influence of Hellenistic and
Iranian art. This expresses not only the cultural heritage of the
Seleucids, the Achaemenids and the Iranian peoples of the steppes,
but also the acceptance of their art to form the basis of Parthian
culture. This heterogeneity can be found in Nisa, the earliest
example of genuine Parthian art.

In the wake of the Seleucid influence in the Near East Greek
craftsmen such as stonemasons and sculptors had been employed to
cater for the Greek and local elite in the Seleucid provinces. In the
contemporary world Hellenistic art expressed status and privilege,
and was thus a fashion sought after by the ruling elite. At the beginning of Parthian rule, Greek art thus continued to provide a
desirable element to be copied by the new rulers. This was done
as much for reasons of fashion as of politics. The desire for things
Greek can be found in art and architecture, as well as in literature.
The Parthians liked Greek designs and copied them in their art,
combining them with Iranian traditions. Thus, Greek Dionysiac

scenes, plant designs, etc., are shown on the ivory *rhytha* from Nisa. In Nisa itself, Greek sculptures and statues are well attested, but they were placed within an architecture which is not purely Greek, but combined Greek, Achaemenid and Central Asian elements.

Most important, however, in the development of Parthian architecture is the move away from using columns to support roofs, and instead to construct a barrel-vaulted rectangular room opening on one side onto a courtyard. This construction, called *ivan*, appears to be an innovation of Parthian architects. Barrel-vaulted constructions have, of course, been found in Mesopotamia as early as the second millennium BC, but never had they been constructed on the scale now found in Parthian monumental art. *Ivans* first are attested in Seleucia–Tigris in the first century AD, when they replaced the doorway which was supported by two columns, and opened onto a court.

Walls were decorated with plaster and stucco work, both externally and internally, using geometrical patterns as well as stylised plant patterns and figures. The main buildings of Old Nisa were decorated with clay and marble statues, distinctly Hellenised in style, but crafted locally. Hellenistic influences were never far away, but neither were Achaemenid/Iranian and Central Asian influences. They all merged into new forms, often locally distinct, but adhering to what will have been a core Parthian art.[2]

The second artistic phase of the Parthians on the plateau shows the Parthians following Achaemenid tradition, with Mithridates II's investiture relief carved at Bisitun, and the innovative design of Gotarzes' equestrian combat adjacent to Mithridates' relief. Both at Bisitun and in Elymais we find scenes of sacrifice carved into the rock, as well as the investiture scene and hunting. These reliefs are also early examples of an innovative feature of Parthian art, frontality.

With the establishment of Parthian power in Mesopotamia, a strong influence of Parthian art can be found in Ctesiphon, Assur, Hatra, Palmyra and Dura-Europos. The rich testimony in architecture and art, especially in sculpture, reveals an adherence to the art of the Parthian elite, with sculptures depicting the embroidered Parthian dress, the distinct high headdress, weapons and jewellery. Wealth of the local elite was characterised by the adaptation of Parthian dress as well as their depiction with horses and camels.

Religious art of these cities also shows an adherence to Parthian couture and style, using frontal depictions.

As discussed above (pp. 111–113), of the Parthian cities Mithradatkert/Nisa yields most information about early Parthian art and architecture. Few reliefs have survived which could be defined as Parthian court art, most notably the Parthian reliefs at Bisitun.

The relief of Mithridates II, now partly destroyed by an inscription carved in the eighteenth century, originally showed a group of four Parthian noblemen standing before the king, probably Mithridates II, who is seen wearing the high *tiara*.[3] In this early relief the figures are still depicted in profile. The adjacent second relief uses an image that we encounter for the first time in Iran, the combat of two adversaries on horseback. The scene is dominated by the king on horseback holding a lance, and crowned by a Nike, a Victory. Opposite him, his adversary is stumbling over his falling horse. An inscription identifies him as 'Gotarzes, son of Gew'. The image of the chivalrous combat, here seen for the first time, became a favoured motif for the Sasanians, but its echo reaches far into medieval Europe and the combat of the lance-bearing medieval knight.

The choice of Bisitun is not without significance. It is, of course, the site known throughout the Achaemenid period for the famous inscription of Darius I, carved shortly after his accession to the throne in 522 BC. The location of the mountain, along the Royal Road leading from Ecbatana to Merv, ensured that it was noticed by travellers. It was a place of historical significance to the Persians, and the Parthians wanted to be seen in a continuous line from their predecessors.

Bisitun itself lay within a park-like space, which included a natural spring. Not far from the reliefs a massive boulder was carved with the image of a dignitary in Parthian dress, flanked on both sides by assistants, placing incense on an altar. The relief, dated to the second century AD, now shows the figure in full frontal position (see Fig. 28).

Ironically it is in the regional kingdoms where Parthian art has been best preserved, a reflection of the fact that the local nobility modelled their architecture, sculpture and fashion on those of the Parthian court. Most rewarding is the Parthian art of Elymais and of Hatra.

Figure 28
Parthian relief
at Bisitun
(photo: MB)

The art of Elymais

The Parthian kingdom of Elymais yields a substantial amount of monumental art which reflects a continuation with Iranian traditions. On the one hand there is the construction of artificial terraces at Masjed-e Soleiman and Bard-e Nisandeh; on the other there are the rock reliefs, most importantly those of Khung-e Nouruzi and Tang-e Sarvak. The terraced platforms in the western Zagros mountains, east of Susa, were constructed from huge blocks of natural stone. These terraces were used as sacred spaces. Masjed-e Soleiman was designed to contain three temples, including a 'Great Temple' for an unknown deity, and a temple of Heracles consisting of a *cella*, *antecella* and a sacristy (Boucharlat 1999: 34). Finds from this site point to regional Parthian art found in Elymais. The upper terrace of Bard-e Nisandeh may have provided space for a fire altar.

The relief at Khung-e Nouruzi provides us with the earliest example of a Parthian–Elymaian rock relief. It is an investiture scene of an Elymaite king, accompanied by three Parthian nobles, receiving the kingship from a royal power seated on horseback and accompanied by an attendant holding a fly-whisk. Above the two kings two flying eagles hold rings of power. It has been thought that the scene depicts the investiture of the Elymaian king Kamniskares, who is installed by the Parthian king, Mithridates. However, as Invernizzi suggested recently, there is reason to believe that the figure on horseback represents not the Parthian king, but the Seleucid king Demetrius II Nikator (Invernizzi 1998b) (see Fig. 29).

The rock reliefs of Tang-e Sarvak, carved on huge boulders, date to the late Parthian period (c. AD 150–224). Various scenes depict a king and his attendants in ritual ceremony, showing the king standing before an altar (III), or reclining in a ritual banquet, holding a wreath (II). The king, identified through an inscription as Orodes, is wearing the Parthian dress, a long tunic and trousers, and a helmet. To his left are two seated figures, also in Parthian dress, holding lances in their right hands. Both wear a typical Parthian hairstyle of a full, curly bob, one covered by a radiate crown,

Figure 29 Parthian relief at Khung-e Nouruzi (photo: MB)

the other by a helmet-like hat. These figures have been identified as two Greek goddesses, Artemis and Athena, or as Athena-Anahita and Mithra, but there is no evidence which supports such a view. Rather, it reflects the Greco-centric tendency to emphasise Parthia's immersion into Greek culture and religion. A more recent suggestion made by Vanden Berghe offers an alternative suggestion which allows a more Iranian view on the interpretation of this scene. In this interpretation the two figures might in fact be male, considering they are wearing trousers under the long tunic, and possibly even sport a moustache (Vanden Berghe, Schippmann 1985: Fig. 9).

Both Tang-e Sarvak and Bisitun provide us with examples of a new artistic motif introduced by the Parthians, the knights' combat. The scene shows two riders on horseback, in full armour, in the moment of attacking each other with their lances at full speed (see Fig. 30).

The latest testimony is a Parthian relief from Susa, dated by an inscription to 14 September, AD 215. It depicts the Parthian king Artabanus seated on a throne, handing the ring, the symbol of power, to Khwasak, the satrap of Susa. The quality of the relief is rather

Figure 30   Chivalrous combat on a Parthian relief at Tang-e Sarvak (with kind permission of H. von Gall)

132

poor, but despite this it shows that certain themes belonged to a catalogue of official motifs which local rulers wanted to follow. The reliefs of Khung-e Nouruzi and Tang-e Sarvak attest to the importance for a local ruler of commemorating his investiture and thereby demonstrating that the Parthian king sanctioned his rule. The best example known is undoubtedly the bronze statue of a Parthian prince from the sanctuary at Shami in Elymais (see Fig. 31). The figure,

Figure 31 Statue of a Parthian nobleman from Shami (courtesy of the Deutsches Archäologisches Institut, Berlin)

more than life-size at 1.90 m, shows a man in Parthian dress, a V-shaped short tunic draped around his waist and held by a belt, his trousers covered in loose-fitting, many-folded riding trousers which were held by garters. His hair is carefully coiffed to result in a bobbed hairstyle. He wears a broad band or diadem, probably a mark of status, and a thick, heavy torque around his neck. He is clean-shaven except for a moustache.

His costume is the standard riding costume of the Parthians, the over-trousers allowing for comfort when riding, and the V-shaped loose jacket allowing for good mobility of the upper body for riding and shooting with bow and arrow.

Hatra

Hatra was founded in the first century BC. It was a wealthy trading city, alongside Nisibis, Dura-Europos and Palmyra. Throughout its history it resisted repeated attempts from both the Romans and the Parthians to take the city, and only collapsed after a Sasanian attack in AD 240. The art and architecture of Hatra has revealed a rich culture influenced by both Hellenistic and Parthian art. Temples dominate the city's architecture, especially the temple for the sun-god Shamash which features five *ivans*, revealing a direct borrowing from Parthian architecture. Of special interest are the numerous statues of the Hatran deities as well as Hatran kings, their families, and members of the local nobility, for these are particularly exquisite examples of art following Parthian models. These statues show that the Hatran aristocracy wanted to be depicted in Parthian fashion, with curly, bobbed hairstyles, elaborately worked headdresses, Parthian dress, i.e. a long, belted tunic worn over many-folded trousers, and jewellery following Parthian designs (see Fig. 32). The headdresses and garments are crafted with considerable care, carefully showing the geometric pattern of the dress, and, with the use of a relief technique, depicting the richness of the embroidery, which consisted of appliqués made of precious material, including precious stones and pearls. The tunics are belted, often showing an elaborate design and beautifully crafted clasps made of metal. They were probably made of very fine material, dyed in fashionable colours which may have given evidence of the wearer's social standing. Textiles were woven in intricate geometrical designs or richly embroidered. Those who could afford it would have woven gold and silver into the cloth, and, as the ultimate demonstration of wealth, had pearls sown onto the garment in geometrical designs. Pearls were also used to decorate the headdresses, which could be similar to the high tiara worn by Parthian kings. Women's clothing also was used to reflect a person's status and wealth. As statues from Hatra show, women wore long, many-folded dresses, fastened with a brooch on one shoulder. High, elaborate headdresses, from which a long veil draped backwards, were adorned with pearls and jewellery. Necklaces would also be worn and earrings, rings and bracelets (see above Fig. 24b). The extravagance of dress, the style of the belt, the headdress, as well as the amount of jewellery worn, indicated the status of the wearer.

Religious sculpture depicting local deities reveals a syncretism of Greek and Near Eastern deities, with artistic elements and religious symbolism of both cultures incorporated into Hatran religious culture.

Figure 32
Statue of the Hatran king Sanatruq in Parthian dress (with kind permission of the Centro Ricerche Archeologiche e Scavi, Turin)

EXCURSUS II: THE PARTHIANS IN THE
EYES OF THE ROMANS

One of the most fascinating and revealing issues in the discussion of artistic representations of Parthians is not the way the Parthians and their subjects wanted to depict themselves in all their heterogeneity, but the way in which the Parthians were depicted by their main enemy, the Romans. Here, recent research has brought to light fascinating evidence of how the Romans created, and fervently fostered, the image of the *alter orbis*, the 'other world', the world of the eastern 'barbarian', standing in total opposition to its own.[4]

A *terminus post quem* for the beginning of the Roman artistic propaganda machine operating against Parthia can be set at 20 BC, the date when Augustus received the lost Roman standards from the Parthian king Phraates. To appreciate the Roman propaganda which was unleashed after this event it has to be emphasised that these standards were recovered in a peaceful act of diplomacy, and without the involvement of military force. Yet in Rome, the event was hailed as a victory of military proportions, and publicly entailed all elements of such a victory, including the erection of a Parthian arch, coins commemorating the event, Parthian Games, and the building of a temple for Mars Ultor to house the standards. According to Rolf Schneider this was one of the most pronounced political events of the principate (Schneider 1998: 97).

The Parthians were depicted as the stereotype of the eastern barbarian. Their otherness was shown physically in their body posture, dress, their hair and beards, and figuratively in the context in which they were used, as supporting figures on public buildings, as leg supports for tables and bronze stands, as support for inscriptions, as defeated enemies, lying on the ground, or with bent heads. In any case, they were depicted in a submissive, subservient and defeatist posture. Distinctive was the V-shaped tunic worn over the many-folded trousers, and made to look untidy and unkempt. The hair was depicted in wild and unruly curls, with and without a soft cap, which became known as the Phrygian cap. The men wore beards and moustaches, adding to their foreignness.

As Schneider revealed, the otherness of the Parthians was signified in a very pronounced manner in Augustan Rome. After 14 BC we find over-life-size figures which decorated public buildings in the city, representing Parthians as supporting figures, either in kneeling or upright positions. In contrast to the white marble used to carve statues of Roman dignitaries, these statues were made from coloured marble imported from Numidia and Phrygia. The marble emphasised the foreignness of the Parthian costume, and clearly identified these figures as 'coloured barbarians'.

On coins, Parthians were easily identified by their distinctive costume. Most notable among the depictions are probably those which show a single Parthian on the reverse of the coin, in kneeling position, offering the Roman standards. The image of the kneeling Parthian was seen on denarii minted in 19/18 BC. Figures of standing Parthians were erected on the Parthian arch, which was erected on the Forum Romanum, and was depicted on several mint series. Trajan minted coins in commemoration of his victory over Parthia, showing the submission of the Parthian king, with a legend reading 'PARTHIA CAPTA' ('Parthia has been conquered'), and the installation of a king with the legend 'REX PARTHIS DATUS' ('A king has been given to the Parthians') (see Fig. 33).

The irony of mints like these was that the Roman emperors claimed victory and hence control over an empire, which they never had. Augustus pretended to have won a military victory when in fact no battle was fought. Even though Trajan took Ctesiphon and some territories east of the Euphrates, it did not amount to a conquest of the Parthian empire. It was inconceivable within Roman propaganda that Parthia could stand on an equal political footing with Rome – which it did. Therefore, in contrast to the political

Figure 33
Sestertius of Trajan commemorating his Parthian victory (courtesy of the Ashmolean Museum, Oxford)

reality, Rome emphasised the image of Parthia as a barbarian country, its inhabitants as uncivilised, without order, culture or political strength. When they were not depicted as bearded barbarians, they were depicted as beautiful youths, still in Parthian garments, but clean-faced, with beautifully symmetrical features. The Parthian youth wearing a Phrygian cap became the image of the foreign, mythical being representing the god Mithra as well as Ganymede.

Curiously, at the same time as the Parthian was depicted as uncivilised, he was also 'orientalised' in traditional fashion, being described as luxury-loving, leading an effeminate lifestyle, and demonstrating excessive sexuality. These traits were not new. The Romans discovered them in history to justify and legitimise their anti-Parthian sentiments. For that reason the Romans regarded themselves as the new Greeks, especially the Greeks of 480/479 BC who had won victories against the Persian army of Xerxes at Salamis and Plataea. To make this connection, Medes, Achaemenids, Persians and Parthians were all conflated. The terms 'Parthian' and 'Persian' became interchangeable; any historical differentiation was denied to present 'the East'. It was no longer Greece versus Achaemenid Persia, it was West versus East, Europe versus Asia, Occident versus Orient, the defence of western values against the despotism of the East. The fact that this image did not stand up to reality was irrelevant. Public spectacles restaging the naval battles of the Greek–Persian wars, the inclusion of Spartan auxiliaries in Trajan's army, Nero's bridge across the Bay of Naples resembling Xerxes' bridge over the Hellespont, the parading of Parthian 'hostages' to show Roman superiority, if not victory – all these were ideologically infused demonstrations of Rome's power and Parthia's weakness. For Rome, there was only one world power; the existence of the other was plainly denied.

4

THE SASANIANS

HISTORICAL SURVEY

Beginnings

In AD 224 the Sasanian dynasty rose in Persis under Ardashir I (AD 224–239/40). Defeating the last Parthian king, Artabanus IV, in battle, Ardashir, the ruler of Istakhr, now claimed the royal title of 'King of Kings'. Ardashir was the son of Papak, who had seized power in Istakhr in 205/6 and had ruled as king under Parthian suzerainty. Their dynasty, however, took their name from Sasan, the guardian of the Anahita sanctuary at Istakhr. His familial relationship to Ardashir is disputed in the sources. According to the Arab historian Tabarī, Sasan was Ardashir's paternal grandfather, who had married a daughter of the noble Bazrangi family, while another source, the *Karnamak-e Ardashir*, claims that Sasan was Ardashir's maternal grandfather and Papak's father-in-law. The Sasanian dynasty was to rule for over four centuries until the collapse of the empire following the Arab invasions and the death of the last Sasanian king, Yazdgird III, in 651.

According to Tabarī, Ardashir had assumed the role of the district governor of Darabgird, a neighbouring district of Persis, at the beginning of the third century AD. Shortly afterwards, in c.205/6 his father seized the kingship of Istakhr, the capital of Persis, from Gozihr. After Papak's death and the accidental death of his son Shapur, the heir to the kingship of Istakhr, Ardashir returned to the city and was proclaimed king. His departure from Darabgird triggered a rebellion against his rule there, but it was short-lived and Darabgird was soon back under Ardashir's control. Over the next few years Ardashir gradually expanded his political influence in the region. From Darabgird he proceeded eastward, taking control of Kerman, where he killed the local Parthian king Balash and installed one of his sons as governor. He then moved his army to the Gulf region where he occupied Bahrain. Following the submission of local rulers of western Persis, he founded the city Ardashir Khvarrah, 'Glory of Ardashir' (modern Firuzabad), and built his own palace outside the city walls.

It was at this point that the Parthian king Artabanus IV became alerted to Ardashir's political ambitions. His self-proclamation as king of Istakhr, which had not received the approval of the Parthian king, his undisguised ambition for political and military power, and the foundation of a new city, a privilege of the King of Kings, directly challenged Parthian authority. Artabanus IV ordered the king of Ahwaz in southern Elymais to lead a Parthian force against Ardashir, but the campaign failed, and Artabanus IV himself gathered an army to confront Ardashir. On 28 April 224 the last Parthian king was killed in the battle of Hormuzjan in Media. Ardashir assumed the royal title of 'King of Kings', declaring himself a king in direct succession from the Parthians. This signalled the beginning of a new political power in Persia, made manifest in the introduction of a new time reckoning, the Sasanid era, which began in 224. It is attested in an inscription found in Bishapur dated to 263/4: 'In the month Fravardin, in the year 58 (of the era) (205/6); in the year 40 of the Ardashir fire (224), in year 24 of the Shapur fire (240/1), the king of fires'. The momentous event of Ardashir's victory over the Parthian king was commemorated in a vast rock relief carved near his royal centre at Firuzabad, depicting the equestrian battle between himself and Artabanus IV (see Fig. 34).

Yet Artabanus IV's death did not immediately signal the demise of the Parthian empire. The local kingdoms were still governed by Parthian rulers, who resisted the new power, especially in the western part of the empire, including Mesopotamia, Media and Armenia, where Ardashir campaigned between c.225 and 227. An attempt to take the city of Hatra failed, and he was forced to retreat from Armenia, when the ruling king, a member of the Arsacid dynasty, received the support of Median forces. But in the autumn of 226 Ardashir was able to take control of the Parthian royal capital

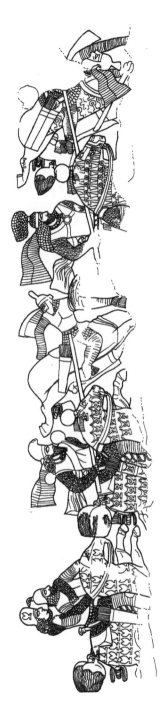

Figure 34 The battle between Artabanus IV and Ardashir I on a relief at Tang-e Ab, Firuzabad (with kind permission of H. von Gall)

Ctesiphon, where he inaugurated his reign as 'King of Kings' in an official investiture ceremony.

Though the dating of Ardashir's eastern campaigns is uncertain, the southeastern kingdom of Sistan, and the provinces of Khorrasan, Merv and Chorasmia, came under Sasanian control early in Ardashir's reign. These conquests seem to have triggered the submission of the kings of Kushan, Turan (*here*: eastern Baluchistan) and Makran. His empire now extended from the River Oxus to the Persian Gulf. In the east it bordered on the River Indus, while in the west the Euphrates remained the border with the Roman empire. The latter was to be contested by the Sasanians throughout their rule, as they laid claim on all the lands which they knew had belonged to Persia in the past (Dio Cassius 80.3.4; Herodian 6.2.2). However, it is thought that the Sasanians no longer possessed any detailed knowledge of these predecessors, and that even the names of the Achaemenid kings had not been committed to their memory. But expansion to the west as far as the Mediterranean, and control of Armenia, determined Sasanian policy towards the Romans over the next centuries.

In the early 230s Ardashir I focused his military efforts on the western expansion of his empire and even challenged Roman power with his attack on Nisibis. This city in Upper Mesopotamia was located at a strategically vital point, the intersection of the trade routes which gave access to the cities of Dura-Europos and Hatra. In the past, Nisibis had been frequently fought over by the Romans, Armenians and Parthians, and now, in a continuation of Parthian policy, Ardashir I upheld the claim for control of the city. His first attempt, however, failed and the Roman emperor Alexander Severus forced his retreat. Likewise, Sasanian raids across the Euphrates and into Roman Syria were repulsed. But Ardashir's fortunes changed in 235, when the death of Alexander Severus led to the destabilisation of Rome and the quick succession of so-called 'soldier-emperors'. Between c.237 and 239 Ardashir conquered Upper Mesopotamia and even took Nisibis and Carrhae. In April 239 Dura-Europos was taken, and a year later Hatra succumbed to Sasanian forces.

In 239 Ardashir's son Shapur I (239–270/3?) was proclaimed co-regent of the empire. He became sole 'King of Kings' in 241, even though Ardashir lived another year, until February 242. The Sasanian military campaigns into Roman Asia Minor, and, more

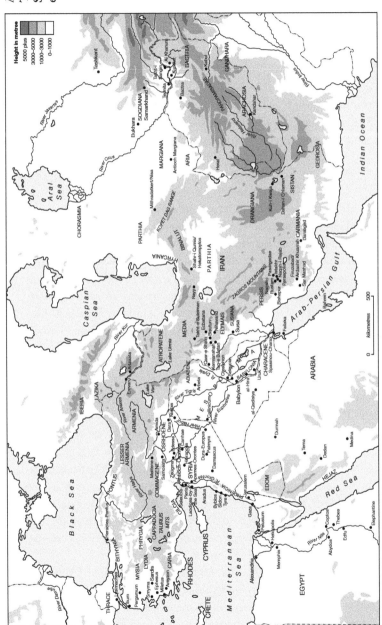

Map 6
The
Sasanian
empire

Height in metres
5000 plus
3000–5000
1000–3000
0–1000

importantly, the military aggression shown in the attacks on Roman Syria had demonstrated that this newly emerged Persian power was intent on the conquest of the former western territories of the Persian empire. Shapur I had to expect a military reaction from the Romans. For them, the loss of these cities warranted a counteroffensive, and the emperor Gordian III commanded an army against Shapur I, regaining both Nisibis and Carrhae. But he then suffered a major defeat in a battle at Misiche, north of Ctesiphon, in 243. In commemoration of his victory, Shapur I renamed the city Peroz Shapur, 'Shapur (is) Victorious'. Gordian III himself was killed, and the Praetorian Prefect, Philip the Arab, was proclaimed emperor.

> When at first We had become established in the empire, Gordian Caesar raised in all of the Roman Empire a force from the Goth and German realms and marched on Babylonia against the empire of Iran and against Us. On the border of Babylonia, at Misiche, a great frontal battle occurred. Gordian Caesar was killed and the Roman force was destroyed. And the Romans made Philip Caesar. Then Philip Caesar came to Us for terms and to ransom their lives, gave Us 500,000 dinars and became tributary to Us. And for this reason We have renamed Misiche Peroz-Shapur.
>
> (ŠKZ 3)

While Shapur I implies in his *res gestae*, inscribed on the walls of the Ka'aba-i Zardusht in Naqsh-i Rustam, that Gordian III died during the battle, the Roman sources insist that he was murdered by Philip the Arab. Even more revealing is the fact that Roman sources completely deny the defeat at the hands of the Sasanian king, and in a blatant reversal of historical truth even claim a Roman victory over the Sasanians. Roman propaganda continued to maintain a strong grip on the dissemination of the facts at the cost of historical reality and the preservation of the image of Rome as the sole (and invincible) world power.

In actual fact, Philip the Arab immediately sued for peace. He agreed to pay a ransom, and probably had to concede Roman territories in Mesopotamia and in Armenia to the Sasanians. However, a few years later, the war between the two powers was resumed when the Armenian king was killed and his son, Tiridates, sought refuge in Rome. Armenia, the buffer zone between the two empires of old, once again played a decisive role in the war between Rome and Persia. In 252 Shapur I led his army along the Euphrates River and won a battle near Barbalissos, a town on the road to Aleppo, annihilating a 60,000-strong Roman army, followed by a brutal campaign into Syria, taking numerous cities and devastating the land. His army advanced even further west and took Antioch-Orontes, one of the strategically most important cities of the Roman empire. Shapur's son Hormizd was dispatched to lead an expedition northward into Cappadocia between 253 and 255. But later in the year 253 Shapur suffered a grave defeat when a contingent of the Sasanian army was annihilated by the ruler of Palmyra, Odainath, who became a Roman ally. In 254 the Roman emperor Valerian continued the Roman campaigns against Shapur I, but the Sasanian army proved more successful. Shapur I took Dura-Europos and Circesion in 256 and in 260 the cities of Carrhae and Edessa. During the battle of Edessa the emperor Valerian was captured and remained in Persia as a prisoner of war. Following his victory at Edessa Shapur took thirty-seven cities in Syria, Cilicia and Cappadocia, including – for the second time – Antioch-Orontes.

The triple victory over the Romans was of such importance that Shapur I commemorated the event in both word and image. His victorious battles were commemorated in the trilingual inscription carved into the walls of the Ka'aba-i Zardusht, written in Parthian, Middle Persian and Greek, the official scripts used in Sasanian administration. The use of the site at Naqsh-i Rustam was deliberate. Although the Sasanians no longer possessed any detailed knowledge of the Achaemenids, they were aware that a previous Persian power had ruled the lands before the Parthians, and the monuments in Persis were testament to their greatness. Naqsh-i Rustam, where the royal tombs of the Achaemenids were located, therefore became the site which the Sasanians now adopted to document their political and military achievements. In doing so, the Sasanians laid claim to a historical succession of Persian dynasties.

Visually the victories over the Romans were commemorated with the creation of three separate rock reliefs, capturing the same scene, the victorious Shapur I on horseback, surrounded by the defeated Roman emperors. The scene on the reliefs depicts the body of

Gordian III lying beneath Shapur's horse, with Philip the Arab supplicating before the king, and Valerian standing beside him, his hand held by Shapur I, symbolising his captivity. The reliefs were carved at Darabgird, probably in honour of Shapur's father Ardashir I, at Bishapur in Persis, the city built by Roman prisoners of war to commemorate Shapur's victories, and – ideologically perhaps most important – at Naqsh-i Rustam,[1] where the tombs of the dynastic predecessors of the Sasanians were testimony to the historical continuity of Persian power.

After Shapur I's death, which should be dated between 270 and 273, three of his sons succeeded to the kingship. Shapur I had selected one of his two younger sons, Hormizd I (c.272–273), as his immediate heir to the throne and invested him during his lifetime: 'It is said that, when Shapur placed the crown on Hormizd's head the great men of state came into his presence and invoked blessings on him' (Tabarī 833).

His brother Bahram I (273–276) succeeded Hormizd a year later. He was Shapur's eldest son, and we can only speculate why he had been passed over by Shapur I in the royal succession. One of the reasons may have been a wariness of Bahram's devout commitment

Figure 35   Relief of Shapur II in Bishapur commemorating the victory over three Roman emperors (with kind permission of S. Mitchell)

to the Zoroastrian religion, which went contrary to Shapur's policy of tolerance towards the different religions practised across the Sasanian empire. Although Zoroastrianism, which had developed its doctrines over the past centuries, was the religion of the Persians, Shapur I, like the Persian kings before him, Achaemenids as well as Parthians, had tolerated other religions unless they conflicted with imperial policy. Thus we find both the chief Zoroastrian priest, Kirdir, as well as Mani, the founder of Manichaean religion, at the court of the Sasanian king. But when Bahram I came to power, possibly with the aid of Kirdir, the religious climate changed. Mani fell out of favour with the king, as well as with his son and successor Bahram II (276–293), and in 276 died in prison. Mostly through Kirdir's influence on Bahram I and Bahram II, the Zoroastrian religion became the sole faith tolerated at the court and across the empire. As a demonstration of his exalted status at court and of his considerable influence over Bahram II, Kirdir was permitted to have his own portrait carved on several rock reliefs. It was carved alongside an inscription at Naqsh-i Rustam and in the nearby site of Naqsh-i Rajab as testament to his devotion to the Zoroastrian religion (see Fig. 36).

Yet, however hard Kirdir tried to eradicate Manichaeism, his own power and influence were linked to Bahram I and his son, and it

Figure 36   Kirdir's relief at Naqsh-i Rajab (photo: MB)

seems that following their deaths Kirdir played a less influential role at the court of their successor, Narseh (293–302). Kirdir's zealous pursuit of Zoroastrianism and his intolerance towards other religions ended with Narseh's accession in 293.[2] Like his father Shapur I, Narseh pursued a more tolerant religious policy. His son Hormizd II (302–309) seems to have reigned with an equal ambition for justice and clemency (Tabarī 835–836).

In 293 the Roman emperor Carus was able to carry a military campaign into Mesopotamia and briefly occupied Ctesiphon, but he died soon afterwards, apparently killed by a bolt of lightning. Then the Romans succeeded in placing their candidate, Tiridates, on the Armenian throne, and Narseh declared war on the new emperor, Diocletian. After an initial defeat in Mesopotamia the Romans under Galerius made an attack further north, winning a decisive victory over Narseh in Armenia. Narseh's wife, his sisters and his children were taken captive (Aurelius Victor, *liber de Caesaribus* 39.33–36). In the Peace of Nisibis of 298 he conceded five territories west of the River Tigris to Rome, relinquished Georgia as a political ally, and recognised Roman-controlled Nisibis as the only city allowed to trade with the two empires.

> The principal points of the (Roman) embassy (*led by Sicorius Probus*) were these: that in the eastern region the Romans should have Intelene along with Sophene and Arzanene, Cordyene and Zabdicene, that the river Tigris should be the boundary between each state, that the fortress Zintha, which lies on the border of Media, should mark the edge of Armenia, that the king of Iberia (*Georgia*) should pay to the Romans the insignia of his kingdom and that the city of Nisibis, which lies on the Tigris, should be the place for transactions.
>
> (Petrus Patricius, frg.14, transl. J.M. Lieu)

Thereupon Narseh's family was set free and allowed to return to Persia. The peace agreement, which was to last for forty years, demonstrated two political issues: Rome did not underestimate Sasanian power, and for both sides the region of Upper Mesopotamia as well as the kingdom of Armenia were crucial geopolitical regions, the control of which would be an ongoing cause of war.

The reigns of Shapur II and his successors

From the fourth century onwards religion became politicised for both the Roman and the Sasanian empires. Constantine the Great (307–337) publicly gave his support to the Christian religion after AD 312. The Christianisation of the Roman empire meant that the Christian religion became synonymous with Roman politics. Followers of the Christian faith were equated with supporters of Rome, a sentiment which had a particular bearing on Armenia, where it divided the nobility between an anti-Christian group which supported Persia, and a Christian group which supported Rome/Byzantium. It also had implications for the Christians living in Sasanid Persia, whose position in the empire became much more vulnerable.

In 309 Shapur II succeeded to the throne, favoured by the Sasanian nobility over three older sons of Hormizd II (John of Antioch, frg.178; FHG 4: 165). Shapur II led a campaign against Arab tribes which had crossed the Persian borders and had even advanced into Persis, and conducted further campaigns on the Arab peninsula across the Persian Gulf (Tabarī 836). A truce with Constantine meant that the two empires enjoyed a period of peace on the Roman–Sasanian border, but hostilities commenced after the death of the Roman emperor in 337. In 338 Shapur II led an army into Armenia and temporarily forced its king Khosrow to leave Armenia and seek Roman protection. From there he marched into northern Mesopotamia. The focus of his raids into Roman territory was Nisibis, which was besieged several times, in 338, 346 and again in 350, but which was able to withstand the Sasanian attacks. The first persecutions of Christian groups began in the aftermath of the first failed siege of Nisibis. The main reason may have been that, in times of crisis, Christians were easily targeted as a political scapegoat, being suspected of acting as Rome's fifth column.

> The pagans (in Persia) slandered the Christians to Shapur, their king, (accusing them) of sending an embassy to the Roman emperor. Shapur became angry and began to oppress the Christians and destroy their churches. Constantine the Victorious wrote to him saying: 'Considering that I keep the divine faith, I dwell in the light of truth, I profess the

true faith etc.' Shapur not only did not accept his words,
but he immediately went up against Nisibis. He withdrew
from there, covered in confusion, thanks to the prayers of
Mar Jacob and Mar Ephrem. In his anger, he took captives
from Mesopotamia.

(Michael the Syrian, *Chron*.VII.3, p. 132;
transl. Vince, revised Brock)

In the course of the constant raids of both Sasanian and Roman
forces into enemy territory, the Sasanians suffered another setback
at Amida (modern Diyabakir) in 344. By 350 Shapur II had to abandon his western campaigns and move his troops to the east, where
nomadic tribes, the Chionites, who probably belonged to the larger
group of the Huns, threatened the northern border of the empire.
Over the next eight years Shapur's military attention seems to have
focused on his eastern campaigns where he successfully defended the
borders of the empire and strengthened his political control. His success allowed him to ignore a Roman peace offering submitted in 356,
and instead he launched a renewed attack on Roman Amida soon
after the end of his eastern campaigns in 359. His army now included
a military contingent under the command of the Chionite king,
Grumbates, and with his aid Amida was taken after a 73-day siege
amidst much slaughter of the city's population (Amm.Marc.19.1–9).

Meanwhile, in Byzantium, Julian contested the throne of
Constantius II, and was proclaimed emperor in 360. He embarked
on a massive campaign against Shapur II, marching directly towards
Ctesiphon. The two armies never confronted one another on the
battlefield; instead Shapur II raided the land and thereby threatened
the food supply for the Roman army. Even though Julian reached
the Sasanian capital, Ctesiphon, he did not besiege the city, but
rather began the retreat. When Julian died in a minor skirmish, the
army found itself without protection in enemy territory and short
of supplies. Jovian was appointed Julian's successor, and he immediately entered into peace negotiations with Shapur II. In a reversal
of the Peace of Nisibis, the Romans ceded Nisibis to the Sasanian
empire, and were forced to relinquish the conquered territories east
of the Euphrates. Armenia also was to return to Sasanian control
(Amm.Marc.25.7.9). However, a few years later, the Roman emperor
Valens opposed the Sasanian control of both Armenia and Georgia.

As a result, each kingdom was divided into a Sasanian and a Roman section, with Roman Armenia being reduced to a mere province.

Shapur's long reign was dominated by wars and raids against the Romans in the west, against Arab tribes in the south, and nomadic invasions in the north and east. But despite suffering initial military setbacks against the Romans, Shapur II successfully defended the empire from attack by invaders, and affirmed Sasanian control of the southern and northeastern borders of the empire. Defence walls built in strategically important parts of the empire demonstrated a long-term strategy for the protection of the empire,[3] while the alliance with the Chionite king, however temporary it may have been, was evidence of his political and diplomatic skills. Yet Shapur's politically most significant triumph must have been the Roman retreat at Ctesiphon and the retrieval of Sasanian territory from Roman occupation.

Over the next 150 years Sasanian political history was overshadowed by succession troubles in which the hold of the Sasanian nobility over the kingship became manifest. Although Shapur II's successors were members of the royal dynasty, the king's dependency on the political and military support of the nobility was reflected in their ability to depose a reigning king in favour of another royal candidate. Successors were found among the king's brothers as well as his sons, leaving the nobility a wide range of candidates to choose from. It was a situation which considerably weakened Sasanian kingship and revealed the growing antagonism between the king and the aristocracy. The problem was not to be addressed, at least to some extent, until the reign of Kavad I, when a social revolt threatened the power of the aristocracy. For now, the nobility exercised their power over the king. They deposed Shapur's successor, his half-brother Ardashir II (379–383), after a four-year reign and replaced him with a son of Shapur, Shapur III (383–388). Five years later, he, too, was dethroned by the nobility, who possibly were also responsible for his murder. His brother Bahram IV (388–399) was able to stay on the throne for eleven years, before he was assassinated in 399, again probably on the orders of the noble class. During Bahram's reign the Sasanians were for the first time threatened by Hunnic peoples who had invaded the empire from the north, crossing the Caucasus mountains, and were able to move as far as Mesopotamia.

Under Yazdgird I (399–421) the Sasanian empire enjoyed a period of relative peace with Byzantium. It was also a period of tolerance towards the Christians of Persia. Under the auspices of Yazdgird I a synod was held in Seleucia in 410, in which the Christian groups of the empire were officially recognised as a religious community, distinct from the western Christians of the Byzantine empire. The head of the church was to be appointed by the Sasanian king. But the most fervent of the Christian groups were unable to tolerate the Persian Zoroastrians and sought to attack these 'pagans', burning down their sacred temples. Yazdgird I immediately retaliated with persecutions. The situation calmed again under Yazdgird's successor Bahram V Gor ('the Wild Ass (Hunter)') (421–439). Peace with Byzantium was maintained, but only because the emperor had to focus his military forces on invaders from the northern borders, while the Sasanian king had to confront eastern invasions of nomadic peoples, who were probably Hephtalites.

We possess little information about Sasanian foreign policy during this period. Although there was no direct confrontation with Rome, conflicts between the two empires arose over Armenia and Georgia. But principally, both powers were occupied with an increasing problem of invading peoples. Rome, which had split into eastern and western empires after the death of Theodosius I in 395, suffered invasions from Goths, Vandals and other Germanic tribes. The borders of Sasanid Persia were increasingly threatened by nomadic tribes invading from the northern steppes. Apart from the Chionites who had invaded Persia at the time of Shapur II, there now appeared a new wave of intruders, known as Kidarites, Alxon and Napki. Bahram's successor Peroz (459–484) fought two long campaigns against the Hephtalites; one, which began in c.465, ended in disaster, when Peroz and his family were taken prisoner. He was forced to pay a ransom for his own freedom, and to make further payments in order to secure the freedom of his son Kavad. A second attack on his eastern enemies ended with a further defeat, during which Peroz himself was killed. His successor Valakhsh signed a peace treaty with the Hephtalites but the payment of an annual tribute remained (Procopius, *BP* 1.4.35). By now the Hephtalites had become a recognised political force which was used in the succession struggles of the Sasanian dynasty. They supported

Kavad I (488–496, 499–531), the son of Peroz, in his bid for the throne in 488 and again eleven years later, in 499, after the Sasanian nobility had temporarily dethroned him in favour of another candidate, Zamasp.

Kavad's reign was marred by an internal threat. A new religion, preached by a Persian named Mazdak, led to social unrest among the population. While the movement was at first tolerated by Kavad, because it curbed the power of the landed aristocracy, the nobles reacted by dethroning the king who, after escaping from prison, sought refuge with the Hephtalite king. With the help of an alliance concluded with the Hephtalite king, which was sealed with a marriage to the king's daughter Niwandukht, Kavad regained his power three years later, in 499. The Hephtalites then supported him in a campaign against Armenia where Kavad succeeded in taking Theodosiopolis in 502 and even took Amida in January 503. For the next ten years Kavad I had to concentrate his military forces in the north of the empire, where once again the incursions of nomads threatened the stability of the empire. It led him to sue for peace with the Romans, which was concluded in 506 (Procopius, *BP* 1.9.24). But war with Rome was resumed in 527 over Georgia. In several battles the Roman Belisarius commanded the Roman army successfully against the Sasanians, but he was finally defeated in the battle at Callinicum in 531. Kavad I himself died before he could turn the success against the Romans to his advantage.

The height of empire: Khosrow I Anoshirvan ('Of Immortal Soul') (531–579)

During the 48-year reign of Khosrow I, son of Kavad I and Niwandukht, the war with Byzantium became more marked. In the terms of the Endless Peace, concluded in 532, Justinian agreed to pay 11,000 pounds in gold (Procopius, *BP* 1.22.3). The peace agreement allowed Justinian to focus on his war against the Vandals in Africa and the Goths in Italy. While Justinian was away in Italy, Khosrow I attacked Roman territory in 540. The pretext for the renewed hostilities was the city of Lazika (ancient Colchis), which asked Khosrow for military support against its Byzantine overlords. The Sasanian army was sent to the Black Sea and occupied Petra. The lack of Roman defences in the east meant that Khosrow could take cities in Mesopotamia and Syria, resulting in the sack of Antioch (Procopius, *BP* 2.7). Khosrow ordered the city to be rebuilt near Ctesiphon as Weh Antioch Khosrow, 'Better-than-Antioch-(is the city built by) Khosrow'. The Sasanians moved against Armenia where they defeated a larger Roman force, killing its general Narses. A five-year treaty was concluded in 545, in which the Romans agreed to pay a sum of 2,000 pounds of gold. But Lazika proved to be too high a price to pay for peace, and in 549 the war over the city was resumed. A second treaty was signed in 551 with a further payment of 2,600 pounds of gold. All the while, the Byzantine–Sasanian conflict still continued in Lazika, and it took until 561 for a peace agreement to be made in which the Sasanians ceded Lazika, but received a further 30,000 pounds of gold from Byzantium (Menander Protector, frg.11 M). The agreement was made between Peter the Patrician, the Byzantine Master of Offices, and the Persian ambassador Yesdegusnaph.

But Khosrow I had to turn his attention once again to the northeast, where the Hephtalites threatened the borders of the empire. He was supported by a new force, the Turks (Chin. *T'u-Küe*), who occupied the region between the Gobi desert and Turfan, as far as Lake Balkhash. Their alliance led to the defeat of the Hephtalites in 560, with the Oxus River as the border between Turkish and Sasanian territory. Until the end of his reign Khosrow was faced with the potential threat of a military alliance between the Turks and the eastern Roman empire. Their united force would pose a serious threat to the Sasanian army, but in addition there were political and economic implications to consider. An embassy of the Turks was sent to the emperor Justin II in 568 to negotiate a commercial alliance in which the Turks offered to take control of the silk trade. This would circumvent the Sasanian realm, thereby inflicting considerable damage to Sasanian trade. In the end, nothing came of such a Byzantine–Turk alliance.

Renewed warfare under Justin II began with an unsuccessful Roman attack on Nisibis, followed by a Sasanian counterattack on Dara, which forced the Romans to end the war in 573. In the 570s Khosrow was able to extend Sasanian power into south Arabia, when he expelled the Roman-backed occupier Ethiopia, and installed a local noble as king of Himyar. Until the end of the Sasanian empire this country, equivalent to modern Yemen, remained under Sasanian overlordship, and provided the Sasanians with a strong foothold for the maritime trade with India.

Khosrow's internal politics were marked by two important measures, the eradication of Mazdakism and the implementation of social and legal reforms. Early in his reign Khosrow I curbed internal rebellion and possible sources for the formation of opposition by extinguishing the religion of Mazdak, whose religious teachings advocated a social policy which undermined the hierarchical structure of Sasanian society. He also pursued a harsh policy against the followers of Manichaeism, though this was apparently limited to certain groups within this religion. Sasanian control over various peoples of the eastern part of the empire was reaffirmed, as in the case of the Bariz, a people inhabiting the region southeast of Kerman, who suffered punitive campaigns and were forced into a humiliating submission. In a military reform he instituted four military commanders, called *spāhbeds*, who held the highest military office, replacing a single supreme commander. Each of them was given the command of one of four geographical quarters of the empire. The decentralisation of military control was probably aimed at curbing the chances of one leader being able to form a military opposition against the king.

According to Tabarī, Khosrow set the tone for his kingship in a letter addressed to the highest officials of his empire:

> The thing that most strikes fear into the hearts of people is the feeling of deprivation felt by those who fear the ending of their state of comfortable living, the eruption of civil disorders, and the advent of unpleasant things to the best of individuals, in regard to their own persons, their retainers, their personal wealth, or what is dearest to them. We know of no cause for fear or absence of a thing that brings more crushing ill fortune for the generality of people, nor one likely to bring about universal disaster, than the absence of a righteous king.
>
> (Tabarī 893)

One of the measures Khosrow undertook to bring peace to the empire was to end the social upheaval which had been brought about, or was a by-product of, the religion preached by Mazdak.

> Among the things he (*Mazdak*) ordained for people, made
> attractive to them, and urged them to adopt, was holding
> their possessions and their families in common. (. . .) With
> those doctrines, he incited the lower classes against the
> upper classes.
>
> (Tabarī 894)

Khosrow extirpated Mazdakism and ordered its fervent followers to be killed. He acted equally harshly in the case of a group of Manichaeans.

In a tax reform Khosrow I ordered the land to be surveyed and harvests properly accounted for in order to determine the exact taxation of the population. He was thereby able to exercise more control over the state's income than previously, when tax collection was controlled at the local level and subject to variation. A new class of small landowners, the *dehkānān*, was created, possibly to balance the power of the landowning nobility. To increase agricultural productivity through irrigation, Khosrow endowed the extension of canals and subterranean water channels by providing financial support. Old bridges were restored and new ones built; care was given to the road system in order to improve the infrastructure of the empire and to facilitate trade. Castles and fortifications were built along the main road network to protect caravans and internal traffic.

With his social legislation, a countermeasure to the situation brought about by Mazdak's reforms, Khosrow decreed that care should be provided for children whose father was not known. Women who had been taken against their will were entitled to claim compensation from their assailant. If the woman was married she was to remain with her husband; if not, she was free to choose whether or not to stay with the man who had taken her. Orphaned children who belonged to the nobility were to be brought up at the royal court and later married to spouses of their own social standing. The king himself guaranteed their bridal goods and dowries, and promised them high offices at court.

Khosrow was a great social reformer, while at the same time he revived the Sasanian court through his support of the arts and sciences. He promoted the literary heritage not only of his own country, but of non-Iranian lands too, as well as science and medicine. Greek medicine was welcomed at the Sasanian court, as was

Indian science and the Buddhist religion. Histories and stories which had previously been committed to memory were written down to be preserved for posterity. It is for these qualities of political and cultural leadership that Khosrow was remembered in the Persian and Arab world as one of the greatest kings of the Sasanian dynasty.

The last kings

Under Khosrow's son and successor Hormizd IV (579–590) Sasanian policy with regard to Rome remained hostile, while the threat of an invasion by the Turks continued to loom, but was averted when the Sasanian commander Bahram Chubin defeated the Turks in 589. But Hormizd soon lost the support of the nobility and was replaced by his son Khosrow II (590–628).

During the reign of Khosrow II the Sasanian empire enjoyed a brief but important military resurgence, during which the Sasanian army advanced as far as Chalcedon, opposite Constantinople, in 615, posing the most imminent threat ever to the Byzantine emperor. He extended his empire in the south with the successful invasion in 619 of Egypt, which was the crucial provider of grain for the Roman/Byzantine world. The Sasanian army even advanced further south into Nubia. But Khosrow's reign also saw what is dubbed 'the last battle of antiquity', the last battle between a Byzantine and a Sasanian army, led by the emperor Heraclius on the one side, and Khosrow II on the other.

Khosrow II ascended to the throne in February 590 with the support of the Sasanian nobles, but his rule was contested by the Sasanian general Bahram Chubin. When a peaceful solution between the two contestants could not be reached a state of war erupted between them, and Khosrow was forced to seek Roman support for his claim to the throne. While Khosrow was staying at Circesium, Bahram crowned himself king. The emperor Maurice declared his support for Khosrow as the legitimate royal heir to the throne (Theopylactus Simocatta 4.14.1–2) and, gathering support, Khosrow prepared his campaign against Bahram VI Chubin, who was finally defeated in a battle near the River Blarathos (Theopylactus Simocatta 5.9.4–11.7).

Maurice's policy of support for Khosrow II ensured a period of peace between Byzantium and Sasanid Persia. The emperor even entrusted his oldest son Theodosius to Khosrow II when Maurice's rule was threatened by Phocas, but Byzantium fell into political turmoil after Phocas proclaimed himself emperor following the death of Maurice in 602. When he was overthrown by Heraclius in 610, the Sasanians once again resumed their war against Byzantium. In 611 Khosrow's army took Antioch, followed by Damascus and Tarsus (613), and even conquered Jerusalem (614), removing the Holy Cross from the city and taking it to Ctesiphon. It was predominantly the Christians who suffered during the plunder of the city.

By 622 Heraclius was ready to go to war against Khosrow. He had secured a fragile peace in the west with the Avars and was therefore able to concentrate his forces on a massive eastern campaign. For this enterprise he also received financial support from the Church, evidently in reaction to the Sasanian occupation of Jerusalem and the persecution of its Christian inhabitants. The first battle between the two armies was fought in February 623, probably in eastern Anatolia, in which Heraclius emerged victorious. Further campaigning, however, was hampered by the constant threat of a renewal of the hostilities with the Avars. Thus it was only in December 627 that Heraclius' army confronted Khosrow II again, this time on Sasanian territory, and fought a decisive battle near Nineveh. Khosrow and his wife fled from Heraclius' advancing army, leaving Khosrow's residence at Dastagird to travel to Ctesiphon. Only by destroying the bridges which gave access to Ctesiphon, as well as by gathering a large military force, did Khosrow stop Heraclius from taking the city.

At this point Khosrow lost control over his own ranks, and he was killed in a palace coup. His son Shiroe succeeded to the throne as Kavad II. But this palace coup signalled the beginning of the end of the Sasanian dynasty, and reigns of Sasanian monarchs followed in quick succession, even including two daughters of Khosrow II, Puran, who reigned for one year (630–631), and her sister Azarmigdukht, whose reign lasted for only four months. The Sasanian empire fell in the reign of the Sasanian king Yazdgird III (633–651). The final blow was dealt not by the Byzantines, but by a new power from the south, the Arabs.

The Arabs had gradually taken control of the Arabian peninsula, taking Bahrain, Yemen and the territory of the Lakhmids. They then forced the Byzantines out of Syria, and in 636 advanced into the

Sasanian empire, taking Babylon. In the spring of 636 the two armies met at al-Qadisiya, and after a bitter battle fought over several days, the Sasanian army was defeated. A few months later the Arabs took the royal capital, Ctesiphon, almost without resistance, and then embarked on the conquest of the lands of the Sasanian empire. In 642 they defeated a Sasanian army at Nihavand in Media in a final battle. Yazdgird himself was killed, probably by members of his own court, in 651. The Arab conquest of the Sasanian empire ended a history of Persian rule which had begun over 1,500 years earlier. With it the world of the ancient Near East had come to an end.

KING AND COURT

> I, the Mazda-worshipping Lord Shapur (I), King of Kings of Iran and non-Iran, whose lineage is from the Gods, son of the Mazda-worshipping divinity Ardashir, King of Kings of Iran, whose lineage is from the Gods, grandson of king Papak, ruler of Iranshahr.
>
> (ŠKZ §1)

In his *res gestae* Shapur I professed to be a follower of Ahuramazda and therefore of Zoroastrian religion. But with the announcement that he was the king of kings 'whose lineage is from the Gods' Shapur's kingship went far beyond a declaration of his creed. The godlike status of the Sasanian king was expressed in the use of the Middle Persian term *bay* (god), which, however, is distinct from the term *yazd* (divinity), used only for deities. Beginning with Shapur I the Sasanians also extended the Parthian royal title of 'King of Kings' as a kingship exercised over 'Iran and non-Iran'. 'Iran', the Middle Persian rendering of the word 'Aryan', described the ethnic descent of all Iranian peoples. As 'King of Kings of Iran and non-Iran' the Sasanian monarch expressed his claim to rule over all the peoples of the empire, were they of Iranian or non-Iranian descent.

The Sasanian king had to be a member of the royal dynasty. Primogeniture was not a necessary criterion for succession to the throne, but the king's descent from the royal dynastic family remained the vital prerequisite for selection to the throne throughout Sasanian rule. In the case of a smooth succession the king selected the heir to the throne, who, on his accession, received the public acclamation of the nobility. However, owing to the powerful position of the noble class at the court, as well as dynastic strife and war, the selection of the king was frequently determined by the nobility. Considering that his accession and, more importantly, his survival, was controlled by the Sasanian nobility, the adherence to the principle of dynastic descent may seem superfluous, but the Sasanian dynasty was blessed with the *khvarrah*, the 'divine fortune', which meant that it was inextricably linked with the kingship. At a practical level, the nobility's consensus on choosing the king from among the Sasanian family prevented the possibility that members of the nobility would compete for the kingship, which would have led to dissent not only between king and nobility, but between the noble families themselves.

In continuation of the ceremonial practices of the Parthians the investiture was celebrated in the presence of the nobility, which, it is important to note, included Persians as well as Parthians. Many of the Parthian noble houses continued to serve in high office under the new dynasty, and their political and military support was acknowledged in the Sasanian royal inscriptions. An innovation of the investiture ceremony was the inclusion of the chief *mōbad*, the priest, who would place the crown on the king's head. His presence may indicate that the official investiture was not followed by a separate religious ceremony.

It is not certain where the royal investiture took place. Ardashir I had proclaimed himself 'King of Kings' on the battlefield of Hormuzjan, but his coronation as 'King of Kings' was celebrated in the royal capital of the Parthians, Ctesiphon. As the royal capital of the Sasanian kings, it may well have served as the place for the royal investiture throughout Sasanian rule. It has been suggested that coronation ceremonies also took place at Istakhr.

The divine inauguration of the king was a central aspect of Sasanian kingship and became manifest in several investiture reliefs which invariably depict the king receiving divine power directly from the god. In these scenes the two figures are arranged antithetically, either standing or on horseback, with the king shown receiving his power, symbolised in a ring, directly from the god. The earliest investiture scene was carved by Ardashir I on a rock surface near Ardashir Khvarrah/Firuzabad which shows the king and the god facing each other, as Ardashir receives the ring of power from Ahuramazda. The scene is witnessed by members of the nobility (see Fig. 37).

Figure 37a   Investiture relief of Ardashir I at Tang-e Ab, Firuzabad (photo: MB)

Figure 37b   Investiture relief of Ardashir I at Tang-e Ab, Firuzabad – close-up (photo: MB)

Historically most important, however, is a second relief which Ardashir carved at Naqsh-i Rustam, which the Sasanians recognised as a historically significant place of their predecessors. Ardashir's relief was the first of several investiture reliefs to be placed here by the Sasanians, who also used the site to commemorate the power struggles between contestants to the throne in depictions of chivalrous combat. In using this site, the Sasanian kings laid claim to a Persian heritage of royal rule, and signified historical continuity.

Ardashir's investiture relief is not only of historical importance, it also is one of the finest artistic executions of a rock relief. The high relief depicts Ardashir and Ahuramazda on horseback, their respective enemies, the last Parthian king Artabanus IV and the evil god Ahriman, lying dead beneath their horses. The message conveyed in this image is all too clear: as the god triumphs over the evil power, so Ardashir triumphs over his enemy; as Ahuramazda vanquishes spiritual enemies, his equivalent power on earth, Ardashir, vanquishes his political foes (see Fig. 38).

A further relief, carved at nearby Naqsh-i Rajab, introduces a new form of depiction, which includes other members of the royal family. Between the standing figure of the king and Ahuramazda we now

Figure 38 Investiture relief of Ardashir I at Naqsh-i Rustam (with kind permission of S. Mitchell)

find two smaller figures, one being the king's son and heir, the other probably the Iranian god Verethragna, who, in a syncretic adaptation, took the guise of the Greek god Heracles, and hence was depicted holding a club. The scene is set under a canopy and takes place in the presence of, yet unobserved by, two female figures, one of whom undoubtedly is to be identified as Ardashir's wife and mother of the heir to the throne. With this relief Ardashir added the image of the royal family to the corpus of royal representations, a feature which was to be continued by his successors.

Shapur I followed his father's practice of commemorating his accession to the throne in two different investiture scenes. While one relief follows the model of the divine investiture between the mounted king and god, a second relief shows King Shapur on horseback, watched by members of the Parthian and Persian nobility – a first visual expression of the godlike king who is separate from the nobility, and the 'secular' approval of the king by heads of the Persian noble houses. Shapur also ensured the loyalty of the noble class through gifts given to them directly from the royal treasury as well as from the treasuries of the kingdoms:

> When the crown was (eventually) placed on his head (*i.e. after his father's death*), he (*Shapur I*) gathered together before him all the great men of state. (. . .) Then he gave orders that the riches in the treasuries were to be lavished on the people (*the landed and military classes who supported the state*), sharing them out amongst those whom he deemed worthy of receiving them – the prominent persons, the troops, and those (of them) who had fallen into indigence. He wrote to his governors in the provinces and outlying districts that they were to do so likewise with the wealth under their control.
>
> (Tabarī 826)

During his investiture the king received the royal insignia, including the king's headdress, a personalised crown worn together with the royal diadem. The image of the king wearing his personal crown was depicted on the royal coinage, and has often been decisive in identifying a ruler. The most distinctive feature of the royal Sasanian headdress was the ball-shaped feature rising above the crown, which may have been a ball of hair covered with a silk-like fabric. The crowns themselves became more elaborate over time, as broadening turreted crowns, often featuring elaborate additional ornaments, such as wings and/or a crescent moon, or deer's antlers, symbols of the kings' *khvarrah*.

At the death of a king the fires which burnt in honour of his reign were extinguished, and only after the official mourning period had been observed were fires lit for the new king. This practice also applied to other members of the royal family. It is somewhat surprising that we know virtually nothing about royal burial customs. So far no evidence has been brought to light which would demonstrate that the remains of the Sasanian kings and their families were buried at a designated site. As followers of Zoroastrian religion, their bodies would have been exposed and their bones placed in an ossuary. Only further excavation might reveal whether a designated royal site, such as Ctesiphon or Istakhr, included a space to house the remains of the king and his family.

The king was the head of the empire. He acted as lawgiver, instituted reforms, and led his army in war. His rule was absolute, though in practice his reign was controlled by the nobility. Only in the early phase of Sasanian kingship, in the transition of power from Ardashir I to Shapur I, did the king appoint a co-regent. This was most certainly intended to secure an untroubled succession and as a measure against any attempt to destabilise the new dynasty.

Kingship was expressed in court ceremony, religious ritual, banqueting and hunting (see Figs. 39, 40, 41). Royal virtues, such as courage and endurance, excellence in horsemanship, skilfulness in archery and javelin-throwing, were practised during the hunt, which was pursued in the enclosed parks of royal estates, as well as on the plains and in the forests outside the palace world. Both banqueting and hunting were the favoured motifs in interior palace decoration, in plaster and stucco work, on stone, in mural paintings, and in textiles. They are most prominent on ceremonial silver dishes, especially on plates, cups and bowls, which might have been displayed at royal feasts and banquets but were also prestigious royal gifts presented to the nobles and dignitaries. Banquet and hunting scenes were also a favoured motif on gems, rings and seals. The hunting scenes depict the king as the hunter, often on horseback, or riding a camel or an elephant, or on foot. His prey includes bears, lions, boars, deer and gazelles. Perhaps the most striking execution of a hunting scene is the carving on the walls of the *ivan* of Khrosrow II at Taq-e Bostan in Media, in which Khosrow is depicted within successive scenes as a boar hunter amidst his hunting party and accompanying musicians.

A further motif to demonstrate the king's courage and fighting skills was the depiction of the chivalrous combat, the fight between the king and an equal opponent on horseback, engaged in a frontal attack with their lances. The chivalrous combat, first encountered in Parthian rock art, is depicted in several reliefs at Naqsh-i Rustam (see Fig. 42), but also appears on gems and finger rings. As the rock reliefs clearly indicate, the accession of the king was a key event, manifested in the chivalrous defence of his throne, or his investiture and public acclamation by Ahuramazda and the Sasanian nobility.

Figure 39 Sasanian silver plate depicting a royal banquet (courtesy of the Walters Art Museum, Baltimore)

Figure 40 Sasanian gold and silver plate depicting a royal
hunt of Shapur II (with kind permission of The
Hermitage Museum, St Petersburg)

Figure 41 Hunting scene of Khosrow II in a relief at Taq-e Bostan (photo:
MB)

The king's immediate officials at court were the *bidakhsh*, the vice-chancellor, who was the king's second-in-command, and the *hazāruft* (Gr. *chiliarch*), the leader of the royal bodyguard, followed by the *asbed*, the master of the cavalry, and the *framādār*, the commander-in-chief. Further high offices were those of the *argbed*, the commander of a fortress, and the *sālār ī darīgān*, the commander of the palace guard. There appears to have been a royal adviser and an adviser of the queens. A master of ceremonies, a chief of services and a chief steward were in charge of different aspects of court life, and probably had immediate access to the king, while the chief scribe and the treasurer were responsible for the court administration. A judge and a priest (*magus*) represented the legal and religious affairs of the court respectively. Matters relating to royal pursuits like hunting were administered by the master of the hunt and the chief of boars. The king had supreme command in war, but there were also two military offices, the head of the infantry (MP *spāhbed*) and the head of the cavalry. When Khosrow I instituted reforms in the sixth century, he divided the empire into four large administrative and military sections; accordingly the single head of administration and the head of the military were replaced by four officials each.

Figure 42   Sasanian relief at Naqsh-i Rustam depicting a chivalrous combat (photo: MB)

Members of the Persian and Parthian nobility acted as advisers to the king or were members of the King's Council. They were admitted to the royal court and enjoyed the privilege of dining at the King's Table. These nobles were allowed to wear *tiaras* which, through colour and individual emblems, distinguished them from one another and ranked their status in relation to the king.

The Sasanian court migrated between different royal capitals. Ctesiphon, the former Parthian royal centre, was taken over as the winter residence and the representational centre of the Sasanian kings. During the Sasanian period it was much rebuilt and extended, and a number of cities were added in its vicinity by several Sasanian kings, leading to its name in Arabic sources as 'al-Mada'in', 'The Cities'. Ardashir I built Weh-Ardashir there, a circular city west of the royal palace, and in the sixth century Khosrow I added Weh Antioch Khosrow, which may have been located southeast of the royal palace. The royal palace (Ivan-e Khosrow) stood on the east bank of the river, featuring a central *ivan* 35 m high, with a span of 25 m, flanked by two smaller *ivans*. In the great audience hall three empty seats stood below the king's throne, ready to receive the Roman emperor, the great Khagan of Central Asia and the Chinese emperor. The audience hall was decorated with mosaics, and the floor was covered with an immense carpet, measuring 27 x 27 m. Its design depicted a garden, creating the illusion that even in winter the king would sit in a spring garden in which 'paths formed figures, the separating parts rivers, the intervals between them hills. On its border earth sown with spring growth out of silk against branches of gold, silver and the like'[4] (Tabarī 2452).

City-foundations were concentrated on Persis and Mesopotamia, less so on other parts of the realm. The first Sasanian royal city was built by Ardashir I in western Persis, when he was still a subject king of the Parthians. Ardashir Khvarrah ('To-the-Glory-of-Ardashir') was built on a round-city plan, a design possibly adapted from Parthian cities, and measured c.2 km in diameter. The city-circle was divided into four quarters, each of which was divided into five sub-sections. The centre point of the city was marked by a square tower 30 m high and may have functioned as a beacon used for communication (see Fig. 43).

Ardashir's palace was built 4 km outside the city. It was situated within a park, next to a natural lake. Built on a rectangular plan,

Figure 43   Aerial photograph of Ardashir Khvarrah (Firuzabad) (courtesy of G. Gerster)

the palace measured 55 x 104 m. Its main feature was a grandiose *ivan* 20 m high, which gave access to three square, domed halls, which probably were for representational use. This architecture established the Sasanians as innovators of the squinch, an architectural feature characterised by three corners, which allowed architects to link the square structure of the room with a round dome. The palace of Ardashir provides the earliest example of such a structure, which remained in use throughout the Sasanian period and became a marked feature of Islamic architecture. Doors built in a keyhole design allowed access to the rear of the palace, where an inner courtyard led to the adjacent rooms. Other architectural features, like the scalloped canopies above doorways and blind windows, resembling a feather design, were a direct borrowing from Achaemenid palaces, ultimately deriving from Egyptian architecture.

The royal cities Bishapur in Persis and Weh Antioch Shapur/Gundeshapur in Khuzestan were built by Shapur I in commemoration of his victories over the Roman armies (see Fig. 44). Bishapur, built by Roman prisoners of war, was based on a rectangular city-plan measuring 1.8 x 0.9 km. A palace complex in the north of the city included a cross-shaped hall based on a square plan (22m²), its floor covered with mosaics, a typically Roman feature which was adapted into Sasanian architecture. Weh Antioch Shapur/Gundeshapur, which measured 3.4 x 1.5 km, was built after the destruction of Antioch-Orontes.

In the later Sasanian period Khosrow II built a city at Dastagird on the Diyala River (64 km east of modern Baghdad). During his reign we also observe a return to the northern part of the empire. At Taq-e Bostan Khrosow II carved his investiture relief in a large *ivan* cut into the rock next to the smaller *ivan* of Shapur III. Further to the west he built a summer palace for his wife Shirin, at Qasr-e Shirin. It is also in the sixth century that the largest fire sanctuary was built in northern Media, Adur Gushnasp (modern Takht-e Suleiman) (see below p. 189 and Fig. 48).

But the Sasanian court was more than just the splendour of architecture, sumptuous interior decorations, lavish feasts, and the dazzling robes of the king and his courtiers. It provided a space for the collection and discussion of art and literature, of sciences and medicine. Court singers, the minstrels, recited stories and legends of the past glory of the Persians. *Magi*, sages and astrologers resided

Figure 44   Aerial view of Bishapur (courtesy of G. Gerster)

at the court to confer with the king on religious and philosophical matters. Most of our information about the Sasanian court as a centre of knowledge and intellectual discussion relates to the court of Khosrow I, and while academic dispute flourished during his reign, there is no reason to believe that arts and sciences were less well regarded under his predecessors. On the contrary, Shapur I's invitation to Mani to stay at his court is a clear indication of the fact that knowledge about other religions and cultures was an integral part of Sasanian court life. Of Khosrow's court it is said that he sought to accumulate knowledge from the east and west. A Persian doctor, Burzog, was sent to India from where he brought back Indian literature, fables from the Pañcatranta, which he translated into Middle Persian. Under the chief *mōbad* Veh-Shapur twenty-one *nasks*, or books, of the Avesta, the Holy Scriptures of the Zoroastrians, were written down. Paulus the Persian, a Nestorian who later converted to Zoroastrianism, was responsible for the translation of Greek philosophy and science. After Justinian closed the philosophical school at Athens in 532, the philosophers travelled to the Sasanian court, encouraged by Khosrow's reputation as a 'philosopher-king'. A university was opened at Gundeshapur, and the king is known to have assembled medical doctors, astrologers and theologians in colloquia. Medicine appears in the sources as a highly regarded profession. In 545 Khosrow asked the Byzantine emperor for the accomplished Palestinian doctor Tribunus to be employed as the chief physician at his court for twelve months. Finally, games like polo, chess and backgammon were introduced at the court, probably from India.

His later successor Khosrow II became the object of legendary stories, the most famous being the story of 'Khosrow and Shirin', a tangled love story based on the life of Khosrow and his love for the Christian princess Shirin. The story entered the famous Book of Kings, the *Shahnameh*, written by Firdowsi, and was adapted in the late twelfth century by Nizami.

Women at the Sasanian court

The king's wife and his mother enjoyed the highest rank among the female members of the royal court, followed by the king's sisters and the king's daughters. The Sasanian kings practised polygamy, but the mother of the heir to the throne took the prominent rank as king's wife. The king's mother bore the title 'Mother of the King of Kings', while the king's wife and mother of the heir to the throne was referred to as 'the Empire's Queen'. A daughter of the king was given the title 'Queen of Queens', and a third rank was constituted by the term 'Queen'. Other royal women were referred to as 'Princess' or 'Lady'. The title of 'Queen of Queens' is attested for the daughter of Papak and sister of Ardashir, Denak, for Shapur's daughter Aduranahid, and for Shapurdukhtak, the wife of Bahram II and perhaps the daughter of Shapur Mesan Shah. This title has in the past been interpreted to imply the woman's status as her brother's consort, but it seems more likely that it indicated an order of rank, in which a daughter or the sister of the king took the highest position among the 'queens', a collective term of reference to the royal women of the court. The term 'lady' was probably a form of address, as is manifested in a reference to Ardashir's wife as 'Lady Murrod, Mother of the King of Kings' (ŠKZ §37), and for the goddess Anahita in Narseh's inscription at Paikuli.

Owing to the assumption that the Sasanian kings were fervent followers of Zoroastrianism, which condones, and even advocates, marriages between immediate family members, there is a general belief that brother–sister marriages occurred as a matter of course between the king and his sisters. In actual fact only a few brother–sister marriages are attested. Narseh was married to a woman, also called Shapurdukhtak, who is assumed to be his sister, and Kurdiyah is referred to as the sister-wife of Bahram VI Chubin. Yet even in these cases it is not known whether these were full-sibling marriages or alliances between half-siblings, in which case the marriage would not be regarded as incestuous. As far as can be gauged from the sources, the king took wives from among the Sasanian nobility as well as from among non-Sasanian dynastic families. Furthermore, foreign women, often captured on campaigns, would also enter the women's quarter of the king's palace, but were not eligible to become royal wives.

According to Shapur's inscription at Naqsh-i Rustam Ardashir's mother was Rodak, who bore the title 'Mother of the King of Kings' (ŠKZ §41), a title which passed on to Ardashir's wife Murrod, the mother of Shapur I. Khoranzim, the first royal woman mentioned in Shapur's inscription, and most likely his wife, was called the 'Empire's Queen'.

As some royal alliances make clear, marriages to non-Persians were also concluded. Yazdgird I is said to have married Shoshandukht, a daughter of the Jewish Exilarch, who became the mother of Bahram V Gor. Kavad I was married to a Hephtalite princess, Niwandukht, the mother of Khosrow I Anushirwan. In a political alliance Khosrow himself married the daughter of the king of the Turks, and their son Hormizd IV was to succeed to the throne. Khosrow II is said to have had two wives, the Persian princess Shirin, a Nestorian Christian, and Maria, a Byzantine princess.

As members of the court royal women had a public profile, appearing in the king's entourage and participating in official duties. They were honoured by royal fires named after them and, as coins demonstrate, performed religious sacrifices alongside the king. They were depicted on royal reliefs, including investiture reliefs and reliefs depicting seemingly private scenes of the royal couple. Their portraits appear on seals, gems and finger rings, and on a variety of silver dishes. In a few cases the portraits of royal women appeared on coins. Their names and official status are mentioned in royal inscriptions and official documents.

Royal women were part of the king's entourage and therefore accompanied the king on campaigns. As happened in the Parthian period, often this placed them in danger and indeed resulted in their being taken captive by the enemy. Thus, when Narseh was captured by the Romans, his wife and children likewise became captives. They were freed only after Narseh agreed to a peace with Rome (Peter Patricius, frg. 13–14.). Similarly, Peroz's wife and his daughter Perozdukht were among the royal women captured by the Hephtalite king after Peroz's defeat, in which he lost his own life. The women, as well as the king's encampment, were released after a Sasanian noble, Sukhra, agreed a peace settlement.

It was even possible for royal daughters to succeed to the throne, as happened in the tumultuous last years of Sasanian rule, when two princesses, Puran and Azarmigdukht, both daughters of Khosrow II, were able to succeed to the kingship. Puran was most noted for her diplomacy with Byzantium, returning the Holy Cross to Jerusalem, which had been plundered during Khosrow's campaigns in 614.

Figure 45a Sasanian seal depicting a royal woman (drawing by Marion Cox)

Figure 45b Seal of Denak (with kind permission of The Hermitage Museum, St Petersburg)

Representations of royal women

Following the depiction of Ardashir's wife in his investiture relief at Naqsh-i Rajab, depictions of the king's wife became an accepted subject in Sasanian art. Bahram II included his wife in his investiture relief at Naqsh-i Rustam, and even extended the genre of rock relief art. A relief at Tang-e Qandil shows a family scene between Bahram II and his wife who is holding up a flower in her right hand, the left hidden in her long sleeve in a gesture of deference. A similar scene is shown at Barm-e Delak, in which the king offers a flower to a female figure, her left hand hidden in the sleeve of her dress. At Sar Mashad Bahram II is depicted protecting his wife and two other members of his family from a lion. Different views have been expressed concerning the identity of the king and his consort on these reliefs, but there is a strong argument to ascribe them to Bahram II, who is thus credited with the introduction of several new designs of royal rock reliefs.

Narseh's relief at Naqsh-i Rustam shows the king facing a female figure to his left, both figures holding a diademed ring, a symbol of imperial power. Between them stands a smaller male figure, dressed like Narseh in flowing robes, consisting of a knee-length tunic and trousers, belt and a sword. Corresponding to the male dress, the female figure wears a long, flowing robe held by a belt tied into a bow, a diadem and turreted mural crown which surrounds her curled hair. Like the king, she wears a heavy pearl necklace. The woman has often been identified as Anahita, and the scene was therefore seen as a divine investiture scene. However, not only is nothing known about Anahita's role in royal investiture, but nothing in her appearance allows us to conclude that this figure is a deity. She is the same height as the king, with their eyes level. But, most importantly, while she holds the ring of power with her right hand, like the king, her left hand is invisible, hidden, in a gesture of respect, in her long sleeve. This is the gesture not of a deity, but of a human figure who accepts her place next to the king, and showing the respect and obedience warranted when in his presence. The woman is most likely Narseh's queen Shapurdukhtak, and the boy standing between them their son and heir to the throne, Hormizd II (cf. Shahbazi 1983: 255–268) (see Fig. 46).

A late Sasanian relief, elaborately carved at Taq-e Bostan in Media, depicts Khosrow II centred between a male and a female figure. Khosrow receives the ring of power from the male figure, who is

Figure 46 Sasanian relief at Naqsh-i Rustam depicting the royal family of Narseh (photo: MB)

probably rightly identified as the god Ahuramazda. The female figure also holds a ring of power and has been identified as the Persian goddess Anahita, who also gives the kingship. But this function of Anahita is unattested in our sources, and not even mentioned in the Avesta. Anahita was the goddess of water and fertility, and is not associated with investiture. One possible solution to the problem is to consider that, following earlier models, in which the king is shown sharing the ring of power with his wife, the female depicted at Taq-e Bostan is in fact Khosrow II's wife Shirin (see Fig. 47).

Vessels made of precious metal show female busts in relief, or worked as complete figures. The scenes of the drinking vessels and jars for pouring wine depict female musicians and dancing girls in flowing robes, arms and legs extended to express movement. The vessels were most likely used for royal banquets, and hence depict themes of celebration and joyous entertainment. Female dancers and musicians were a natural occurrence at the royal court and as part of the king's entourage accompanied the king on his migrations between royal capitals and on hunting parties. In the hunting scene at Taq-e Bostan in which the king is depicted as a boar hunter, some female musicians can be seen performing in a boat, while another

Figure 47   Detail from the relief at Taq-e Bostan depicting Khosrow II and his wife (photo: MB)

scene shows them seated on an artificially raised platform, playing music in the presence of the king.

The Sasanian nobility

As is emphasised in Sasanian royal inscriptions, the noble class included the aristocracy of the new Persian royal power based in Persis, as well as that of the previous Parthian empire. The lords and knights of both groups are named as the core of the noble class, which supported the Sasanian king. It is therefore not surprising that the heads of the old Parthian families of the Suren and Karen, as well as of the Varaz and Andegan, were directly named in the royal inscriptions.

> Then Shapur the commander of the fortress and Prince Peroz and Prince Narseh son of Sasan and Papak the *bidakhsh* and Ardashir Suren and Hormizd Varaz (. . .) and Kirdir the Ahuramazda *mōbad* and Narseh Karen and (. . .), and Rakhsh, commander of the army and Ardashir Tahmshapur and Shapur (. . .) the scribe of the accounts of the realm and Zodkard, the cupbearer, and similar prince(s) and lord(s) and knight(s) and village chief(s) and satraps and accountants and shop keepers and other Persians and Parthians who (were influential in?) Babylonia (. . .) to Our presence came.
>
> (NPi C)

A hierarchical structure divided the noble class into four groups. The first group were the *shahrdārān*, which comprised the sons of the Sasanian king and the local kings, followed by the members of the wider Sasanian clan, the *vāspuhragān*. A third group were the *vuzurgān*, the 'great ones', who were the heads of the noble families in the empire, and finally the large group of the free population, the *āzādān*, living in the empire as small landowners.

As regional kings, as satraps and as estate owners the nobility exercised considerable power at the royal court. Even though the heir to the throne was in many cases selected by the king, his reign was only secure as long as he had the backing of the noble class. Their ability to withdraw their support for a reigning king in favour of another candidate led at times to considerable dynastic upheaval.

The sometimes rapid succession of rulers damaged the king's ability to implement long-term reforms which would affect internal stability. The nobility's power increasingly eroded the power-base of the Sasanian kings, a process which was further encouraged by the large number of royal brothers and sons who were prepared to ally themselves with the nobility against the ruling king. In a way one may compare this political dilemma with the situation in the late Roman empire, where the acclamation of the emperor by the army likewise encouraged the quick succession of emperors.

Over the centuries noble alienation from the king led to his resentment of the nobility, which in part explains Kavad I's initial tolerance of Mazdak's attack on the wealthy and advocacy of the equal distribution of property. Only in the later part of his reign did he interfere with the social unrest which occurred as a consequence of Mazdak's ideas, and began to stabilise the situation. In order to do so Kavad I instituted a new group of small landowners, the *dehkānān*. Their existence curbed the power of the nobility and their concentration of land-based wealth. Kavad's tax reforms, which were continued under Khosrow I, further undermined the nobility's ability to control the money of the royal treasury.

ORGANISATION OF THE EMPIRE

The lands of the Sasanian empire were ruled by kings and satraps, continuing the political organisation of the empire of the Parthian period. As far as can be established the regional kings were appointed from amongst the brothers and sons of the king of kings. The kingdoms were put under the control of members of the royal family in order to ensure their loyalty, and, for all its turbulent history, it has to be said that threats to Sasanian royal power came from the noble class or from external forces, while we hear nothing of internal rebellions of local kingdoms.

After Ardashir's conquest of the kingdoms of the Parthian empire, his son Shapur I could list the following lands under Sasanian rule:

> Persis, Parthia, Khuzestan, Mesene, Assyria, Adiabene, Arabia, Azerbaijan, Armenia, Georgia (*Iberia*), Segan, Arran (*Albania*), Balasakan (*Derbend*), up to the Caucasus mountains and the Gates of Albania, and all of the mountain

chain of Pareshwar (*Alburz mountains*), Media, Gurgan, Merv, Herat and all of Aparshahr (*Khuzestan*). Kerman, Sistan, Turan, Makran, Paradan, Hindustan (*India/Sind*), the Kushanshar up to Peshawar and up to Kashgar, Sogdiana and to Tashkent, and on the other side of the sea, Oman.

(ŠKZ §2)

The order of the list is not accidental. In mentioning Persis and Parthia as the primary kingdoms, Shapur I deliberately gave weight to the political centres of Persian power, Persis as the homeland of the Sasanian dynasty, and Parthia as the former centre of the Arsacids. It is the view of the victor, but Parthia's mention as the second kingdom in the empire also expresses recognition of the previous power. The two core lands are followed by the lands of Upper and Lower Mesopotamia, the northern kingdoms from Azerbaijan and Armenia to Herat, and the kingdoms in the south-east and south of the empire, from Kerman to Sogdiana. In addition to the lands ruled during the Parthian period, the empire at the time of Shapur I has taken control of the Kushan region, and has added Oman to its possessions.

Perhaps more strongly than the Parthians, the Sasanians emphasised their claim on the lands which had formerly been controlled by the Persians. Thus, they claimed the territory west of the Euphrates River which had come under Roman control, as well as the region of Asia Minor, which remained the *casus belli* of Persia's wars with Rome, and later Byzantium, throughout the Sasanian period. But only under Khosrow II was this goal achieved, when the Sasanians led a successful campaign into Syria, taking Damascus and Jerusalem, and even advanced to Egypt. At this point, the Sasanian empire had reached its greatest extent, the closest it ever had been to restoring power over the territories once held by the Achaemenids. Furthermore, the Sasanians' political influence in Yemen gave them a stake in the south Arabian maritime trade which provided commercial access to the Far East, to India and even Sri Lanka.

In continuation of the political division of the Persian empire into kingdoms, the Sasanian king appointed his brothers and sons, as well as other members of the Sasanian family, as regional kings. The office of satrap, or governor, is still attested, though a satrap was primarily assigned to govern royal cities like Gundeshapur and Weh

Ardashir, or provincial centres like Qom and Kashan. Perhaps this meant that the satrapal office was reduced to an administrative office in royal cities, with the king himself as the effective ruler.

To administer the empire, the kingdoms and satrapies were divided into smaller districts with local administrators.

Among those who live under the rule of the king of kings Shapur: Ardashir king of Adiabene, Ardashir king of Kerman, Denak queen of Shapur, ward of Shapur, Hamazasp king of Georgia, Prince Balash son of Papak, Prince Sasan who is adopted by the Farrak family, Prince Narseh son of Peroz, Prince Narseh son of Shapur, Shapur *bidakhsh*, Papak *chiliarch*, Peroz chief of the cavalry, Ardashir Varaz, Ardashir Suren, Narseh lord of Andegan, Ardashir Karen, Vahnam *framādār*. Frik satrap of Weh-Antioch-Shapur, Sritoy son of Shahimust, Ardashir 'joy of Ardashir', Pazihr, valiant of Shapur, Ardashir satrap of Qom, Chashmak 'brave of Shapur', Vahman 'joy of Shapur', Tir-Mihr, chief of the fortress of Shahrkert, Zik master of ceremonies, Artaban of Damavand, Gundifarr Abgan 'who seeks combat', Pabish 'Perozshapur' son of Shanbit, Varzin satrap of Isfahan, Kirdisro *bidakhsh*, Papak Vaspurigan, Valash son of Seleucus, Yazdbad counsellor of queens, Papak swordbearer, Narseh satrap of Rind. Tiyanik satrap of Hamadan, Vardbad chief of services, Yoymard son of Rastak, Ardashir son of Vifar, Abursam-Shapur head of the harem, Narseh son of Barrak, Shapur son of Narseh, Narseh chief steward, Hormizd chief scribe son of Hormizd chief scribe, Naduk, chief of prison, Papak, gate keeper, Pasfard son of Pasfard, Abdagash son of the castle lord, Kirdir *magus*, Rastak, satrap of Weh Ardashir, Ardashir son of the *bidakhsh*, Mihrkhwast treasurer, Shapur commander, Arshtat Mihran of Rayy secretary, Sasan, the eunuch son of Sasan, Virod chief of markets, Ardashir satrap of Neriz, (. . .) Sasan the judge, (. . .) Gurik chief of boars.

(ŠKZ §§44–50)

Over time the administrative, legal, financial and clerical offices became more defined as a hierarchical structure emerged within each main office. The priestly office of the *mōbad* was divided between a 'great *mōbad*' and a 'priest of priests' (MP *mōbadān mōbad*). Commanders-in-chief appear on a local level, as do so-called advisers (MP *handarzbed*) who operate at the court as well as in the kingdoms. A 'protector of the poor and judge', instituted under Khosrow I, operated in the provinces to serve the lower classes of Sasanian society.

Economy and trade

The economic prosperity of the Sasanian empire depended on two main sectors, trade and agriculture. Royal income was secured through taxation and through money obtained as fines and ransom in war.

When the Sasanians came to power in AD 224 the overland routes of the Silk Road had long been established. Silk remained the most important Chinese export, valued by the Sasanian as well as the Roman aristocracy. Even though the fall of Dura-Europos, Palmyra and Hatra must have affected the prosperity of Upper Mesopotamia, it does not seem to have had a long-term effect on trade.

Part of the trade was conducted by sea, leading from the Euphrates into the Persian Gulf, along the coast of the Arabian peninsula to Oman and Yemen, and eastward along the coast to the River Indus and even reaching as far as Sri Lanka. From Yemen and Oman Persian ships carried myrrh and frankincense, and from the east the Persians imported spices, perfumes and wild animals. Apart from silk, the most sought-after luxury items of the Sasanian aristocratic classes were pearls, which were worn as jewellery, but also used to embroider fabrics for their elaborate dresses and costumes.

Trade relations between Sasanid Persia and Rome played an important role in the political and diplomatic exchanges between the two empires. This is apparent in Rome's attempt to curb the trading power of the Sasanians in the peace treaty of 298, and in its later endeavour to gain direct access to Chinese silk in order to exclude Sasanian middlemen.

In the peace treaty of 298 between Diocletian and Narseh, the Sasanian king was forced to agree that the only city of the trade exchange between Rome and Sasanid Persia was to be Nisibis, since the emperor refused to negotiate this point of the treaty (see p. 148).

The principal points of the (Roman) embassy (*led by Sicorius Probus*) were these: that in the eastern region the Romans should have Intelene along with Sophene, and Arzanene along with Cordyene and Zabdicene, that the river Tigris should be the boundary between each state, that the fortress Zintha, which lies on the border of Media, should mark the edge of Armenia, that the king of Iberia should pay to the Romans the insignia of his kingdom and that the city of Nisibis, which lies on the Tigris, should be the place for transactions. Narses heard these things and since the present fortune did not allow him to refuse any of them, he agreed to them all, except, in order to seem to do everything under constraint, he refused only that Nisibis should be the place of transactions. Sicorius, however, said: 'This point must be yielded. Moreover, the embassy has no instructions on this point from the emperors.'

(Peter Patricius, frg.14; transl. J.M. Lieu)

In the mid-sixth century AD, in their attempt to undermine the Sasanian profits gained from the silk trade with China, the Romans investigated other trade routes and alliances, including a treaty with the Turks, as well as the theft of silkworm eggs which introduced the production of silk to the West.

At about this time (*AD 551*) certain monks, coming from India and learning that the Emperor Justinian entertained the desire that the Romans should no longer purchase their silk from the Persians, came before the emperor and promised so to settle the silk question that the Romans would no longer purchase this article from their enemies, the Persians, nor indeed from any other nation; for they had, they said, spent a long time in the country situated north of the numerous nations of India – a country called Serinda (*China*) – and there they had learned accurately by what means it was possible for silk to be produced in the land of the Romans. Whereupon the emperor made very diligent enquiries and asked them many questions to see whether their statements were true, and the monks explained to him that certain worms are the manufacturers of silk, nature

being their teacher and compelling them to work continu-
ally. And while it was impossible to bring the worms here
alive, it was still practicable and altogether easy to convey
their offspring. Now the offspring of these worms, they said,
consisted of innumerable eggs from each one. And men bury
these eggs, long after the time when they are produced, in
dung, and after thus heating them for a sufficient time they
bring forth the living creatures. After they had thus spoken,
the emperor promised to reward them with large gifts and
urged them to confirm their account in action. They then
once more went to Serinda and brought back the eggs to
Byzantium, and in the manner described caused them to be
transformed into worms, which they fed on the leaves of the
mulberry; and thus they made possible from that time forth
the production of silk in the land of the Romans.

(Procopius, *Goth.* 8.17.1–8)

We have no indication of the growth or decline of the population of the Sasanian empire during more than four centuries of
Sasanian rule. While the population increased through deportations
from conquered cities, and through the addition of the women and
children who were taken prisoners of war in campaigns, the constant
warfare with Rome and invading hordes must have led to a decline
in the population. In addition, raids of invading peoples, bad
harvests, droughts, and periods of famine will have affected the
survival of the population in different parts of the empire.

The land was cultivated in large estates owned by the noble class,
as well as on smaller farms. The gap between the wealthy landowners
and the farmers, many of them perhaps tenant farmers, must have
been considerable, and by the sixth century reached a point where
Khosrow I had to take countermeasures to stop the imbalance
between rich and poor farmers and created the class of the *dehkānān*,
independent landowners who provided a strong enough class to curb
the power of the landed aristocracy.

Grains like barley, rye and emmer were part of the staple diet of
the Persians. Date palms, fig and apricot trees were cultivated in
orchards, and in addition grapes, nuts and olives. To maintain the
fields and orchards and to increase the crops, irrigation systems had
to be improved and extended. Yet whatever precautions were taken

to ensure good harvests, the Persian population endured great loss and suffering in the reign of Peroz, when an extensive drought lasting seven years caused bad harvests and famine.

> During his (*Peroz's*) reign a great famine came over the land for seven years continuously. Streams, qanats, and springs dried up; trees and reed beds became desiccated; the major part of all tillage and thickets of vegetation were reduced to dust in the plains and the mountains of his land alike; bringing about the deaths there of birds and wild beasts; cattle and horses grew so hungry that they could hardly draw any loads; and the water in the Tigris became very sparse. Dearth, hunger, hardship, various calamities became general for the people of his land. He accordingly wrote to all his subjects, informing them that the land and capitation taxes were suspended, and extraordinary levies and corvées were abolished, and that he had given them complete control over their own affairs, commending them to take all possible measures in finding food and sustenance to keep them going.
>
> (Tabarī 873)

It was probably the most devastating disaster which ever befell the Sasanian empire. Efforts made under Khosrow I to increase agricultural growth through irrigation in Mesopotamia, a cadastral survey and a tax reform may have been in response to the catastrophe.

> Khosrow chose some men of sound judgment and wise counsel, and ordered them to investigate the various types of crops the cadastral survey had revealed for him, the number of date palms and olive trees, and the numbers of heads of those liable for the poll tax. On that basis they were to fix the rates of taxation by the yardsticks of what they perceived would ensure the well-being of his subjects and ample means of sustenance for them. They were to report the results of this to him. (. . .) They discussed the matter among themselves at length and finally agreed to base the land tax on the products that kept alive men and

beasts, these being: wheat, barley, rice, grapes, trefoil and clover, date palms and olive trees.

(Tabarī 962)

The army

The most powerful office was that of the *spāhbed*, the commander of the army, which had an estimated size of 50,000–80,000 men. The army division followed the decimal system, in which one regiment was made up of 10 companies of 100 soldiers each, with 10 regiments forming a division.

One of the most famous commanders was Mihr Narseh, who became a member of the king's court and was appointed grand vizier (MP *vuzurg framādār*), to act as regent for Bahram V when the king left on an eastern campaign. In 421 he led the Sasanian army against the Romans, entering Constantinople and negotiating a truce. He remained in office under Bahram's successor Yazdgird II.

The army's main force was the mailed cavalry, which was divided into two sections, the heavily mailed cavalry and the lighter mailed cavalry used in close combat. The horsemen were equipped with lances, as well as with bows and arrows. The simple bow was eventually replaced by the composite bow. The cavalry was recruited from the wealthy noble class who could afford the horses and armour.

> The equipment that a cavalryman of the army had to take along with him comprised horse mail, soldier's mailed coat, breastplate, leg armour plates, sword, lance, shield, mace, and fastened at his waist, a girdle, battle axe, or club, a bow case containing two bows with their strings, thirty arrows, and finally, two plaited cords, which the rider let hang down from his helmet.
>
> (Tabarī 964)

Other soldiers were recruited from within the empire, and provided through political alliances with nomadic groups, like the Chionites and Hephtalites, who then offered contingents of their armies to be included in the Sasanian army. In addition, foreign mercenaries were also found. Ammianus Marcellinus describes the power of the Sasanian army as follows:

Their (*the Persians'*) military training and discipline, and their constant practice of manoeuvres and arms drill, which I have often described, make them formidable even to large armies. They rely especially on their cavalry, in which all their nobility and men of mark serve. Their infantry are armed like gladiators, and obey orders like soldiers' servants. (. . .) Most of them are dressed in garments of various gleaming colours, which are open in front and at the sides and flutter in the wind, but never expose any part of their bodies from head to heel.

(Amm.Marc.23.6.83)

Elephants were also used in battle, mostly for frightening the enemies' horses. However, elephants became unpredictable in a panic and thus were a risk for their own army. Siege instruments were used against cities, having been adapted from Roman siege operations.

In his report on the approach of the Roman army on Ctesiphon in 362 Ammianus Marcellinus provides the following account of the Sasanian army:

The Persians opposed us with squadrons of cuirassiers drawn up in such serried ranks that their movements in their close-fitting coats of flexible mail dazzled our eyes, while all their horses were protected by housings of leather. They were supported by detachments of infantry who moved in compact formation carrying long, curved shields of wicker covered with raw hide. Behind them came elephants looking like moving hills. Their huge bodies threatened destruction to all who approached, and past experience had taught us to dread them.

(Amm.Marc.24.6.7)

RELIGION

The multi-ethnic empire of the Sasanians included many different peoples who all followed their own cultural and religious customs. Alongside Persian religion the Greeks living on Persian soil upheld their religious cults, while the Jewish community continued to practise its religion as it had done under the Parthians. By the second century AD Christianity had attracted a large following and had found its way into the Persian empire. During the reign of Shapur I some of the Christian population had been resettled, not as Christians, but as craftsmen and traders. A new religion was founded under the leadership of Mani, a Persian, who practised his religion at the time of Ardashir I and Shapur I. In the east, Buddhism found its way into Iran, and established itself as a major religion there.

As Zoroastrians the Sasanian kings were followers of Ahuramazda. Yet the long-held view that Zoroastrianism became the 'state religion' has to be met with caution. The Sasanian dynasty celebrated religious rituals according to the Zoroastrian doctrine. Sacrifices were made before fire altars, and the kings' burials will have followed Zoroastrian practices. But Zoroastrianism was the religion of the Sasanian kings, and, while followed by most members of the Sasanian nobility, it was not imposed on the peoples of the empire, who continued to follow their own religious beliefs. Their ability to do so may have been dependent on the tolerance of each individual king, as well as on political circumstances, but the temporary persecutions do not sufficiently support the argument that the Zoroastrian religion became a 'state religion' under the Sasanians. The Sasanian empire experienced the strongest imposition of the Zoroastrian religion during the reign of Bahram I and his son, when the zealous Zoroastrian priest, Kirdir, was able to exert considerable influence at the court (see above Fig. 36). But despite his efforts to eradicate other religions in the empire, and elevate Zoroastrianism as the only accepted creed, subsequent kings did not adopt his policy. Written sources do not allow the conclusion that the kings regarded themselves as the head of a 'state church'. Furthermore, in a revision of the previous interpretation of the archaeological evidence which identified numerous buildings as religious architecture, these identifications have been cast into doubt, if not discarded. As a result, scholars suggest that the dissemination of Zoroastrianism across the empire was not as extensive as has previously been thought. It is more likely that there was a separation between a royal religious cult and the religious cults celebrated by the peoples of the empire. This view does not exclude the possibility that Zoroastrianism may have become more widespread among the Persian population, but it dismisses the idea of a religion imposed on the people.

The Persians' belief in the divinity of the sun and moon, and in the four natural elements, earth, sky, water and fire, had been upheld over centuries. It had entered the Zoroastrian religion, which forbade the pollution of these elements by prohibiting, for example, earth burials, and the exposure of the sacred fire to the open air. Kings and priests sacrificed before fire altars which were constructed inside so-called *chahar taqs* ('Four-Arch-(buildings)'). The *chahar taq* was built on a square ground plan, with a domed roof. Inside the *chahar taq* stood a stone altar on which the fire was brought from an adjacent room where a fire was kept burning by the priests of the fire temple. The most formidable example of such a building is the late Sasanian site of Adur Gushnasp (modern Takht-e Suleiman) in northern Iran. It is the largest religious site dated to the Sasanian period which attests to the significance of the Zoroastrian fire cult (see Fig. 48).

Fires were also lit for the king and for other members of his family. The king's fire was extinguished upon his death and new fires were lit with the accession of the new ruler. In further honour of the royal fires animal sacrifices were made by the order of the king:

> And here by this inscription (*at Naqsh-i Rustam*) we founded a fire Khosrow-Shapur by name for our soul and to perpetuate our name, a fire called Adur-Anahid by name for the soul of our daughter Aduranahid, queen of queens, to perpetuate her name, a fire called Khosrow-Hormizd-Ardashir by name, for the soul of our son Hormizd-Ardashir, great king of Armenia, to perpetuate his name, another fire called Khosrow-Shapur by name, for the soul of our son Shapur king of Mesene, to perpetuate his name, and a fire called Khosrow-Narseh by name, for the soul of our son, the Mazda-worshipping Narseh, king of Sind, Sistan and Turan to the edge of the sea, to perpetuate his name. And that which we have donated to these fires, and which we have established as a custom, all of that we have written upon the document. Of those 1,000 lambs, of which custom gives us the excess, and which we have donated to these fires, we have ordered as follows: for our soul each day a lamb, one and a half measures of bread and four quantities of wine.
>
> (ŠKZ §§33–35)

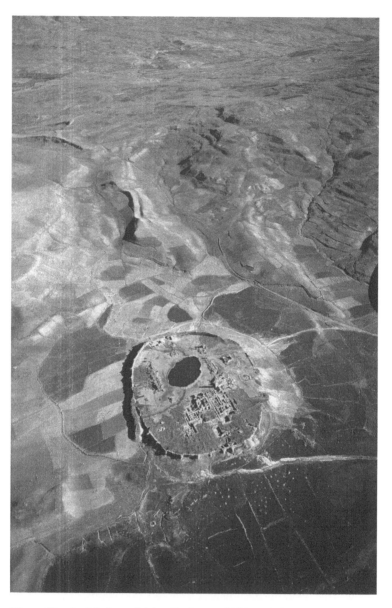

Figure 48   Aerial view of Adur Gushnasp (Takht-e Suleiman) (courtesy of
             G. Gerster)

Shapur's concern for the souls of members of his family, including those who had passed away, reflects the Sasanian practice of honouring and commemorating one's relations. As the above passage shows, this could be expressed in the king's foundation of fires 'for our soul and to perpetuate our name', as well as for the souls of his daughter and his sons, and by offering sacrifice for a religious ceremony. Charitable donations given to the poor, or offered for the benefit of public services, such as the maintenance of roads and canals, were also regarded as acts which enhanced the well-being of the soul of the deceased.

The importance of the royal fires is manifest in Sasanian coinage, which depicts the king's portrait on the obverse, and on the reverse the figure of the king and his wife, or another member of his family, sacrificing before a fire altar.

Further problems in our understanding of the importance of the Zoroastrian religion for the Sasanian kings arise from an interpretation of the archaeological evidence which is based on the idea of the union between 'state' and 'church'. While those investiture reliefs which show the king receiving the ring of power from Ahuramazda demonstrate beyond dispute the king's emphasis on the god's endorsement of his kingship, as well as the godlike status of the king himself, investiture reliefs which show a female figure together with the king have been interpreted to represent the goddess Anahita as a goddess of investiture. As we have seen above, this interpretation has more recently been challenged (Shahbazi 1983), and the idea of a connection between the goddess Anahita and royal investiture will have to be dismissed.

Considering the current state of research it can be established that under the Sasanians Zoroastrian religion was followed by the Persian kings, and in the later part of the empire its doctrines were written down for the first time. But by no means can it be ascertained that Zoroastrianism became the only religion of the Sasanian kings, or indeed, that Zoroastrianism determined Sasanian politics. Rather we must allow the same acceptance or 'tolerance' towards other religions in the multicultural and multi-ethnic empire of the Sasanians, although this acceptance was subject to internal and external political circumstances. The exclusion of other religions in favour of Zoroastrianism was at its strongest point when Kirdir exercised his influence over Bahram I and his son. Persecutions of other religions

191

did not happen as a matter of course, but were intrinsically linked to the political climate at the time of individual rulers. As the religions, especially Christian and Manichaean religion, became politicised they were used by Romans and Sasanians to justify their wars against one another.

Christianity

The religious undertone of politics became most apparent when the Roman emperor Constantine I the Great (307–337) declared his support for the Christian religion. It meant that he regarded himself as the protector of all Christians, regardless of their geographical location. Thus Christians who lived in Sasanid Persia, or indeed in Armenia and Ethiopia, became pawns in the political game between the Roman/Byzantine empire and Sasanid Persia.

Christian communities can already be found in the Persian empire at the time of the Arsacids. In the second century AD these were only small groups with centres in Upper Mesopotamia, at Arbela and Edessa. The influx of Christians increased following the Sasanian victories in Roman Syria and Asia Minor, and the subsequent deportation of the population under Shapur I to be resettled in Mesopotamia. As entire city-populations were resettled, so were their Christian communities, including their bishops. They adhered to their own languages, Syriac and Greek. The different communities based in Nisibis, Seleucia-Ctesiphon and Susa, were far from united, until one of their bishops, Papa bar Aggai of Seleucia-Ctesiphon, became head of the Persian Christians. With the support of Yazdgird I a synod was held in Ctesiphon in 410, during which the Christian Church of Persia established itself as an organised church distinct from the western Christian Church. This declaration of allegiance to the Sasanian empire did not prevent a group of fanatical Christians from destroying Zoroastrian fire temples (Theodoret, *HE* 5.31.1), a crime against which Yazdgird immediately retaliated with persecutions.

But the Christian Church itself was deeply disunited, split between those who followed the view of Nestorius, patriarch of Constantinople in 428, and that of Cyril of Alexandria. While Nestorius represented the view of the two natures of Christ, the human and the divine, and regarded Mary as the mother of Christ, but not as the mother of God, Cyril was a monophysite, for whom Christ had only one side, the divine. The synod of 484 saw the birth of the Nestorian Church, which continued to develop in Persia in opposition to Constantinople. Nestorius built a religious school in Nisibis and in Gundeshapur.

Persecution of Persian Christians was politically motivated, as they were an easy target in times of war. When Christianity had become the state religion of the Roman emperors at Constantinople, being a Christian was easily equated with being pro-Roman. Like the Manichaeans the Christians were persecuted under Bahram II. The Christians themselves were not a homogeneous group but were divided into different sects. But as the organisation of the religion became an issue, the division between the various groups became obvious and by the end of the third century led to internal problems. With the Armenians' conversion to Christianity and Constantine's assumed role as the protector of all Christians, religious loyalty became a politically charged issue. The Persian Christians were eyed with suspicion, as they potentially supported the Roman emperor against the Sasanians. The justification for such an attitude was provided by the case of Armenia. After the death of the Christian, pro-Roman king Tiridates, members of the Armenian nobility who were non-Christian and anti-Roman supported Shapur's campaign in Armenia. This caused Constantius, Constantine's successor, to send military aid to the Christian Armenian group and to reinstall the Christian king Chosroes on the Armenian throne. The repercussions for the Christian groups in Persia were felt after Shapur II's unsuccessful attack on Nisibis in 338, after which he ordered the first persecutions of Persian Christians.

The persecution of Christians came to a halt with the synod of 410 in Seleucia-Ctesiphon at which the Sasanid Christians decided to found their own church and their own religious laws. This step was undertaken to demonstrate their independence from the Byzantine Christians and therefore from the Byzantine emperor. Eventually, these Christians became followers of Nestorianism, and Sasanid Persia saw itself in the surprising role of being the prime protector of the religion. A new wave of persecutions only occurred during the later Sasanian empire, during Khosrow I's war with Byzantium between 540 and 545.

Manichaeism

Shapur I's tolerance of Mani's religion was part of the Persian kings' policy of practising religious tolerance as long as a religion was not used to question or undermine political power. Mani, who probably belonged to a noble Persian family in Babylon, had returned to Persia after the accession of Shapur I. At the time of Ardashir's reign he had travelled to the southeastern parts of the empire and to India. It was during this journey that he was introduced to Buddhist religion, which was practised in the Kushan empire. Probably under the protection of Shapur's son or brother Peroz, and Shapur's brother Mihrshah, Mani was admitted to an audience with the king, and was subsequently allowed to teach his religion at the royal court, and even accompanied the king on campaigns. Mani shared this privilege with Kirdir, the Zoroastrian high priest at court, who, however, regarded Mani as a rival to his own religious ambitions.

The principles of Mani's religion combined aspects of Zoroastrian, Christian and Buddhist religion. Truth was central to his belief, expressed in acting morally good and rejecting evil. In the dualistic world man found himself in, he was endangered by evil, the opposite of good, threatened by darkness, as the opposite of light, and tempted to believe in Matter rather than in God. But by listening to those who lived an exemplary life, the so-called elect, they, the hearers, would find final redemption. The dualism between good and evil, light and darkness is also present in Zoroastrian belief. Manichaeism was opposed to aggressive behaviour and war. It was a religion of peace, asking believers to respect the life of animals and not to kill them for their meat. People should act for the good of society.

Under the influence of Kirdir, Shapur's successors, Bahram I and Bahram II, attempted to extirpate Mani's religion.

> And in all the provinces, in every part of the empire, the acts of worshipping Ohrmazd (*Ahuramazda*) and the gods were enhanced. And the Zoroastrian religion and the magi were greatly honoured in the empire. And the gods, 'water', 'fire', and 'domestic animals' attained great satisfaction in the empire, but Ahriman and the idols suffered great blows and great damage. And the (false) doctrines of Ahriman and

of the idols disappeared from the empire and lost credibility. And the Jews, Buddhists, Hindus, Nazarenes, Christians, Baptists, and Manichaeans were smashed in the empire, their idols destroyed, and the habitations of the idols annihilated and turned into abodes and seats of the gods.

(KNRm)

Summoned to the court of Bahram I, Mani was arrested and imprisoned in Gundeshapur, where he died a few weeks later, on 14 February 276. Under Bahram II the followers of his religion suffered severe persecutions, but Narseh, who succeeded to the throne in 293, ended Kirdir's fanatical ambition and returned to the more tolerant religious policy of Shapur I. By then Manichaeism had spread westward into the Roman empire, and to the east, where the religion was taught in eastern Iran, Central Asia and even in China. It survived for several centuries in the cities along the Silk Road. In fact, the most important documents recording Manichaean beliefs and doctrines were found in Turfan. In the West, the religion was threatened in 297 by the edict of Diocletian, to whom the Persian origin of the religion was sufficient to declare it a danger to Rome: its advocates were to be burnt, and its followers killed and their property confiscated.

Mazdakism

During the reign of Kavad I (488–496 and 499–531) a certain Mazdak advocated a radical religion, which seemingly aimed at undermining the religious and social basis of the Sasanian empire. Men should share their possessions equally within their local community, so that each had an equal share in food and property and none was above the other. Women also were to be shared within a community. Such sentiments would have found support among the poorer peasant class, while posing an immediate threat to the upper classes, especially the large landowners. With his reform Mazdak must have intended to decrease the class distinctions within Sasanian society and improve the lot of the lower classes. Since his religion became popular in a time of economic hardship, after several years of drought and famine suffered during the reign of Peroz, there must have been a great need for social and economic aid. As for the sharing

of women, it is difficult to reconcile such a practice with the importance of family life and legitimacy. It might, however, allude to the
polygamous marriages practised by the royal family and possibly the
nobility, but upon which, for financial reasons, members of the lower
classes could not enter. That was a limitation which they could never
improve, unless their social standing rose. It has also been suggested
that Mazdak might have proposed that marriages between partners
from different social classes should be permitted. On the surface his
religion looked more like a social doctrine, but it was based on the
religious ideas of good and evil. It is difficult to assess what effect
it had on Sasanian society and to what extent it was responsible for
the social uprisings which occurred during this period. Followers of
his religion were persecuted, but never entirely eradicated in Iran
until the early Islamic period.

ART AND ARCHITECTURE

The art and architecture of the Sasanians evolved from those of their
predecessors, the Parthians. City-foundations following a circular
city plan and palace buildings dominated by imposing *ivans* are
testimony to the Parthian legacy. As in the Parthian period, rock
reliefs continued to be used to depict investiture scenes and chivalrous combat. The rich material evidence of silver objects, such as
cups and vessels, bowls and plates worked in relief, and Sasanian
glassware may well have been modelled on Parthian prototypes.
Sasanian art is further evident in sculpture, stucco decorations, as
well as in a wealth of coins, and in minor arts, such as seals, gems
and finger rings. Hardly any jewellery has come down to us, though
its designs and splendour can be grasped through depictions on
reliefs and sculpture, as well as in written descriptions.

There appears to be a relative consistency in the execution of
Sasanian art over the four and a half centuries of Sasanian rule, but
it must be remembered that we are focusing on a very limited corpus
of Sasanian court art. Artistic themes concentrate on representations
of the king, and they remain unchanged throughout Sasanian rule.
Individuality rests with the identification of each king represented
on silver vessels, busts worked in stucco, or in precious metal, sculpture, as well as coins, with his personalised crown. In addition, there
is a disparity in the distribution of the material culture. For example,

most rock reliefs are located in Persis and concentrate on the early Sasanian period. A resurgence of this art appears at Taq-e Bostan in Media, during the reigns of Ardashir II and Shapur III, and in the late Sasanian relief of Khosrow II. Yet within this corpus of reliefs artistic developments can be determined.

Palaces and city-foundations are manifestations of Sasanian monumental art. Among the most important foundations were Ardashir Khvarrah/Firuzabad and Bishapur, as discussed above (see pp. 168–70). The cities' royal palaces were situated at the edge of the city or even outside the city walls. Their distinctive feature was the central *ivan*, the vaulted space open to one side, which was used as a reception hall of the king. Palaces and official buildings were built with mud bricks, the most important building material, while plaster and stucco were used for internal and exterior wall decorations. In Ardashir Khvarrah the large central *ivan* led to another representative space, a domed hall. This hall was built on a square ground plan, but roofed by a round dome, an architectural innovation which was achieved by introducing a three-cornered element, the squinch.

Fire temples, so-called *chahar taqs* or *atashgadehs*, were erected across the empire. The fires burnt in honour of the king and members of his family, though it appears that members of the Sasanian nobility also ordered fires to be burned for their family. For example, Mihr Narseh, the grand vizier under Bahram V, is said to have built fire temples for himself and one each for his three sons:

> he constructed there (*at Jirih*) for himself a fire temple, which is said to be still in existence today (. . .). It is called Mihr Narsiyān. In the vicinity of Abruwān he founded four villages, with a fire temple in each one.
>
> (Tabarī 870)

One of the most important Sasanian fire temples is the temple of Adur Gushnasp in northern Iran, known today as Takht-e Suleiman. This temple complex, dated to the late Sasanian period, c. sixth century AD, features at its centre two rooms, built on a square plan, with a cross-shaped interior, the centre of which formed the altar. In the smaller room the eternal fire was kept, attended by the priestly community which inhabited the site. From here, the fire was carried to the larger chamber for the celebration of religious rites. The site of the complex was chosen because of a natural lake whose spring lies c. 60 m below its surface. Adur Gushnasp was surrounded by a high fortification wall, 4 m thick, with thirty-eight towers and one entrance gate.

Also of the late Sasanian period is a *chahar taq* at Qasr-e Shirin in Media, part of the palace complex built as a summer residence by Khosrow II for his wife Shirin. The *chahar taq*, which was destroyed during the Iran–Iraq war of the 1980s, was built on the same square plan with a cross-shaped interior. The remains of the layers of the sacred ash are still visible today.

A more difficult question is the identification of temples of the goddess Anahita. The vast complex at Kangavar, on the Royal Road leading from Ecbatana to Ray, has, until recently, been thought to be a temple of Anahita, but it is now interpreted as a palace complex of the late Sasanian period.

Another alleged Anahita temple is the square subterranean hall at Bishapur. Built from hewn stones, and featuring four central doorways leading to a narrow corridor with a water channel, it has been assumed that this was a sanctuary for Anahita. While the architecture undoubtedly suggests that the central space of this square building served as a water-filled basin, with a surrounding stepped floor, the space does not allow for the performance of religious ritual or sacrificial offerings. Ultimately the idea of temples built for Persian gods is a view expressed in Greek sources, while nothing suggests that the Sasanians worshipped their gods in such a fashion. As in the Achaemenid period, sacrifices to the gods continued to be made before a sacred fire placed on a fire altar. These sacred fires were kept in closed chambers.

Sasanian court art

There is rich evidence from Sasanian silver dishes, which epitomise the art of the court. These dishes, cups and vessels were used in a royal ceremonial context, and as gifts. Elaborately worked in relief, these dishes depict scenes of court life, most notably the king's hunt, or royal banquets, with the king attended by his queens, attendants, and dancers and musicians. Another category of silver vessels shows female dancers between vine leaves, a motif adapted from Roman art.

Seals and gems provide a rich source for the study of Sasanian art. Most of the motifs used on them are animals or flower designs, with fewer objects portraying royal and high-ranking nobles depicted in profile.

The depiction of the kings and members of the royal family on the different media used in Sasanian court art allows some conclusions about dress and fashion. Sasanian kings and nobles wore a many-folded riding costume, consisting of trousers and a tunic which was held by a belt. An additional belt held his sword. The king wore a heavy necklace or torque, and earrings, possibly made of large pearls. In addition to his personal crown the king wore a ribboned diadem, which was always depicted on reliefs as a waving band. Sasanian kings were bearded and their long, curly hair cut in a bobbed hairstyle. The Sasanian nobles are seen wearing a similar riding costume, though it will have differed from the king's in the quality of the fabric and in colour. The different designs of their belts may have indicated their hierarchical rank. Certainly the head-dress (MP *kolah*), which was a cap with a top in the shape of an animal, such as an eagle or a bull, and could bear the emblem of the noble house from which they descended, marked their status amongst their peers. Royal women wore long, flowing robes with long, wide sleeves, huge pearl necklaces and earrings. Early Sasanian reliefs show women with their hair tightly bound together, but they then are depicted with long hair coiffed carefully in individual curls.

Sasanian art and culture did not abruptly end with the Arab conquest. Architectural designs, artistic styles and motifs in decorative art, metalwork, textiles, glass and jewellery, gradually underwent adaptations by Muslim Persian artists. Likewise Sasanian literary tradition continued into the early Islamic period. Middle Persian texts, including written histories, were translated into Arabic, and became part of the historiography of the new Muslim era. Persia's pre-Islamic roots were revived under the Abbasid dynasty (749–1258/1050) in Iran and under the Samanids (AD 819–1005) who ruled in parts of Khorasan and Central Asia.

Turning away from the capital of the Arabs, Damascus, the Abbasids founded a new centre, Baghdad, close to Ctesiphon, in 762, basing their city plan on the round design used by their Parthian and Sasanian predecessors. Palatial structures, including Sasanian-style *ivans* and courtyards, were adopted, and the elaborate stucco work which decorated palace interiors was based on Sasanian designs. Banquets and royal hunts were still regarded as exclusive pursuits of kings and continued to be depicted on gold and silver vessels, pottery and textiles.

The Abbasids modelled their court and court ceremony on the Sasanians and adapted Persian administrative practices. Shadows of royal Sasanian diplomacy can be glimpsed in the gifts sent in 802 and 807 by Harun al-Rashid to Charlemagne to honour the recently crowned king of the western empire. Among the gifts were a Persian cloak and a tent, centuries-old Near Eastern symbols of royal power and kingship; the gift of an elephant, while satisfying the curiosity of the western king, was also a symbol of military strength. The world of ancient Persia had come to an end, but far from disappearing, its influence can be traced to the new eastern powers, and through their contact with the Holy Roman Empire, to western Europe.

APPENDICES

THE ACHAEMENID DYNASTY

Cyrus II the Great	c.559–530 BC
Cambyses II	530–522
Bardiya/Gaumata	522
Darius I	522–486
Xerxes I	486–465
Artaxerxes I	465–424
Xerxes II/Sogdianus	424–423
Darius II	423–404
Artaxerxes II	404–359
Artaxerxes III	359–338
Artaxerxes IV (Arses)	338–336
Darius III	336–330

THE ARSACID DYNASTY

Arsaces I	c.247/38–217 BC
Arsaces II	c.217–191
Phriapatius	c.191–176
Phraates I	176–171
Mithridates I	171–139/8
Phraates II	139/8–128
Artabanus I	128–124/3
Mithridates II	124/3–88/7
Gotrarzes I	91/0–81/0
Orodes I	81/0–76/5

Sinatruces	c.78/7–71/0
Phraates III	71/0–58/7
Mithridates III	58/7
Orodes II	58/7–38
Phraates IV	38–3/2
Phraates V	2 BC–AD 2
Orodes III	4–6
Vonones I	8/9
Artabanus II	10/11–38
Vardanes	38–45
Gotarzes II	43/4–51
Vonones II	51
Vologeses I	51–76/80
Pacorus	77/8–108/9
Vologeses II	77/8
Artabanus III	79–81
Osroes	108/9–127/8
Vologeses III	111/2–147/8
Vologeses IV	147/8–191/2
Vologeses V	191/2–207/8
Vologeses VI	207/8–221/2 or 227/8
Artabanus IV	213–224

THE SASANIAN DYNASTY

Ardashir I	AD 224–239/40
Shapur I	239/40–270/2
Hormizd I	270/2–273
Bahram I	273–276
Bahram II	276–293
Bahram III	293
Narseh	293–302
Hormizd II	302–309
Shapur II	309–379
Ardashir II	379–383
Shapur III	383–388
Bahram IV	388–399
Yazdgird I	399–421
Bahram V Gor	421–439

Yazdgird II	439–457
Hormizd III	457–459
Peroz	459–484
Valakhsh	484–488
Kavad I	488–496; 499–531
Zamasp	496–498
Khosrow I Anoshirvan	531–579
Hormizd IV	579–590
Khosrow II	590–628
Bahram VI Chubin	590–591
Kavad II	628
Ardashir III	628–630
Shahrbaraz	630
Khosrow III	630
Puran	630–631
Azarmigdukht	631
Hormizd V	631–632
Khosrow IV	631–633
Yazdgird III	633–651

NOTES

FOREWORD

1 Most notably, here, one must mention the book by Josef Wiesehöfer, *Ancient Persia*, (2nd rev. edn London 2001) as well as the contributions appearing under his editorship in the series *Oriens et Occidens*, which provide new and stimulating approaches to the study of the ancient Persian empires, as well as to the intercultural contacts between East and West.

1 INTRODUCTION

1 See especially the new study by Rollinger (2003a).

2 THE ARCHAEMENIDS

1 Against the recent suggestion by Summers (2000) that Kerkenes Dağ should be identified with Pteria see Rollinger (2003b: 322–326).
2 For his possible burial site at Persepolis, where an unfinished tomb was modelled on Cyrus' tomb at Pasargadae, see Kleiss (1971).
3 The tombs of Artaxerxes II and Artaxerxes III, as well as an unfinished tomb, are located at Persepolis.
4 Although Herodotus remarks on the reform of the empire under Darius I (Hdt.3.89–97), it is doubtful that it was implemented in the way he suggests.
5 A gold *daric* weighted 8.41 g, a silver *siglos* 5.60 g. The coins depicted a running Persian archer.
6 See, for example, the representation of a satrap on the so-called Harpy-tomb from Lycia.
7 On this observation see especially Sancisi-Weerdenburg (1995).
8 For the finds from the Oxus Treasure, now in the British Museum, see O.M. Dalton (repr. 1964), *The treasure of the Oxus*, London. For those

from Pazyryk see S.I. Rudenko (1970), *Frozen tombs of Siberia: The Pazyryk burials of Iron Age horsemen*, transl. M.W. Thompson, London.
9 On the effect of the wars on Greece see especially Hölteskamp (2001).
10 Spawforth (1993).
11 See the excellent discussion by Wiesehöfer (1992).
12 Edward Said's study *Orientalism* (1978) is still fundamental here.

3 THE PARTHIANS (ARSACIDS)

1 A Parthian date for the construction of the wall has been suggested by Kiani (1982), against the traditional view which suggests a Sasanian date.
2 '[So] scheint es eine übergeordnete formative Komponente gegeben zu haben, die eine Art Leitmotiv für die zahlreichen lokalen Sonderformen gewesen ist' (von Gall 1998: 80).
3 For a drawing of the relief see Colledge (1967: fig. 4).
4 The fundamental study has been carried out by Schneider (1986).

4 THE SASANIANS

1 The relief at Naqsh-i Rustam depicts only Philip the Arab and Valerian, not the body of Gordian III.
2 Narseh recorded his accession to the throne in a bilingual inscription on a tower-like structure at Paikuli, now in modern Iraq.
3 Defence walls were built in western Iraq against invading Arab tribes, and in the north against nomadic invaders.
4 When Ctesiphon fell in 637, the carpet was cut into small pieces by the conquering Arabs.

SELECT
BIBLIOGRAPHY

ELAMITES AND MEDES

Boucharlat, R., (1994), 'Continuités à Suse au 1er millenaire av. J.-C.', *AchHist* 8: 217–228.

Carter, E., Stolper, M. (1984), *Elam. Survey of political history and archaeology*, Berkeley, Ca.

Genito, B. (1986), 'The Medes. A reassessment of the archaeological evidence', *East & West* 36: 11–81.

Hansman, J. (1972), 'Elamites, Achaemenians and Anshan', *Iran* 10: 101–124.

Helm, P. (1981), 'Herodotus' Medikos Logos and Median History', *Iran* 19: 85–90.

Henkelmann, W. (2003), 'Persians, Medes and Elamites. Acculturation in the Neo-Elamite period', in: Lanfranchi et al. (2003): 181–231.

Lanfranchi, G.B., Roaf, M., Rollinger, R. (eds), (2003), *Continuity of empire? Assyria, Media, Persia*, Padua (History of the Ancient Near East, Monographs V).

Miroschedji, P. de (1985), 'La fin du royaume d'Anshan et de Suse et la naissance de l'empire perse', *Zeitschrift für Assyriologie* 75: 265–306.

Miroschedji, P. de (1990), 'La fin d'Élam. Essai d'analyse et d'interpretation', *Iranica Antiqua* 25: 48–95.

Potts, D.T. (1999), *The archaeology of Elam. Formation and transformation of an ancient Iranian state*, Cambridge.

Rollinger, R. (2003a), 'The western expansion of the Median "empire": a re-examination', in: Lanfranchi et al. (2003): 289–319.

Sancisi-Weerdenburg, H. (1988), 'Was there ever a Median empire?', *AchHist* 3: 197–212.

Sancisi-Weerdenburg, H. (1994), 'The orality of Herodotus' Medikos Logos or: the Median empire revisited', *AchHist* 8: 39–55.

Summers, G.D. (2000), 'The Median empire reconsidered: a view from Kerkenes Dağ, *Anatolian Studies* 50: 55–73.

Vallat, F. (1997), 'The history of Elam', *Encyclopaedia Iranica* 8: 301–312.

THE ACHAEMENIDS

Briant, P. (2002), *From Cyrus to Alexander. A history of the Persian empire*, Winona Lake, Ind.

Brosius, M. (1998), *Women in Ancient Persia (559–331 BC)*, Oxford.

Brosius, M. (2000), *The Persian empire from Cyrus II to Artaxerxes I*, London (LACTOR 16).

Frye, R.N. (1983), *The history of ancient Iran*, Munich.

Garrison, M., Root, M.C. (2002), *Persepolis Fortification Tablet seal impressions and Fasc. I: Images of heroic encounter*, Chicago.

Hallock, R.T. (1969), *Persepolis fortification tablets*, Chicago.

Hansman, J. (1972), 'Elamites, Achaemenians and Anshan', *Iran* 10: 101–124.

Hölteskamp, K.-J. (2001), 'Marathon – vom Monument zum Mythos', in: *Gab es das griechische Wunder?*, ed. by D. Papenfuss, V.M. Strocka, Mainz: 329–353.

Kleiss, W. (1971), 'Der Takht-i Rustam und das Kyros-Grab in Pasargadae', *AA*: 157–162.

Kuhrt, A. (1996), *The Ancient Near East*, 2 vols, London.

Miller, M. (1997), *Athens and Persia in the 5th century BC*, Cambridge.

Miller, M. (2003), 'ii. Greco-Persian cultural relations', *Encyclopaedia Iranica* 11: 301–319.

Miroschedji, P. de (1985), 'La fin du royaume d'Anshan et de Suse et la naissance de l'empire perse', *Zeitschrift für Assyriologie* 75: 265–306.

Niebuhr, B.G. (1847), *Vorträge über Alte Geschichte*, vol. 1, ed. U. Niebuhr, Berlin.

Rollinger, R. (2003b), 'Kerkenes Dağ and the Median "empire"', in: Lanfranchi et al. (2003): 321–326.

Root, M.C. (1979), *The king and kingship in Achaemenid art: Essays on the creation of an iconography of empire*, Leiden (Acta Iranica 3rd ser., Textes et Mémoires 9).

Said, E.W. (1978), *Orientalism*, London.

Sancisi-Weerdenburg, H. (1995), 'Persian food: stereotypes and political identity', in: *Food in antiquity*, ed. J. Wilkins, D. Harvey, M. Dobson, Exeter: 286–302.

Schmitt, R. (1991), *The Bisitun inscriptions of Darius the Great. Old Persian text*, London (Corpus Inscriptionum Iranicarum, Part I, vol.1).

Seipel, W. (ed.), (2000), *7000 Jahre persische Kunst. Meisterstücke aus dem Iranischen Museum in Teheran*, Milan, Vienna.

Spawforth, A. (1993), 'Symbol of unity? The Persian-Wars tradition in the Roman empire', in: *Greek Historiography*, ed. S. Hornblower, Oxford: 233–247.

Spycket, A. (1980), 'Women in Persian art', in: D. Schmandt-Besserat (ed.) *Ancient Persia: Art of an empire*, Malibu: 43–46.

Stronach, D. (1978), *Pasargadae*, Oxford.

Walker, C. (1997), 'Achaemenid chronology and the Babylonian sources', in: *Mesopotamia and Iran in the Persian period. Conquest and imperialism 539–331 BC*, ed. J. Curtis, London: 17–25.

Wiesehöfer, J. (1992), '"Denn es sind welthistorische Siege. . .". nineteenth- and twentieth-century German views of the Persian wars', in: *The construction of the ancient Neat East*, ed. A.C. Gunter et. al., Copenhagen: 61–83 (Culture and History 11).

Wiesehöfer, J. (2001), *Ancient Persia*, 2nd, revised edn, London.

Wiesehöfer, J. (2002), '"Griechenland wäre unter persische Herrschaft geraten. . .". Die Perserkriege als Zeitenwende?', in: *Zeitenwenden. Historische Brüche in asiatischen und afrikanischen Gesellschaften*, ed. S. Sellmer, H. Brinkhaus, Hamburg: 209–232.

Young, Cyler T. (1967), 'The Iranian migration into the Zagros', *Iran* 5: 11–34.

THE PARTHIANS

Alram, M. (1998), 'Stand und Aufgaben der arsakidischen Numismatik', in: Wiesehöfer 1998: 365–388.

Boucharlat, R. (ed.), (2002), *Les Parthes*, Dijon.

Brock, S. (1984), *Syriac perspectives on Late Antiquity*, London (Variorum Collected Studies).

Colledge, M.A.R. (1967), *The Parthians*, London.

Colledge, M.A.R. (1977), *Parthian art*, London.

Debevoise, N.C. (1938), *A political history of Parthia*, Chicago.

Gall, H. von (1990), *Das Reiterkampfbild in der iranischen und iranisch beeinflussten Kunst parthischer und sasanidischer Zeit*, Berlin.

Gall, H. von (1998), 'Architektur und Plastik unter den Parthern', in: Wiesehöfer 1998: 75–94.

Invernizzi, A. (1994), 'Die hellenistischen Grundlagen der frühparthischen Kunst', *AMI* 27: 191–203.

Invernizzi, A. (ed.), (1995), *In the land of the gryphons*, Florence.

Invernizzi, A. (1998a), 'Parthian Nisa. New lines of research', in: Wiesehöfer, 1998: 45–60.

Invernizzi, A. (1998b), 'Elymaeans, Seleucids, and the Hung-e Azhdar relief', *Mesopotamia* 33: 219–259.

Invernizzi, A. (2000), 'The Square House at Old Nisa', *Parthica* 2: 13–53.

Kiani, M.Y. (1982), *Parthian sites in Hyrcania. The Gurgan Plain*, Berlin (AMI Ergbd 9).

Kugler, F.X. (1907–35), *Sternkunde und Sterndienst in Babel*, Münster.

Leslie, D.D., Gardiner, K.H.J. (1996), *The Roman empire in Chinese sources*, Rome (Studi orientali).

Posch, W. (1998), 'Chinesische Quellen zu den Parthern', in: Wiesehöfer 1998: 355–364.

Schafer, E.H. (1985), *The golden peaches of Samarkand. A study of T'ang exotics*, Berkeley, Los Angeles, London.

Schneider, R.M. (1986), *Bunte Barbaren. Orientalenstatuen aus farbigem Marmor in der römischen Repräsentationskunst*, Worms.

Schneider, R.M. (1998), 'Die Faszination des Feindes. Bilder der Parther und des Orients in Rom', in: Wiesehöfer 1998: 95–146.

Schuol, M., Hartmann, U., Luther, A. (eds) (2002), *Grenzüberschreitungen. Formen des Kontakts zwischen Orient und Okzident im Altertum*, Stuttgart.

Sherwin-White, S., Kuhrt, A. (1993), *From Samarkand to Sardis. A new approach to the Seleucid empire*, London,

Sonnabend, H. (1986), *Fremdenbild und Politik. Vorstellungen der Römer von Ägypten und dem Partherreich in der späten Republik und frühen Kaiserzeit*, Frankfurt, Bern, New York (Europäische Hochschulschriften III 286).

Strassmeier, J.N. (1893), 'Zur Chronologie der Seleuciden', *Zeitschrift für Assyriologie* 8: 106–113.

Vanden Berghe, L., Schippmann, K. (1985), *Les reliefs rupestres d'Elymaïde (Iran) de l'époque parthe*, Ghent.

Wiesehöfer, J. (1996), '"King of Kings" and "Philhellen": Kingship in Arsacid Iran', in: *Aspects of Hellenistic kingship*, Aarhus: 55–66 (Studies in Hellenistic Civilizations VII).

Wiesehöfer, J. (ed.), (1998), *Das Partherreich und seine Zeugnisse, The Arsacid empire: Sources and documentation*, Stuttgart (Historia EZ 122).

THE SASANIANS

Back, M. (1978), *Die sassanidischen Staatsinschriften*, Leiden (Acta Iranica 18).

Boucharlat, R. (1999), 'Villes, palais, temples', in: *Empires perses d'Alexandre aux Sassanides*, Dijon: 30–34 (Les dossiers d'Archéologie 243).

Brown, Peter (1989), *The world of Late Antiquity*, London.

Cameron, A. (ed.), (1995), *The Byzantine and early Islamic Near East, III. States, resources and armies*, Princeton (Studies in Late Antiquity and Early Islam 1).

Cereti, C.G. (1997), 'Primary sources for the history of inner and outer Iran in the Sasanian period', *Archivum Eurasiae Medii Aevi* 9: 17–71.

Dodgeon, M.H., Lieu, S.N.C. (1991) (eds), *The Roman eastern frontier and the Persian wars AD 226–363. A documented history*, London.

Fowden, E. Key (1999), *The barbarian plain. Saint Sergius between Rome and Iran*, Berkeley, Los Angeles, London.

Girshman, R. (1962), *Iran, Parthes et Sassanides*, Paris.

Greatrex, G., Lieu, S.N.C. (eds), (2002), *The Roman eastern frontier and the Persian wars, pt. II: AD 363–630*, London.

Grinaschi, M. (1966), 'Quelques spécimens de la littérature sassanide, conservés dans les bibliothèques d'Istanbul', *Journal Asiatique* 254: 1–142.

Gyselen, R. (1989), *La géographie administrative de l'empire sassanide*, Paris.

Gyselen, R. (ed.), (1999), *La science des cieux. Sages, mages, astrologues*, Bures-sur-Yvette (Res Orientales 14).

Hartman, U. (2002), 'Geist im Exil. Römische Philosophen am Hof der Sasaniden', in: Schuol, Hartmann, Luther: 123–160.

Herrmann, G. (1977), *The Iranian revival*, London.

Hillenbrandt, R. (1999), *Islamic art and architecture*, London.

Howard-Johnston, J.D. (1995), 'The two great powers in Late Antiquity. A comparison', in: Cameron 1995: 157–226.

Huyse, Ph. (ed.), (1999), *Die dreisprachige Inschrift Šābuhrs I. an der Ka'ba-i Zarduŝt (ŠKZ)*, 2 vols, London (Corpus Inscriptionum Iranicarum Pt. III, vol. I, texts I).

Kettenhofen, E. (1995), *Tirdād und die Inschrift von Paikuli*, Wiesbaden.

Lewis, B. (1996), *The Middle East*, London.

Maenchen-Helfen, O. (1973), *The world of the Huns*, Berkeley.

Rubin, Z. (1995), 'The reforms of Khosro Anushirwan', in: Cameron 1995: 227–297.

Rubin, Z. (2000), 'The Sasanian monarchy', in: *CAH² XIV: Late Antiquity: empires and successors AD 425–600*, ed. Av. Cameron, B. Ward-Perkins, M. Whitby, Cambridge: 638–661.

Schippmann, K. (1990), *Grundzüge der Geschichte des Sasanidischen Reiches*, Darmstadt.

Shahbazi, Sh.A. (1983), 'Studies in Sasanian prosopography I', *AMI* 16: 255–268.

Vanden Berghe, L. (1978), 'La Découverte d'une sculpture rupestre a Darabgird', *Iranica Antiqua* 132: 135–147.

Vanden Berghe, L., Overlaet, B. (1993), *Hofkunst van de Sassaniden. Het perzische rijk tussen Rome en China [224–642]*, Brussels.

Whitby, M. (1988), *The emperor Maurice and his historian. Theopylact Simocatta on Persian and Balkan warfare*, Oxford.

Wiesehöfer, J., Huyse, Ph. (eds), (in press), *Erān ud Anerān. Beiträge zu den Beziehungen zwischen Ost und West in sasanidischer Zeit*, Stuttgart.

Winter, E., Dignas, B. (2001), *Rom und das Perserreich. Zwei Weltmächte zwischen Konfrontation and Koexistenz*, Berlin.

INDEX

Also in the Ancient Peoples series

The Egyptians
Robert Morkot

Widely published author on the subject, Robert Morkot presents
a clear introduction to the origins, history and culture of Ancient
Egyptian civilization.

This excellent addition to the popular family of books on ancient
peoples offers a broad coverage of Egyptian life and Morkot also
addresses a number of important questions dealing with race and
colour, Eqypt's relationship with Africa and Egypt's 'legacy'.

The Egyptians includes chapters on:

- dynasties and empires
- society
- daily life
- religion
- art and architecture
- languages and literature.

This engaging and accessible book provides students with the
ideal introduction to this fascinating civilization.

ISBN10: 0–415–27103–7 (hbk)
ISBN10: 0–415–27104–5 (pbk)
ISBN10: 0–203–48653–6 (ebk)

ISBN13: 987–0-415–27103–5 (hbk)
ISBN13: 987–0-415–27104–2 (pbk)
ISBN13: 987–0-203–48653–5 (ebk)

Available at all good bookshops
For ordering and further information please visit:
www.routledge.com